INSIGHT GUIDES

The world's largest collection of visual travel guides

Taiwan

Update Editors: Bernd Hans-Gerd Helms
and Linda Chih-Ling Hsu

Executive Editor: Scott Rutherford

Editorial Director: Brian Bell

APA PUBLICATIONS

Part of the Langenscheidt Publishing Group

L

INSIGHT GUIDES

Taiwan

CONTACTING THE EDITORS: Although every effort
is made to provide accurate information in this
publication, we live in a fast-changing world and would
appreciate it if readers would call our attention to any
errors or outdated information that may occur by
writing to us at Apa Publications,
P.O. Box 7910, London SE1 8ZB, England.
Fax: (44) 171-620-1074.
e-mail: insight@apaguide.demon.co.uk.

First Edition 1983
Third Edition (Updated) 1998

Distributed in the UK & Ireland by
GeoCenter International Ltd
The Viables Centre, Harrow Way
Basingstoke, Hampshire RG22 4BJ
Fax: (44 1256) 817988

Distributed in the United States by
Langenscheidt Publishers Inc.
46–35 54th Road
Maspeth, NY 11378
Tel: (718) 784 0055
Fax: (718) 784 0640

Worldwide distribution enquiries:
APA Publications GmbH & Co. Verlag KG
Singapore Branch, Singapore
38 Joo Koon Road
Singapore 628990
Tel: 65-8651600
Fax: 65-8616438

Printed in Singapore by
Insight Print Services (Pte) Ltd
38 Joo Koon Road
Singapore 628990
Fax: 65-8616438

Reid

The book you are holding is part of the
world's largest range of visual travel
guides. Its purpose is to help you have
the most valuable travel experience possible,
and we try to achieve this not only by providing
information about Taiwan but also genuine
insight into the island's history, cul;ture, institutions and people.

Since the first Insight Guide was published
in 1970, the series has been dedicated to
the proposition that, with insight into a destination's people and culture, visitors can
both enhance their own experience and be
accepted more easily by their hosts. Now, in
a world where ethnic hostilities and nationalist conflicts are all too common, such attempts to increase understanding between
peoples are more important than ever – not
least in a destination such as Taiwan where
political sensitivities are very apparent.

Zach

Insight Guide: Taiwan is carefully struc-
tured both to convey an understanding of
the island and its cultures and to guide
you through its attractions:

♦ To understand Taiwan today you need to
know something of its past. The History
section explains the complex story, while the
Features section introduces the reader to the
land and its people, with topics ranging from
the legacy of Confucius and traditional medicine to Chinese opera and contemporary
cuisine.
♦ The main Places section provides a run-
down of all the places worth seeing, divided
by geographic area.
♦ The listings in the Travel Tips section give
easy-to-find information on such things as
transport, hotels, restaurants, shops and
outdoor activities. Information may be located
quickly by using the index printed on the back
cover flap, which can also serve as a convenient bookmark.

Wassman

Taiwan has long been a problem for travel writers, just as it is for the international political community. To the government leaders in Taipei who have made the
island one of the four economic tigers of Asia,

Taiwan is the Republic of China. To the government in Beijing, Taiwan is a renegade province. Nomenclature and politics aside, Taiwan has developed its own personality, one of the world's great exporting economies located on an island of unexpected beauty. Here is a living museum of Chinese culture, including a storehouse of treasures moved from the mainland when Chiang Kaishek established his exile government in Taipei.

Anderson

At the core of *Insight Guide: Taiwan* is a manuscript written by **Daniel Reid**, an American scholar of Chinese culture. Born in San Francisco in 1948, Reid has opted for Taiwan and the Chinese way of life since 1973. He holds a graduate degree in Chinese language and civilization from the Monterey Institute of International Studies, and an undergraduate degree in East Asian studies from the University of California, Berkeley. Reid speaks Mandarin fluently, is proficient in reading and writing Chinese and pursues an interest in classical Chinese literature at his hideaway outside of Taipei. Reid's wife, Michelle, was born in Taiwan of Chinese parents.

Lee

Keeping this new edition updated were **Bernd Hans-Gerd Helms** and his wife, **Linda Chih-Ling Hsu**. Helms studied geography and history, and has written several travel books. Hsu worked in the travel industry. Both frequently visit Taiwan.

John Gottberg Anderson, former Apa managing director, developed the working structure for this guide. A former newspaper reporter in Honolulu and Seattle, Anderson studied Asian culture at the University of Hawaii. He contributed to the first editions of several other Insight Guide titles, including Burma, Nepal and Sri Lanka.

Paul Zach took on the task of turning an assortment of words and pictures into a well-rounded Insight Guide. A native of Cleveland and a graduate of Ohio University, Zach has written extensively about Asia for the *Washington Post*, *International Herald-Tribune*, *Los Angeles Times*, *Business Week* and *Asian Wall Street Journal*.

Rocovits

Keith Stevens's exploration of Taiwan's religions is an outgrowth of his long interest in Chinese folk religions. Born in England, he studied Chinese at universities in London and Hong Kong. He spent nearly a quarter of a century in Asia, first with the British Army and later with the British government.

Andy Unger penned this volume's chapter on Chinese art. He studied the psychology of language at Harvard, and painting in Florence and London before moving to Taiwan to pursue Chinese calligraphy.

Jon-Claire Lee, a graduate of New York University's drama program, contributed his insights to a short essay on film in Taiwan. He lives in his native Taiwan as a faculty member of the Chinese Cultural University.

The principal photographer for this volume was **Bill Wassman**, a resident of New York whose work first attracted international attention in early editions of *Insight Guide: Nepal*. Wassman spent two months poking his Leicas into every part of Taiwan. Wassman is a graduate of Indiana University in comparative literature and anthropology,

Frank Salmoiraghi spent several weeks photographing Taiwan between assignments in Singapore, Malaysia and Indonesia. A resident of Hawaii, his fine images also enhance the pages of *Insight Guide: Hawaii*.

Dan Rocovits is a long-time resident of Taiwan. He first steamed into Keelung Harbor in 1968 and settled in the island as a freelance writer, but soon discovered it was more lucrative to market his stories along with photos. Rocovits speaks Mandarin fluently and lives near Taipei.

Other photographs in *Insight Guide: Taiwan* are the work of Taiwan's **Chi Feng Lin** and **Chyou Su-liang**, Germany's **Heidrun Guether**, Hawaii's **Allan Seiden**, Holland's **Paul van Riel**, France's **Pierre-Antoine Donnet**, England's **Nick Wheeler**, Singapore's **Eric Oey**, and **Kal Müller**, an American in Indonesia.

Wrangling all the new updates, text and photographs for this revamped edition of *Insight Guide: Taiwan* was **Suriyani Ahmad**, in Insight's Singapore office. The new maps were created by Ahmad and **Kathy Wee**, also in the Singapore office.

CONTENTS

Places

Maps

TRAVEL TIPS

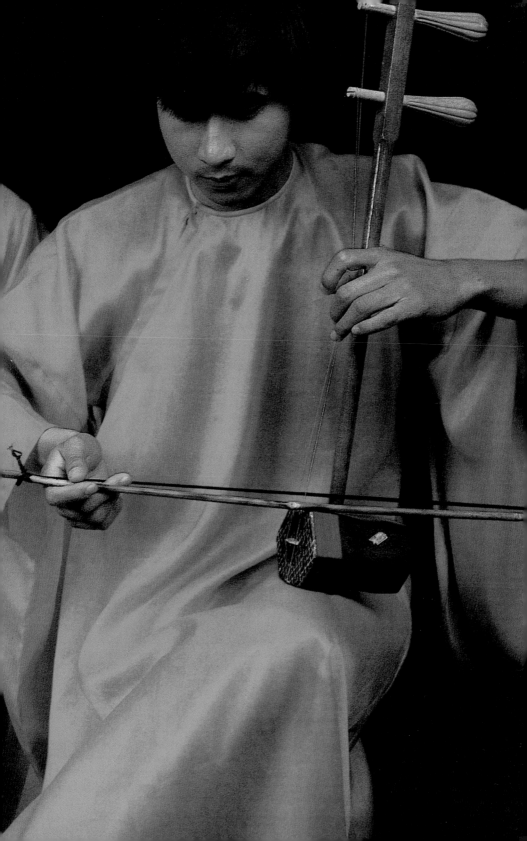

Bao Dao – Treasure Island. Tales of the untold riches of this island, just off the east coast of mainland China, ignited an endless exodus centuries ago. Pirates and political exiles, traders and adventurers, farmers and fishermen left behind the crowded coastal areas of China – often the southern region of Fujian province – to follow the proverbial rainbow.

Taiwan's rugged beauty, crowned by mountains and carved with valleys, satisfied the Chinese sensitivity towards aesthetics and the rhythms of nature. Its forests – thick with camphor, cedar, rattan, oak, fir, pine and other woods – were at once beautiful and commercially valuable.

The Chinese also found that food grew abundantly and rapidly in the soils of Taiwan, a significant concern for a people accustomed to the frequent famines and chronic food shortages of the mainland. Furthermore, the island was fat with mineral resources – coal, sulfur and iron – for building a modern society, not to mention jade, opal and coral for creating and savoring works of beauty.

Finally, Taiwan was a safe haven for enterprising émigrés blown to the island by the political storms of the mainland. Disgruntled mandarins and merchants, fed up with the factional vagaries and chronic interference of court politics, made their way to the island. The minority Hakka came from the Guangdong coast to escape persecution; Ming loyalists came to defy Manchu rule. Later, not so many years ago, Taiwan would become a refuge for those opposed to the Communist regime on the mainland.

Taiwan is frequently papered with a label as one of Asia's economic tigers – or dragons, if you will. And, indeed, so it is, not that far behind Japan in providing an engine of growth for Asia. Since World War II, the Chinese of Taiwan have nurtured a dynamic, modern society with a thriving economy and an enthusiasm for entrepreneurial skills.

Yet, despite the industrialization of the island, the essential features of the world's oldest continuous and most culturally-accomplished civilization are all preserved in Taiwan, both in the arts and in temperament.

Culture is the glue that has held Chinese civilization together for 50 centuries. It has cemented its social systems and traditions into a tough resilient fabric that has withstood history's convulsions. It has produced a written language that has been used, with only minor modifications, since the time of Egypt's pharaohs.

In fact, the notion of Chinese is more of cultural designation than racial or political. There are many ethnic differences between a Manchu and a Cantonese, but both are considered Chinese because they embrace common cultural foundations, practices and written language – even if the spoken dialects of China's vast regions are often mutually incomprehensible.

Preceding pages: Wenwu Temple, Sun Moon Lake; reforestation project; traditional music; Chiang Kaishek Memorial, Taipei. Left, image of Jade Emperor, Kaoshiung.

Throughout Chinese history, religion has taken a back seat to culture. No religious sect – discounting the social philosophy of Confucianism – has imposed its arbitrary views on the secular state and society. Buddhism, Daoism, Islam, Christianity and other faiths have coexisted in China for centuries, because their proponents – for the most part – have been required to stay out of secular and pragmatic concerns.

Given the historical and cultural context of the unifying nature of being Chinese, why the current animosity between Taiwan and the mainland government?

For the past half century, ever since the Nationalists cut their losses against the Communists and retreated to Taiwan, political ideology has divided China. One might also argue that the force of personalities, on both sides, has helped fuel the division. Both Taiwan, the Republic of China, and mainland China, the People's Republic of China, consider Taiwan to be a province of China. The difference in perspective is the mutual claim of both governments to be the legitimate government of China.

Beijing considers Taiwan to be a renegade province, but Taipei considers itself the temporary refuge of a government in exile. Despite their overwhelmingly similar roots, Beijing and Taipei seem unable to reconcile their squabble. And, slowly, this half-century of separation has led to a cultural gap of differing political, economic and social systems.

The unique social trait the Chinese call *ren chingwei*, the flavor of human feeling, permeates all social relationships in Taiwan and China. No matter what the occasion – whether business or pleasure, public or private, important or trivial – human considerations always take precedence. Indeed, in personal relationships, feelings are more important than logic or legality. Whether ren chingwei helps to resolve the governmental differences between Taipei and Beijing is a question of both profound interest and necessity.

Notes about spellings: Over the recent centuries, several systems to romanize the Chinese language have been used. Currently, there are two: Wade-Giles and pinyin. Wade-Giles is the older, and is the only system used in Taiwan. In mainland China, however, pinyin is the predominate and official system, and is used in our guides to China and Beijing.

Names and places mentioned in this book refer sometimes to Taiwan, sometimes to mainland China, especially in an historical context, and sometimes to both. In this guide, references to people, dynasties and places unique to mainland China – and to ancient Chinese history – are in pinyin; references to people and places unique to Taiwan use the Wade-Giles spellings.

A few exceptions are necessary. The goddess of mercy is, in pinyin, Guanyin, and is the spelling used in *Insight Guide: China*. For this book, however, use of this spelling might create confusion, as there are many temples to the goddess in Taiwan, with her name in a temple's name. Thus, the Wade-Giles transliteration – Kuanyin – is used. In such cases and on first reference in a chapter, the pinyin will follow in parentheses.

Guard at National Revolutionary Martyrs' Shrine, Taipei.

L'EMPIRE
DE LA CHINE
d'après l'Atlas Chinois,
AVEC LES ISLES DU JAPON.

Par M. Bonne
Hydrographe
au Bureau de la Marine.

A PARIS
Chez Lattré Graveur ruë St. Jacques
à la Ville de Bordeaux
Avec Priv!

OCEAN ORIENTAL

ISLES DU JAPON

NIPHON

SICOCO

XIMO

MER JAUNE

COREE

FORMOSE

LEQUEO

QUANTONG ou LEAOTONG

TCHE KIANG

KINGKITAO

Nangasaki

Jedo

Osaca

Pinghai

Pmang

NANKING

Ningpo

FUCHEU

Tayoan

Detroit de Diemen

I. des Pigmées

I. d'Oufou

140   145   150   155

140   145   150

.23

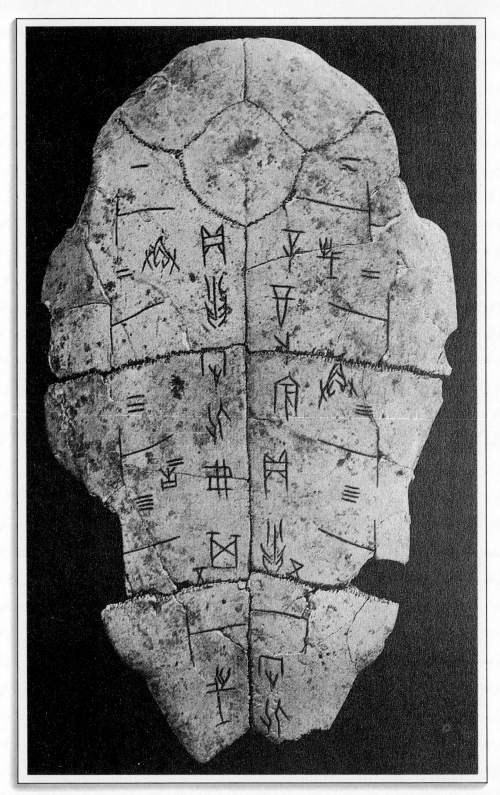

ISLAND SETTLEMENT

"Isla formosa. Isla formosa!" Portuguese sailors shouted with admiration from their ships as they sailed past Taiwan, en route to Japan during the sixteenth century. The island thus became known to the West by the Portuguese word *formosa*, or beautiful.

This island in the East China Sea has lured successive waves of Chinese immigrants from the mainland, explorers and exploiters from the West, and aggressive imperialists from Japan. All desired to possess the island of Taiwan.

But of all Taiwan's suitors, China proved to be the best match for the feisty and fertile island. The marriage of China's sophisticated and aesthetic culture with Taiwan's bountiful beauty and rich natural endowments has produced one of the most dynamic lands in Asia. Like *yin* and *yang*, ancient Chinese heritage and the island's indigenous charms are the inseparable elements that define Taiwan.

Little is known about Taiwan's earliest history. Radioactive carbon-dating of primitive utensils found in caves has indicated prehistoric people first appeared on the island at least 10,000 years ago. Archaeologists believe Taiwan's links with mainland China may be just as old. They have identified four stages of prehistoric tool development that match those of the mainland. They have also identified two later stages of development suggesting that other prehistoric Southeast Asian cultures arrived on the southern and eastern coasts of Taiwan. The early aborigines, whose descendants now form an important part of Taiwan's culture, are believed to have come from Malaysian and southern Chinese Miao ancestry.

The most ancient Chinese historical record referring to Taiwan indicates that the island was called the Land of Yangchow, before the rise of the Han dynasty, in 206 BC. There even may have been an attempt at that time to explore the island, according to the *Shihchi,* which referred to the island of Taiwan as

Yichow. The earliest attempt to establish a Chinese claim to Taiwan apparently occurred in AD 239, when the kingdom of Wu sent a 10,000-man expeditionary force, according to the ancient *Sankuochi*, or the *History of the Three Kingdoms.*

In the early 1400s, a eunuch magistrate and navigator from the Ming court, Zheng He, reported his "discovery" of the island to the emperor of China. The name used went down in the record books as *Taiwan*, which means terraced bay. But despite the obvious

fertility of the island's land, an imperial rule prevented the Ming empire's populace from emigrating to Taiwan – or elsewhere.

Two distinct groups of aborigines were living on Taiwan at the time of the Chinese arrival. One group lived sedentary agricultural lives on the rich alluvial plains of the center and southwest. The others were violent people, roaming the mountains, fighting incessantly among themselves, and practicing ritual tattooing and head-hunting, right up to the present century.

Although it is not known exactly when the Chinese first began to settle on Taiwan, the first mainland immigrants came from an ethnic group called the Hakka – literally guests, or strangers. The Hakka, a minority group relentlessly persecuted in China since ancient times, were driven from their native home in Hunan province about 1,500 years ago and forced to flee south to the Fujian and Guangdong coasts of the mainland. There, they successfully engaged in fishing and trading, activities that eventually brought them to the Pescadores Islands, now known as Penghu, and then later to Taiwan. By AD 1000, the Hakka had probably established themselves in the southern part of Taiwan, driving the indigenous aboriginal tribes from the fertile plains and up into the mountains. The Hakka grew sugar cane, rice and tea, and

Fujian refer to themselves as bendi ren, thereby distinguishing themselves from the 1949 influx of mainland refugees, whom are called *waisheng ren,* or outer-province people, by the old-timers.

Still, the only true natives of Taiwan are the ethnic minorities. Like the first nations of America and the aborigines of Australia, they have been shunted off to special reservations, located in the mountains of central and southern Taiwan. The majority of Taiwan's populace, in contrast, is descended from various groups of mainland Chinese immigrants. Even the Taiwanese dialect of Chinese is a direct offshoot of Fujianese.

During the fifteenth and sixteenth centu-

engaged in active trade with the mainland. Today, the Hakka rank among Taiwan's most enterprising people.

Other Chinese also set their sights on Taiwan. During the Ming dynasty (1368–1644), immigrants from Fujian province began to cross the Taiwan Strait in ever-increasing numbers. They pushed the Hakka further inland and usurped the rich western plains. Chinese settlers adopted the term *bendi ren,* which means this-place person, or native, to differentiate themselves from both the Hakka and the original indigenous peoples, whom they called "strangers". Even today, the descendants of these early immigrants from

ries, Taiwan became a haven for marauding pirates and freewheeling traders plying the eastern Chinese coast, from both China and the Japanese archipelago.

The distinction between pirates and traders was gratuitous, as both groups operated freely in Taiwan's waters. In fact, because it was close to the trading centers and shipping lanes of China and Japan, yet free of outside political control – the populace governed itself along clan and village lines, without interference from Beijing or elsewhere – Taiwan turned into a pirates' paradise. When times were good, they traded. When times were bad, they raided. In 1590, the Portuguese arrived on the north coast of Taiwan, where they established a trading settlement and port facilities.

All the while, the island's industrious inhabitants produced abundant food and other supplies for whoever could pay the price.

Colonial interests: The Japanese first attempted to annex Taiwan in 1593, after the warlord Hideyoshi Toyotomi unsuccessfully tried to conquer China by way of Korea. Hideyoshi's designs on Taiwan fared no better, as it proved too unruly to control.

This did not seem to put off the Europeans, however. The Dutch turned to Taiwan after they failed to wrest Macao from the Portuguese. At first, in the early 1600s, they were island, importing opium from Java, then a part of the Dutch East Indies. The Dutch taught the islanders to mix tobacco with opium and smoke it. The habit rapidly took root in Taiwan, later spreading to the mainland. (Two centuries later, opium would play a notorious role in the fall of the Qing dynasty, and would become the catalyst for war between China and Britain.)

Meanwhile, in 1626, the Spanish took control of a cape in the northeast, close to Keelung and later building a fort in Tanshui. The jealous Dutch, wishing to maintain complete control over the island's foreign trade, drove the Spanish out of Taiwan in 1642. Two years later, the Manchu conquest of the main-

primarily interested in the Pescadores, but they had to give in to an ultimatum from the Chinese court; in 1624, they established a fort and settlement on the southwestern coast of Taiwan.

In classic colonial fashion, the Dutch imposed heavy taxes and labor requirements on the island's inhabitants, and imported zealous missionaries to convert them to Christianity. The Dutch East India Company gained exclusive commercial rights to the

Left, bronze pitcher from Spring and Autumn Period (722–481 BC). **Above**, the Dutch Fort Zeelandia, Taiwan, early 1600s.

land began, an event that exerted lasting impact on Taiwan.

For a while, the Dutch lived in relative harmony with both local residents of Taiwan and immigrants from the mainland. But the Dutch then sought to collect a poll tax; frustrated Chinese revolted in 1652. The revolt was easily suppressed, but nearly 6,000 locals were slaughtered.

China's Ming dynasty reigned for 276 years, under 16 emperors. The creative arts and sciences flourished. But its glory faded under an administration that became increasingly corrupt. At the same time, Manchu leaders built a strong base of support and a huge army in the northeastern provinces. They swept south, advancing against the crumbling Ming armies. Before the Manchu reached Beijing, the last Ming emperor appointed a Taiwan-based pirate named Cheng to command the remnants of the Ming forces, hoping to deflect the Manchu assault on the imperial capital. Nevertheless, large bands of marauding bandits eventually stormed Beijing and opened the gates, allowing the Manchu armies to overcome Beijing's defenses and seize control of the government. The emperor hung himself, a humiliating final act in the saga of a glorious era.

Cheng, meanwhile, managed to keep the Ming army together. He also took a Japanese

wife, who bore him a son. The son inherited the Ming banner from his father. With it came a new name for the son: Koxinga – Lord of the Imperial Surname.

With an army of 100,000 men and an armada of 3,000 boats, Koxinga carried on the mainland fight against the Manchu, from 1646 until 1658. At one point, he almost recaptured the capital of Nanjing. But the Manchu finally forced Koxinga to retreat to the island bastion of Taiwan, an event that eerily foreshadowed the manner in which Chiang Kaishek would retreat across the Taiwan Strait three centuries later.

In Taiwan, Koxinga encountered the Dutch,

who discounted him as a mere pirate, incapable of mounting a serious threat. But Koxinga's spies, aided by Dutch deserters, provided valuable intelligence. In 1662, Koxinga sailed down the coast with 30,000 armed men, engaging 600 Dutch settlers and 2,200 Dutch soldiers at the three coastal forts. Koxinga captured Fort Zeelandia, near present-day Tainan, and graciously permitted the Dutch governor and his surviving men to leave the island. Thus, Dutch rule in Taiwan ended four decades after it began.

Taiwan became the personal domain of Koxinga. He gave the island its first formal Chinese government, turning it into a Ming enclave that, until his death, defied the Manchu, who had by now established firm control over the mainland.

Koxinga's reign was brief but influential. He set up his court and government at Anping, near Tainan, and developed transportation and educational systems. Great strides were made in agriculture. Tainan became the political and commercial center, and Anping grew into a prosperous harbor.

Perhaps Koxinga's greatest and most lasting contribution to Taiwan was his love for most things Chinese. His entourage included more than 1,000 scholars, artists, monks and masters of every branch of Chinese culture. He ushered in a renaissance of numerous ancient Chinese laws, institutions, customs and life-styles.

Koxinga died suddenly in 1683, at the age of 38, only a year after his conquest of Taiwan. Centuries later, he was named a national hero and is venerated in Taiwan as a *chuntzu*, perfect man.

Koxinga's son and grandson maintained rule over Taiwan until 1684, when the Manchu finally succeeded in imposing sovereignty over the island, snuffing out the last pocket of Ming patriotism. Taiwan officially became an integral part of the Chinese empire, when the Qing court conferred the status of *fu*, or prefecture, on the island. But Qing rule remained nominal at best. The Manchu magistrates sent to govern Taiwan usually succumbed to intrigues and self-indulgent decadence.

Left, porcelain jar, Qing dynasty, in the National Palace Museum, Taipei. Right, portrait of Taiwan's first Chinese ruler, Koxinga, painted by one of his descendants.

老光手畧

為憑

惠

甘

阿比手畧

為憑

惠

甘

差兄 阿比如妹等緣我蕃自歸化以來既沐 皇上之休風效不效張家九世同居以慕先代之遺風我覺無如各

立分管公議將先父遺下水田財物家器等件定作參房均分配搭均平當塲招閭為定各掌各業不得

分管日後世代蕃日富有萬金保各房之造化亦無憑草立有憑合仝立閭分約字壹樣參紙各蔵各分各執

分圖字叁紙是定再照了

一段入葺葺卜埔土坤東西四至界填愼各面踏分明留為公葉逐年按方輪當合應批照

一段土在武军庄界内其東西四至界址同公親塲見到地面踏分明水為阿比應得之業各房

一段土在武军庄界内其東西四至界址同公親塲見到地面踏分明該業永為老吻應

一段址在武军庄界内其東西四至界址同公親塲見到地面踏分明該業永為差兄應得之

一越界混爭合應批照了

一不得越界混爭合應批照了

歲拾壹月

立閭分約字武军社蕃婦

老吻

差兄

启終���

日仝立閭分約字武军社蕃婦 阿比

老吻

公親 武礼沙簡

建 打万

知見 打那美打其万加觧

本社土目武礼亀刘

本社土目九仔邑列

在塲佳孫

宠吹

板搖

菅社人上仝合癸

代書人李 元吉

保

Despite strict prohibitions from the imperial court against further emigration to Taiwan, colonists continued to pour across the strait from the mainland. During the first 150 years of Manchu rule, the island's population increased seven-fold. Karl Gutzlaff, a Prussian missionary visiting Taiwan in 1831, observed: "The island has flourished greatly since it has been in the possession of the Chinese. The rapidity with which this island has been colonized, and the advantages it affords for the colonists to throw off their

crews from Taiwan, and dealt directly with the islanders rather than with Beijing.

One of the first foreigners to recognize Taiwan's economic potential, and to advocate the island's outright annexation, was Dr. William Jardine, cofounder of the powerful British trading firm Jardine, Matheson, and Company. Jardine was alarmed when China took up arms in 1839 to suppress the British opium trade in Guangzhou (Canton). He informed the British foreign secretary that "we must proceed to take possession of

allegiance, have induced the Chinese to adopt strict measures… The colonists are wealthy and unruly…"

One early point of contention between China and the West concerned the fate of shipwrecked European sailors washed ashore on Taiwan. These involuntary visitors were routinely beaten, imprisoned and often beheaded, either by the Chinese authorities or by aboriginals. Whenever the Western powers sued the court of Beijing to intervene in such incidents, they discovered that Beijing had little real authority over island affairs, and even less interest. So Western nations resorted to gunboat diplomacy to rescue their

three or four islands, say Formosa, Quemoy and Amoy (Xiamen), in order to secure new markets and new footholds in China."

When the first conflict, or Opium War, broke out between China and Britain, it further antagonized the strained relations between China and the West. Crews of British vessels subsequently shipwrecked off the coast of Taiwan met with even harsher treatment. The ships were plundered, then burned. The crews were stripped naked and forced to walk painful distances to captivity.

The British were not the only foreign power to show an interest in Taiwan during the nineteenth century. Several American traders and diplomats also advocated annexation of the island. They included Commodore Matthew Perry, who understood Taiwan's strategic importance in East Asia. Gideon Nye, a wealthy American merchant and a leading member of his country's expatriate community in Guangzhou, proposed in 1857 that "Formosa's eastern shores and southern point… in the direct route of commerce between China and California and Japan, and between Shanghai and Canton, should be protected by the United States of (Kaohsiung) in the south. During the ensuing decade, foreign trade in Taiwan grew rapidly, involving British and American firms. Primary export products included camphor, tea, rice, sugar, lumber and coal. The sole import, which sometimes exceeded exports in value, continued to be opium.

By 1867, 25 foreign traders lived in northern Taiwan at Tanshui and Keelung, and another dozen lived in the south at Tainan. Trade boomed, doubling in volume by 1869 and doubling again by 1870. Colorful expa-

America." Nye also had personal reasons for his proposal: he suspected that his brother, who mysteriously disappeared on the opium clipper *Kelpie* in 1849, had been captured and killed in Taiwan.

The treaty ending the first Opium War, in 1858, opened four Taiwanese ports to foreign trade: Keelung and Suao in the north, and Taiwanfoo (Tainan) and Takao

Preceding pages: a tribal member used his handprints to transfer property to new Chinese settlers, Tungshih, 1866. **Left,** Chinese rendering of Dutch fort on Taiwan. **Above,** British negotiated opening China's ports to trade.

triate communities flourished around Taiwan's ports. They maintained close ties with their counterparts in Hong Kong, Guangzhou and Xiamen.

A negative aspect of the trade boom was the increased frequency of violent incidents, corresponding to the greater number of foreign trading vessels that called at the island's ports. Brawls between drunken foreign merchants and the local Chinese usually ignited the violence. Vendettas followed. Local magistrates refused to act in such cases, insisting that the foreigners petition authorities in Beijing. But because of Beijing's lack of influence and interest in the island's affairs, nothing was accomplished through such "legal channels". The situation was further aggravated by the arrival of foreign missionaries, in the early 1870s.

Zealous missionaries from the various sects of Christianity fanned out over the island and staked out exclusive territorial domains, which created more confusion than the tenets of their conflicting religious doctrines. The missionaries, backed by their home countries, competed for exclusive territories in much the way traders competed for monopolies of major exports.

Periodic attacks on foreign missionaries and their Chinese converts led to the same futile wrangling between local magistrates rest were slaughtered by Botan aborigines. When the news of the killings reached Tokyo, Japan immediately prepared to launch a punitive expedition against the Botan tribe. Only Foreign Minister Soyeshima Taneomi held back the impending attack, deciding first to try to work out a diplomatic resolution in Beijing.

Soyeshima was accompanied by Charles Le Gendre, an advisor to the planned military expedition to Taiwan, and who had earlier resigned as American consul to Xiamen (Amoy), in 1872, in order to enter the service of Japan's new Meiji emperor.

Le Gendre had extensive experience in the island, negotiating settlements involving sev-

and foreign officials, as did the incidents in the commercial sector. Only displays of force produced settlements.

Yet one thing was clear to all the squabbling parties: Taiwan was indeed an alluring beauty. It was rich in resources and strategically located, but it was also untamed. There was a need for law and order that Beijing could not provide. Expatriates clamored for foreign governments to step in. The Japanese did just that.

The Japanese: In 1872, a Japanese ship foundered and sank off the coast of Taiwan. Three of its crew drowned, but only 12 of the remaining crew eventually survived. The eral American ships wrecked there, in some cases dealing directly with ethnic minority tribes. But Washington always ignored Le Gendre's calls for greater American vigilance in Taiwan. Now he advised Tokyo it should prepare for war if its foreign minister's mission to Beijing failed.

Soyeshima managed to obtain a formal audience with the Chinese emperor, a significant accomplishment. The emperor tacitly admitted that the minorities inhabiting parts of eastern Taiwan were beyond his political control. All of Japan hailed that disclosure as a diplomatic victory, but Soyeshima's return to Tokyo was marred by factional fighting over the military's long postponement of intervention in neighboring Korea, another Chinese protectorate. The disgusted foreign minister wiped his hands of the Taiwanese affair; Le Gendre stepped in. A violent revolt of samurai protesting Meiji reforms in February 1874 impressed upon the Japanese government the urgent need for a foreign adventure to vent frustrations of dissatisfied – and now masterless – samurai. So on 27 April of that year, 2,500 troops, 1,000 coolies and several foreign advisors, led by Le Gendre, boarded warships bound for Taiwan.

The military expedition landed at two points in southern Taiwan, one clearly within

withdrew from Taiwan and returned to Tokyo in triumph.

China continued to run Taiwan as a prefecture of Fujian province for more than a decade after the departure of the Japanese. It was declared the 22nd province of China in 1886. The population surpassed 2.5 million.

But the repercussions of the Japanese occupation continued to resound through Taiwan. For one thing, Japan's bold military move, for the first time in the island's history, had created a semblance of law and order on the island.

In fact, some foreign traders even seemed to welcome the Japanese occupation of 1874, as it forced Chinese authorities to take greater

Chinese jurisdiction. Japanese troops made a few forays into the mountains to punish the offending tribal groups.

But their continued presence in the south prompted strong Chinese protests and a willingness to negotiate. After protracted talks in Beijing, the Chinese government agreed to pay Japan to compensate the families of the dead crewmen, and four times as much additionally for the expenses incurred by the military expedition. In return, Japanese forces

Left, Qing emperor receives a foreign envoy in Beijing. **Above**, civil war on the mainland was convoluted, involving men from all backgrounds.

interest in the island's affairs and virtually eliminated attacks on its foreign settlements. Meanwhile, militarists back in Tokyo soon began rattling their swords and demanding outright annexation of Taiwan, Korea and the Ryukyu Islands (Okinawa).

Full-scale war between Japan and China again broke out in 1895, when the Japanese invaded Korea, long a loyal Chinese ally. China sent battleships to Korea's aid, but the Japanese sunk them in a blatant effort to fuel hostilities. Earlier, China had managed to buy off Japan to avert war, but, this time, nothing short of territorial gains would satisfy Japan's burning desire for an overseas empire. In the 1895 war, China suffered total and ignoble defeat at the hands of a nation it had considered inferior and barbaric. China's navy had been a mockery in the war. Not long before, vast sums of money that had been earmarked for modernizing China's navy had, in fact, been diverted by the Empress Dowager Cixi to restore the Summer Palace, north of Beijing. The out-gunned, humiliated and decimated Chinese navy was annihilated by Japan.

The Treaty of Shimonoseki, written by Japan, ceded Chinese possession of both the Ryukyu Islands and Taiwan to Japan. It marked the start of half a century of Japanese rule over Taiwan, and over much of North

Asia, giving Japan a decisive role in Korea that would culminate in annexation 15 years later, following the Russian-Japanese War.

Japan's takeover of Taiwan did not go down well with some locals, who resisted for several months; over 7,000 Chinese soldiers and several thousand civilians were killed during early resistance. (Later, in 1915, around 10,000 Chinese lost their lives during the Tapani revolt against the Japanese, but again without any success.)

The Japanese undertook an intensive modernization of Taiwan's infrastructure. A domestic network of railways and roads was constructed, linking major points of the is-

land for the first time. The Japanese also built schools, hospitals and industries and updated agricultural methods. Most importantly, strict Japanese rule ended the factional bickering and futile debates that had always marked island politics and commerce. Still, occupation proved oppressive and ultimately unpopular.

Between 1918 and 1937, Japan consolidated its regime in Taiwan, exploiting Taiwan's rich natural resources exclusively for the benefit of Japan.

Resident Japanese officers and magistrates enjoyed elite privileges denied to local citizens, not unlike that of the European colonial powers in nineteenth-century China. In the last stage of occupation, the naturalization of all Taiwanese as Japanese was forced. As was done in occupied Korea, the Japanese required everyone to adopt Japanese names and speak the Japanese language. In effect, Japan tried to remold Taiwan in its own image by forcing Taiwan to sever its ancient Chinese cultural roots. But, as in Korea, such cultural brutality would fail.

Taiwan toiled under Japanese occupation until Japan's defeat in World War II. After Japan surrendered, Taiwan was restored to Chinese sovereignty on 25 October 1945, an event still celebrated annually on the island as Restoration Day.

Following Taiwan's return to Chinese sovereignty, hordes of adventurers from mainland China stormed across the Taiwan Strait, systematically dismantling the extensive industrial infrastructure left by Japan and shipping items of value back to Shanghai for sale.

Meanwhile, civil war had broken out on the mainland. The struggle for control of the vast country matched the Communist Party of Mao Zedong and Zhou Enlai against the Nationalist Party, or Kuomintang (KMT). At the head of the KMT was a fiery leader named Chiang Kaishek. The struggle for control of the mainland had preceded World War II for decades, but both sides had reluctantly joined efforts to defeat the Japanese. With both the Japanese and the earlier colonial powers gone, China had the opportunity to set its own course.

Left, Empress Dowager Cixi, whose misuse of funds caused China's naval defeat against Japan. **Right**, Chiang Kaishek (standing) with his mentor, Dr. Sun Yatsen, 1924.

民國十一年

德國將校大尉楷里格將

清敵孫傳芳謀刺孫大元

民國十年中華革命成功大元帥攝於蘇中

敬呈孫大元帥

春光以留紀念

中華民國二十五年秋月

Chiang Kaishek's association with Taiwan bears striking similarities to the saga of Koxinga centuries earlier. Both men fought to preserve the traditional order in China, and both established a bastion of that order in Taiwan, in defiance of their adversaries on the mainland.

Most significantly, both men successfully launched a renaissance of classical Chinese culture, which has made Taiwan a living repository of China's most ancient and cherished traditions.

Chiang participated in Sun's revolutionary forays into China, completing his military studies in 1912. That same year, Dr. Sun Yatsen became the first provisional president of the Republic of China, when Puyi abdicated as emperor, ending the Qing dynasty and closing the history books on China's 50 centuries of imperial rule. Chiang returned to China shortly after his second son, Chiang Wei-kuo, was born.

Two episodes left permanent imprints on the character of young Chiang after his re-

Chiang Kaishek was born on 31 October 1887, in Zhejiang province. His mother was a devout Buddhist; his father, a salt merchant, died when Chiang was only eight. Then when he was at the tender age of 14, Chiang's mother arranged for him to marry Mao Fu-mei. In 1908, she gave birth to Chiang's first son, Chiang Ching-kuo. At the same time, the Chinese imperial system was disintegrating. Nationalism became the dominant force, and revolution was in the air. Caught up in the rapidly-changing swirl of events, young Chiang took up military studies, in Japan, ironically. It was there that he first met a revolutionary, Sun Yatsen.

turn. For 10 years, he had resided in Shanghai, where he socialized with wealthy merchants and bankers of that city of commerce. Those contacts helped him to forge a political power base that would carry Chiang through two decades of warfare, and also provide him the backbone for Kuomintang successes on Taiwan. He loved Shanghai; Taipei was largely built in its image. The second influential episode occurred in 1923, when Sun Yatsen sent Chiang to Moscow as his emissary. Chiang returned with a deep distrust of the Russians and Communism.

Chiang Kaishek could be labeled a conservative revolutionary. His concept of changing China was to foster nationalism and end China's humiliation at the hands of foreign powers. But his vision of a modern China remained grounded in traditional Confucian social values. A born-and-bred Confucian, he cherished values like loyalty and obedience. He believed that the rebirth rather than the destruction of traditional culture was the answer to China's woes.

After the successful Northern Expedition against the warlords who had partitioned China into personal fiefdoms, Chiang rode

to Christianity. His new wife and his conversion were important influences during the remainder of his life.

The story of Chiang Kaishek's campaigns against the Chinese Communists, and his war against the invading Japanese, is well documented. The Japanese occupied Manchuria in 1932. In 1937, they took Tianjin and Beijing, captured Chiang's beloved Shanghai, and then overran Nanjing, at that time the capital of China. Their advance was bolstered by bombing raids conducted from

into Shanghai to consolidate his power. In 1927, Soong Mei-ling became his second wife. She was the daughter of Shanghai's most powerful banking family, and younger sister of Sun Yatsen's widow. (Dr. Sun had died in Beijing, at the age of 59.) Madame Chiang, as she became known in the West, was an American-educated Christian. Prior to their marriage, Chiang Kaishek converted

Japanese airfields in Taiwan. In 1943, the Generalissimo, as Chiang came to be called, met with American president Franklin Roosevelt and Britain's prime minister, Winston Churchill, in Cairo. The trio pledged the return of Manchuria and Taiwan to China after the war.

Japan surrendered in 1945, but Chiang's problems continued. The Communists seized the opportunity of postwar chaos – and quantities of abandoned Japanese arms – to turn against Chiang's Nationalist army. Civil war raged across the vast Chinese landscape for four long years. His administration was plagued by corruption and incompetence,

Preceding pages: statue of Chiang Kaishek overlooking Sun Moon Lake. **Far left**, Chiang in 1930. **Left**, Dr. Sun Yatsen. **Above**, Lukang in 1934. The Japanese tried to eliminate Taiwan's Chinese identity.

but Chiang himself was as uncorruptible as the severest Confucian. Nor was Chiang insensitive to the sufferings of his people. While on his habitual stroll one afternoon in the summer of 1944, he stumbled upon an officer leading a row of recruits through the woods, roped together like animals. Infuriated, Chiang beat the officer. Only the intervention of an aide prevented Chiang from killing the man outright. The following spring, after continued reports of the roping practice, Chiang had the general in charge of recruit conscription summarily executed.

Chiang Kaishek was elected president of the Republic of China in 1948. But by then, the war was swinging in favor of the Communists as they took Tianjin and Beijing. On 21 January 1949, Chiang Kaishek resigned from the presidency.

Retreat: After nearly a year of self-imposed solitude, in December 1949 he returned to lead an exodus of Nationalist soldiers and a rambling entourage of merchants, monks and masters of classical arts across the Taiwan Strait to Taiwan. Still calling his retreating government the Republic of China, Chiang's army defeated pursuing Communists in a last-stand battle on Quemoy, holding that island ever since.

Chastened by defeat on the mainland, Chiang was determined to reform Kuomin-

tang policies on Taiwan. One of his first acts was to execute the rapacious governor-general, responsible for the looting of Taiwan's wealth and the bullying of its people since 1945. Next, Chiang initiated a land-reform policy, as sweeping as the one instituted by the Communists on the mainland, but with one vital difference. Instead of vilifying and killing landlords, the Kuomintang government paid them for their land, then offered them matching funds and tax breaks. That move helped launch the industrial revolution that would become the catalyst for the island's phenomenal economic growth. Overnight, Taiwan found itself with an entrepreneurial elite of former landlords, who now had the

money and the motivation to invest in Taiwan's future. Other reforms followed. The educational system was overhauled and students were sent abroad to absorb new technology and training.

Although national affairs remained firmly in the hands of the Kuomintang, democratic institutions were established at local levels.

Chiang governed the island according to Sun Yatsen's Three Principles of the People, *Sanminchui*. Revered today in both Communist China and Taiwan, Dr. Sun built his framework for sensible government on three points: *mintsu*, nationalism, or the liberation of China from foreigners; *minchuan*, democracy; and *minsheng*, livelihood, or economic security for people. Of the three principles, Dr. Sun considered nationalism the primary goal, and that the fastest way of obtaining that goal was through a democratic system that provided for the livelihood of the people. Chiang amplified on his interpretations of the Three Principles in his book, *China's Destiny*, published in 1943.

With the outbreak of the Korean War in 1950, Taiwan was placed under the American protective umbrella from possible Communist attacks, and received substantial economic aid, too. In 1955, the United States and Taiwan ratified the Sino-American Mutual Defense Treaty.

The year 1965 proved a critical test of strength for Taiwan and its leadership. Financial aid from the United States, which had provided a springboard for economic development, was terminated. Nevertheless, industrialization, modernization and economic progress accelerated.

Chiang's last years: Throughout his later life, Chiang Kaishek maintained an austere personal life-style. He never smoked, drank or gambled. While at home, he favored the long gowns and Mandarin collars of traditional Chinese scholars. His only indulgences were long walks in the mountains.

Chiang kept a diary that was as colorful as his island republic. But the diary also re-

Chiang Kaishek continued to maintain strict political discipline and social order, but he gave entrepreneurs free reign in the economic sphere. Enthusiasm for capitalism propelled the private sector from less than 50 percent of Taiwan's economy in 1953 to 75 percent in 1974, at the expense of state monopolies. At the same time, the island's population doubled to 16 million people.

Left, Chiang Kaishek and his wife at Cairo Conference, 1934, with Franklin Roosevelt and Winston Churchill. **Above**, Chiang broadcasts the news of his Nationalist government's retreat to Taiwan, 1949.

flected a humble man acutely aware of both his own shortcomings and his responsibilities, in sharp contrast to his portrayal in the Western press as an arrogant, stubborn man. His last testament, in 1975, one week before his death, reveals his concern:

"Just at the time when we are getting stronger, my colleagues and countrymen, you should not forget our sorrow and our hope because of my death. My spirit will always be with my colleagues and countrymen to fulfill the three people's principles, to recover the mainland, and to restore our national culture."

Chiang died shortly after midnight, on 5

April. He was succeeded by the vice-president, Yen Chia-kan. In the next presidential elections the following year, Chiang Kaishek's son, Chiang Ching-kuo, was elected president.

In 1971, a few years before Chiang's death, the Republic of China – Taiwan – a founding member of the United Nations, lost its membership in the organization and was replaced by the People's Republic. In 1978, the United States announced the recognition of the People's Republic of China, and ceased official diplomatic relations with Taiwan.

Chiang Ching-kuo died in 1988. His successor as interim-president was Lee Teng-hui. The National Assembly officially elected

Lee Teng-hui as president in 1990; he was the island's first Taiwanese-born president.

Despite political setbacks, Taiwan continued to thrive and survive. Its gross national product grew steadily by maintaining foreign trade through cultural contacts and trade associations, a remarkable achievement in the wake of diplomatic ostracism.

Lee reinstated parts of the constitution placed in abeyance decades before, amended certain articles and added other new articles. Perhaps most important was the free election of the second National Assembly, which assumed office in 1992. (One the new articles added to the constitution was that the president and vice-president of the Republic of China "will be directly elected by the entire voting population in the Taiwan area".)

Tension rises: The first official governmental contacts between Taipei and Beijing took place in 1993, in Singapore, and several agreements were signed. But Beijing postponed indefinitely the second set of talks, which it had been scheduled to host in 1995. The uneasy truce fell apart in 1996, when Taiwan held its first totally democratic elections for the presidency. Beijing held military maneuvers intended to shake the confidence of Taiwan's voters; these included launching three ballistic missiles into the sea near the important ports of Keelung and Kaohsiung, threatening vital trade routes. The provocative action caused the United States to despatch two aircraft carriers to the Taiwan Strait.

The threats didn't work, and the Taiwanese voted in their first popularly-elected president, 73-year-old Lee Teng-hui (branded as a "sweet-talking chameleon" by the Beijing government) with 54 percent of the ballots cast. A candidate favoring independence for the island came second.

Taiwan's status remains the explosive issue. Officially, Beijing considers the island a misbehaving province, whilst Taiwan has never officially declared independence from the mainland, claiming instead that it is the legitimate government of all China. But Beijing made it clear that, it Taiwan were to declare itself an independent nation, the mainland would not hesitate to use force against it.

Since the late 1980s, despite the posturing on both sides, there have been openings between the two. Residents of Taiwan are allowed to visit relatives on the mainland. Taiwanese businesses have invested US$20 billion on the mainland, mostly in the south – from where many Taiwanese originally came, and Taiwan is now the second-largest investor in mainland China.

But the uncertainties remain. When the American president, Bill Clinton, made a high-profile visit to China in 1998, the pundits were once again assessing what this meant for the future security of Taiwan.

<u>Left</u>, girls on parade with Sun Yatsen posters during Double Ten festivities. <u>Right</u>, changing of the guard, National Revolutionary Martyrs' Shrine, Taipei.

The island of Taiwan straddles the Tropic of Cancer, separated from the mainland Chinese province of Fujian by the Taiwan Strait, 160 kilometers (100 mi) wide at its narrowest point. Taiwan lies 355 kilometers (220 mi) north of the Philippines, and 595 kilometers (370 mi) southwest of Japan's Okinawa.

Taiwan is shaped somewhat like a tobacco leaf, with its tip pointing toward Japan. It stretches 390 kilometers (250 mi) in length and is about 140 kilometers (90 mi) wide at its broadest point. Its total area of nearly

36,000 square kilometers (14,000 sq. mi) makes Taiwan about the size of Holland. Also controlled by Taipei are the Penghu archipelago, or Pescadores, lying midway between the mainland and Taiwan, and the islands of Kinmen (Quemoy) and Matsu, with Kinmen only 2,310 meters (about 1.5 mi) from the mainland.

The central core of Taiwan is a range of forest-fringed mountains – hard rock formations forged from ancient centuries of volcanic activity. The range bisects the island from north to south, covers two-thirds of the island, and is almost impenetrable because of its extreme ruggedness. More than 200 of the island's peaks rise 3,000 meters (10,000 ft) or more in altitude. Taiwan's tallest peak is Yu Shan (Mount Jade), at 3,952 meters (12,966 ft). Heavy rainfall has deeply scarred its face with gorges and valleys.

A narrow valley of rich alluvial soil, 160 kilometers (100 mi) long, separates the middle bulge of mountains from a smaller crest that fronts the east coast. Its cliffs drop sharply to the sea, forming the island's most spectacular scenery. The Central Cross-Island Highway dramatically slices its way through the central range to these east-coast escarpments.

Primeval volcanoes pushed the island up from under the sea, witnessed by coral from prehistoric seabeds that has lodged in igneous rock formations, up to 610 meters (2,000 ft) high in the foothills. While such fiery activity ended eons ago, bubbling pools of hot sulfurous water and hissing steam vents still punctuate the terrain.

The broad, sea-level plains that spread across the western portion of Taiwan give it a decided tilt away from the cliffs that wall the eastern shores. Short, winding rivers bring rain water and alluvium from the mountains to the west, making the plains extremely fertile. Taiwan boasts more agriculturally useful and level land than all the myriad islands of the Philippines and Japan. Most of the island's population lives on the western plains.

Climate: Taiwan's weather is subject to sudden change. The climate is as diverse as the landscape – semi-tropical in the north and at mountain altitudes, with a touch of snow, and totally tropical in the south's flat lands.

There are two distinct seasons: hot (May through October) and cool (November through March). Unfortunately, the island's excessive humidity exaggerates these seasonal changes. During the summer, with average temperatures in the north of 35°C (95°F) and humidity seldom dropping below 75 percent, the entire island seems a giant sauna. Likewise, winter temperatures usually do not fall below 5°C (40°F), but the dampness can chill the bones.

The most pleasant times of the year are the brief spells of spring and fall, during April and May, and October and November. Skies are generally clear, nights are cool and days moderate. But at any time of year, Taiwan's weather may change dramatically. High and low temperatures can vary as much as 10°C (15°F) from one day to the next.

Nature wrings an average annual rainfall of more than 1,000 millimeters (40 in) from the cloak of humidity that hangs over Taiwan. In higher elevations, the average rainfall can be five times as much. The northeast winter monsoon and the southwest summer monsoon provide the moisture. The north-

through the Philippines and storm northwards toward Japan – usually via Taiwan.

The season lasts from mid August until early October. During that time, no less than a half-dozen typhoons may cross or skirt Taiwan annually. At three- to four-year intervals, a typhoon of major proportion crashes into Taiwan, with wind speeds of 160 kilometers (100 mi) per hour or more. Such storms can capsize enormous ships, flood low-lying cities, trigger massive landslides, uproot trees and blow down dwellings.

east monsoon moves in from late October to late March, causing rain in the windward reaches of northeast Taiwan. The southwest monsoon takes its turn from early May until late September, causing wet weather in the south while the north enjoys drier spells.

The most feared aberrations in Taiwan's moody weather are typhoons. *Chufeng*, as the Chinese call them, are also known as the "supreme winds". They swell up in the Indonesian archipelago to the south, then sweep

One of the worst typhoons to hit Taiwan occurred in August 1911. Barometric pressure at the southern part city of Kaohsiung fell below 28 inches, reportedly the lowest reading ever recorded in Taiwan. Winds of 250 kilometers (150 mi) per hour battered the island. In 1968, a typhoon drowned downtown Taipei in four meters (13 ft) of water and made rowboats the only transportation.

Visitors caught in Taiwan during a typhoon need not panic, however. Taiwan's new steel-and-concrete structures and modern hotels are generally immune to serious damage. It's safe to watch from the windows, but risky to walk the streets.

Preceding pages: above Sun Moon Lake. **Left,** Taroko Gorge. **Above,** flooded rice paddy, central foothills of Taiwan.

THE LEGACY OF CONFUCIUS

When friends visit from afar,
Is this not indeed a pleasure?

– Confucius

For more than 2,000 years, Chinese scholars aspiring to government office were required to memorize *The Analects,* or *Lunyu,* the most hallowed of all classics attributed to Confucius. Today, copywriters with Taiwan's tourism bureau often borrow the opening lines of the *Lunyu,* for obvious reasons. The fact that Confucius began his great work with such a disarmingly simple and welcoming maxim emphasized the importance the philosopher placed on friendship and social etiquette.

Confucius believed that true pleasure cannot be found in selfish, sensual abandon or in personal gain, but rather in generosity to friends and in social intercourse – and in social hierarchy. Thus, hospitality has been one of China's most consummate arts.

Confucius, known to the Chinese as Kong Fuzi, or Master Kong, was born in the kingdom of Lu, near modern Shandong and south of Beijing, in 551 BC. As a child, he demonstrated profound interest in ancient rites and rituals, and he often would dress up in formal robes to perform traditional ceremonies that had been all but discarded in his time.

People who knew Confucius admired him for his erudition and his sincerity, but because he lived in a time of internal chaos – the Warring States Period (476–221 BC) – few men of influence were willing to adopt his pacifist ideas.

Without a platform from which to address the masses, Confucius set out to peddle his ideas on his own.

He set forth from Lu while still a young man and traveled throughout the Chinese empire, taking his message of peace, friendship and reform to the various petty princes. Most received him with great interest and hospitality, but few showed intentions of changing their warring ways in deference to

Preceding pages: worshippers reflect Taiwan's Confucian traditions by conducting rites honoring the local god of agriculture. Portraits of Confucius (<u>left</u>) and Laozi (<u>right</u>).

his philosophy of social harmony. While traveling, Confucius also gathered and studied materials that revealed the secrets of the earlier golden ages of Chinese culture – the Xia, Shang and Zhou dynasties. One of the men who assisted him in that task was Lee Dan, known to posterity and philosophy as Laozi, the Old One.

Laozi was the founder of Daoism and composer of the beguiling doctrines of the *Daodejing (Tao Te Ching).* He was also in charge of the imperial archives of the Zhou

dynasty, which housed all the surviving documents detailing events from the twenty-third century BC up until his time. The records were preserved in archaic script on tiles, bamboo and tortoise shells. Laozi permitted Confucius to use the archives and copy as many records as he wished. The ancient documents formed the basis for his so-called Confucian classics.

"I never created or wrote anything original," Confucius claimed. Instead, he considered himself an interpreter and transmitter of the profound ideas and deeds of the ancient kings of China's golden age. Confucius admired numerous venerables from that time, and his own interests in these men won for them a continued following in China.

Although some modern scholars question the attribution of certain works to Confucius, he is generally credited with putting the documents of the imperial archives into a common, contemporary language, and with publishing them. The five classics of Confucianism, known as the *Wujing*, consist of the *I Ching* (Book of Changes), *Shijing* (Book of Poetry), *Shujing* (Book of History), *Liji* (Book of Properties) and *Chuzu* (Spring and Autumn Annals).

Later, lesser works published by Confucius or his disciples and believed to contain the original philosophies of the master were the *Great Learning, Doctrine of the Mean* and *Classic of Filial Piety*.

The *Lunyu* consists of a collection of the notes and journals of the master's conversations, teachings and journeys, told in some 496 chapters. Believed to have been compiled by the disciples of his school, it is often regarded as the basic "scripture" of Confucianism. Publication in itself was a bold move for Confucius. Never before in Chinese history had anyone but kings and ministers published books. But Confucius was a commoner, or at most, a member of an impoverished family of nobility. His years of writing and interpretation of hallowed doctrines were followed by 44 years of teaching, yet another revolutionary course. Before he arrived on the scene, only aristocrats and royalty received formal education. Confucius, however, welcomed to his school of thought anyone who demonstrated a keen intellect and a sincere desire to learn.

By the time of his death at the age of 72, some 3,000 students had been attracted to the teachings of Confucius. Around 70 disciples are believed to have carried on his work, further expounding upon his ideas during the period of great intellectual fervor known as the One Hundred Schools Period. Thousands of books were published, and tens of thousands of students educated, as a direct result of the example set by Confucius.

Among them was Mencius. Considered second only to Confucius among the great sages of ancient China, Mencius further advanced the concepts of his predecessor and reaffirmed basic Confucian principles, particularly the notion that government should be for the good of the people and not the ruler, and that human nature was basically good.

In 221 BC, the enlightened age of Confucius and Mencius was buried under the militant Qin, who swept down from the northwest. Led by founding emperor Qin Shi Huangdi, China was united for the first time under a bureaucratic government. But Qin Shi Huangdi was contemptuous of learning. "I conquered the empire from the saddle of a horse. What need have I for books?" he argued rhetorically.

Qin viewed the contending schools of philosophy as potential sources of sedition and a threat to his empire. He ordered the executions of hundreds of scholars, who were

often buried alive or sent to work on the Great Wall. He also ordered most books in China to be burned. Only tomes on agriculture, divination and medicine were spared from the infamous fires of Qin Shi Huangdi.

It is a testimony to the strength and endurance of Confucian doctrines that his works somehow survived the conflagration. Private editions of his works were secreted in walls and underground vaults. After the demise of the Qin dynasty, the subsequent Han dynasty collected the hidden works of Confucius during the second century BC, and declared the Confucian writings as the official canons of a new state philosophy.

Until Confucian studies were formally abandoned in 1905, the Confucian classics remained the most sacrosanct source of knowledge and moral authority for every ruler and bureaucrat of China.

Etiquette and people: Confucianism is far too complex to cover in detail here. But a few highlights reveal its wisdom. Confucius' most celebrated concepts were those of *li* and *ren*. Li has been translated by various scholars as rites, ceremonies, etiquette and propriety. Its combined implications underline all social behavior in the Chinese system, providing the appropriate behavior for every single situation a person may face in life. If li conflicts with the law, a superior man will

number two. Ren thus dictates social relations. It can be roughly interpreted in English by benevolence, kindness or human-heartedness. Confucius advised his followers: "Be strict with yourself, but be benevolent towards others."

He emphasized a blend of the virtues of self-discipline and generosity. If all humankind conducted itself according to the virtues of ren and li, all social behavior would become appropriate and benevolent, and the sources of friction among people would be eliminated. In his utopian prescription for humanity, Confucius promoted peace and social harmony.

Confucius established the Five Cardinal

not hesitate to follow the dictates of li. Such a concept has driven many of humankind's subsequent philosophical leaders, from Jesus to Gandhi. Li also incorporates the many formal rituals by which a person symbolically expresses propriety and confirms his commitment to them, like the sacrificial rites that honored deceased ancestors.

Even more important is the Confucian concept of ren. Its written form or character consists of the symbols for person and the

Left, Qin Shi Huangdi, who suppressed Confucianism. **Above**, aristocratic life during the Ming dynasty.

Relationships as a guide to the social behavior that would motivate followers to his utopia. These rules governed relations between subject and ruler, husband and wife, parent and child, elder sibling and younger sibling, and between friends. The last is the only social relationship of equality possible in a Confucian society. The rest demand the absolute obedience of inferior to superior.

Such common and continuing traits of Chinese society as authoritarian government, filial piety, patriarchal family structure, primogeniture and the importance of personal friendships – all still important within the social life of Taiwan today – can be traced to the Five Cardinal Relationships. Consider, for example, the case of a woman in Taiwan who gets divorced. The civil code of 1931 (revised in 1985) clearly favors men in divorce-related matters, a practice following Confucian rules for the patriarchal pattern of family structures. But in 1994, the courts ruled that articles of the civil code (which also gave men priority in regards to parental rights) violated the constitution. Such articles may be revised and rewritten soon.

Social order: Sun Yatsen was well aware of the influence of these teachings of Confucius. In the early twentieth century, he was concerned with developing a nationalistic spirit among the Chinese, to enable them to unite

is a reasonably accurate translation of the Confucian version. To "do unto others", as the West does, would be far too aggressive and presumptuous for the Confucian gentleman. The practice of actively performing good deeds is considered a form of social interference in Chinese society. Instead, the Chinese prefer simply to refrain from doing bad deeds.

Any individual who successfully followed the precepts of Confucian teaching could attain the goal of the master's philosophy – becoming the superior man. Confucius stressed that the superior man was not necessarily an aristocrat or powerful politician, but simply a person of virtue. He taught that

for the overthrow of the decadent Qing dynasty. "The Chinese people have shown the greatest loyalty to family and clan, with the result that, in China, there have been familyism and clan-ism but no real nationalism," Dr. Sun lamented. He believed that while loyalty to family and clan should be preserved, the traditional loyalty that a subject held for his emperor should be redirected to the best interests of the state in general.

Confucius also formulated a version of the universal Golden Rule. But like many things Chinese, it takes an opposite tack from the Western concept. "Do not do unto others what you would not have them do unto you"

anyone aspiring to become a gentleman must strive for virtue and cultivate it. Learning was the key to that process. "The superior man makes demands on himself; the inferior man makes demands on others," Confucius is said to have concluded.

In practice, this concept led to the system of appointing learned Confucian scholars to administrate China on behalf of the emperor, thus diminishing the role of hereditary princes and royal relatives. The system was later bolstered by civil-service examinations, which were open even to the humblest peasant. (Although, in fact, given the time and resources needed to prepare for the exams, only the aistocracy could take the years necessary for study.)

Rule by men of knowledge and virtue managed to hold the unwieldy empire together from the second century BC until the birth of the republican form of government, in 1912. The Confucian concept of the superior man also explains the respect that the Chinese have always had for those of scholarly accomplishment.

Practice over philosophy: Confucianism, as practiced by the Chinese, is not a religion in the strict sense of the word. Technically, it is not even a philosophy. It is a way of life with equal importance on theory and practice. Confucius himself rarely expounded on

The people of his day were extremely superstitious, spending an inordinate amount of time and energy on formal sacrifices that invoked myriad spirits. They practiced divination, prayed for rain, and pursued other quasi-religious activities.

When Confucius insisted that humanity's most pressing concerns lay in this life, religious matters receded and social issues moved to the forefront. Since Confucius' time, the Chinese have never felt the need for a single omnipotent god or an exclusive, all-embracing religion. They have simply referred to the powers above as "heaven", an impersonal and inscrutable force that drives the world and universe.

religious subjects, despite repeated inquiries from his disciples. "Not yet having understood life, how can we possibly understand death?" was his retort. Confucius did not deny the existence of gods and lesser spirits. He obviously felt that there was some universal force on the side of right. But he felt that people should steer away from spiritual concerns and concentrate on creating a harmonious society in this world.

Left, youth take part in a ritual ceremony honoring the birthday of Confucius. **Above**, children performing classical music at a festival honoring the sage.

Meanwhile, they have welcomed any and all religious faiths to their land – as long as they did not interfere with social or governmental concerns. Still, to be on the safe side, many Chinese continue to pay homage to a variety of gods. Although Confucianism is not generally considered a religion, temples to the great sage abound. September 28 has been designated Teachers' Day, a national holiday honoring Confucius. Elaborate ceremonies are held at Taiwan's many Confucian temples. Taiwan's other testament to Confucius is Kung Teh-cheng, a teacher of philosophy. Born in 1920, he is the 77th direct descendant of Confucius.

Contemporary influences: The most lasting of the legacies of Confucius has been the perseverance of the primacy of family and friends. This legacy persists in Taiwan, mainland China and far-flung Chinese communities throughout the world. Family and friends provide the individual with many of the social and economic services typically performed by courts, police, banks and lawyers in the West.

It is the family, not the individual, that has been the basic unit of social organization in China since the Zhou dynasty established the system of *bao-jia,* during the twelfth century BC. Society was divided into units of 10, 100, 1,000 and 10,000 families, ac-

tive responsibility for the behavior and welfare of each of its members. When a man, for example, became a high-ranking official in dynastic China, his whole family was honored with gifts and titles. But if he committed treason or other serious crimes, his whole family shared the punishment, whether it was death, mutilation or distant exile.

Today, the laws of the Republic of China hold families responsible for the welfare of their elderly. Reverence for parents is one of the highest virtues in Chinese ethical relations, and care for the elderly is a strong moral obligation.

A family loses face if its elderly members are forced to rely on government welfare

cording to neighborhoods and districts. Each unit chose a leader from its ranks who was responsible for the behavior and welfare of all the families under his jurisdiction. This leader reported directly to the one of the next highest bao-jia unit.

If someone committed a crime, the head of his own household would initially be held accountable, followed by the head of the 10-family unit, then the leader of the 100-family group and so on. Thus, minor crimes rarely were reported beyond the bao-jia organization. A twentieth-century version of the bao-jia system persists in rural Taiwan today.

Thus, the entire family commands collec-

payments or other handouts. Nevertheless, there is a broad range of services for people over 70 – from subsidized transportation and entertainment to free medical care and housing. For those without family to take care of them during the day – not unusual in urban Taipei – there are day-care centers throughout Taiwan, so the old folks have a place to spend their time.

Guan-hsi: In Chinese society, family comes first, state and occupation second. Close connections are maintained with all family members, even those who have moved halfway around the world. Such extended networks provide sources of warmth and comfort, as well as a secure form of social welfare and future business links.

One example of the significance of these ties is built right into the Chinese language. The Chinese have distinct words for elder brother *(geh-geh)*, younger brother *(di-di),* elder sister *(jie-jie)* and younger sister *(mei-mei).* There are different words for grandparents, cousins, uncles and aunts, depending upon their age and the side of the family that they represent. Talk to a Chinese person about your Aunt Sarah, and she or he will undoubtedly inquire whether she's *gu-ma,* your father's sister, or your mother's *ah-yi.*

Friends form the other half of the Chinese social equation. Every Chinese person has a

– *tung ren* – for people with whom you have something in common.

Westerners often view the cultivation of such connections as a discriminating form of cronyism, but the Chinese believe it is perfectly natural to perform favors for friends. Years of experience have taught the Chinese to trust personal friends and relatives to get things done, but they feel uneasy asking favors of strangers. Most of the time, favors are never requested unless owed, and are always repaid in kind.

The Chinese do not make friends easily. But when they do, the friendship lasts for life and is constantly reinforced by exchanges of gifts and favors. The betrayal of a per-

network of carefully cultivated friendships, his *guan-hsi,* or connections. Good guan-hsi in the right places often helps get things done on both sides of the Taiwan Strait. It can open doors and help cut through red tape in government offices. There is an expression for classmates, *tungsywe,* implying that two people attended the same school no matter how many years apart, and another expression for colleagues, *tungshih,* for people who work in the same office. There is even a term

Left, old men imitate art at Confucian temple in Lukang. **Above**, modern ritual: the daily morning flag-raising ceremony at Tainan's city hall.

sonal friend is regarded as a heinous social offense, which can have serious repercussions throughout the offender's network of guan-hsi. That network is only as strong as its weakest link, so each new relationship is given careful consideration.

Confucian-style relationships proliferate in the Chinese business world – and virtually prevent it from unraveling. The Chinese routinely select business associates from among established family members and family friends, unlike Westerners, who tend to choose their friends from among business associates or professional groups.

A Westerner who loses his or her job often

loses most friends as well – until a new position is found with new acquaintances. A Chinese who loses a job or goes bankrupt has family and friends to help obtain new employment or build a new business. Afterwards, he or she continues to deal almost exclusively with the same group of people, rather than with new associates.

Likewise, a Chinese businessperson can invoke the social pressures of a guan-hsi network whenever an associate defaults on payments or contracts. That practice eliminates the need for expensive, protracted court actions that can exhaust participants and clog the legal system. Courts of law are also influenced by the Confucian ethics of Chi-

nese societies. Since the creation of the bao-jia system, people have been encouraged to settle personal disputes within their own families, neighborhoods and occupational groups, rather than impose their problems on the public. The court is always the last resort.

Indeed, by the time a case gets to the court, both parties are automatically considered guilty of failing to resolve their conflict according to the precepts of li. Judges, incensed by the imposition of private squabbles upon the public domain, have been known to render decisions not ideal for either party.

In any case, the Chinese believe that family and friends are in a much better position to understand a member's behavior and motivations than a court. And since the family holds collective responsibility for a member's misdeeds, it has motivation to resolve disputes quickly, to the full satisfaction of all parties involved. In the end, the family also avoids losing face by having its problems unveiled in public.

Not so perfect: Taiwan and Chinese communities overseas often appear to be paradigms of peace and lawfulness. In truth, they suffer their share of criminal activities.

The peaceful appearances are in part a result of the Chinese preference to settle matters among themselves, and to avoid police involvement and press coverage. Even cases of assault and involuntary manslaughter have been settled in Taiwan directly between families of the victim and the perpetrator, with the police acting as mediators and with the absence of court involvement. When the two families agree on the compensation for the victim's injuries or death, the case is considered closed.

Banks are another Western innovation frequently bypassed by the guan-hsi system. In Taiwan, most people participate in small private investment associations, called *biaohui*. A group of friends, relatives and colleagues pool their money to form a mutual fund, from which each member may take turns borrowing.

The borrower has access to large loans from the group depending upon need and the amount of money available in the pot. As with commercial banks or loan institutions, they must be repaid with interest. The Chinese rely on the personal closeness of the group to minimize fraud or default. Such private loans occasionally involve quite large sums of money.

Taiwan is among the most densely-populated places in the world. But had it even 50 times the land, the people would still live close to each other – *re nau*, they say, literally noisy warm. Similarly, they can become appalled at the enormous space requirements that a single foreigner may consume. Not only is it not frugal, but probably more importantly, it must be very lonely.

Modern evidence of Confucius' influence on the Chinese of Taiwan: morning foxtrots in Taipei (left) and a new family joins Taiwanese society (right).

RELIGION

The clatter of wooden divining blocks tossed upon stone floors punctuates murmured prayers. White wisps of fragrant smoke curl from hundreds of incense sticks, disappearing into the aged ceiling beams above. Under the tranquil gaze of ornate images, offerings of fresh fruit and cake adorn the altars. Children frolic while their mothers pray for another son. Old men in T-shirts smoke cigarettes and engage in animated conversation.

Traditional religion has flourished in Taiwan, despite the rapid development from a rural society into an industrialized complex of urban enclaves. Indeed, the temples of Taiwan are as much a feature of the skylines as are factories and office buildings.

Ancestor worship: The ancestor worship of the Chinese is based upon the assumption that a person has two souls. One of them is created at the time of conception, and when the person has died, the soul stays in the grave with the corpse and lives on the sacrificial offerings. As the corpse decomposes, the strength of the soul dwindles, until it eventually leads a shadow existence by the Yellow Springs in the underworld. However, it will return to earth as an ill-willed spirit and create damage if no more sacrifices are offered. The second soul only emerges at birth. During its heavenly voyage, it is threatened by evil forces, and is also dependent upon the sacrifices and prayers of the living descendants. If the sacrifices cease, then this soul, too, turns into an evil spirit. But if the descendants continue to make sacrificial offerings and look into the maintenance of graves, the soul of the deceased ancestor may offer them help and protection.

Inscriptions on oracle bones from the Shang dynasty (16–11th century BC) and inscriptions on bronze, dating from the Zhou period (11th century–221 BC), reveal that an ancestor worship of high nobility, a cult of a high god called *Di*, and an animistic belief in numerous gods of nature had existed early in Chinese history. Originally, ancestor wor-

ship had been exclusive to the king. Only later did peasants too begin to honor their ancestors. At first, people believed that the soul of the ancestor would search for a human substitute and create an abode for the soul during the sacrificial ritual. It was usually the grandson of the honored ancestor who took on the role of substitute. About 2,000 years ago, genealogical tables were introduced as homes for the soul during sacrificial acts. Up until that time, the king and noblemen had used human sacrifices for

ancestral worship. Even today, the Chinese worship their ancestors and offer the deities sacrifices of food. This is widely practiced, for example, during the Qingming Festival.

The original religion of the people actually focused on the worship of natural forces. Later, the people began to worship the Jade Emperor, a figure from Daoism who became the highest god in the popular religion after the fourteenth century. Kuanyin (Guanyin), the goddess of mercy, originated in Mahayana (Great Wheel) Buddhism. Among the many gods in popular Chinese religion, there were also earth deities. Every town worshipped its own unique god. Demons of illness, spirits of

Preceding pages: the classic lines of Tainan's Temple of the Holy Mother at Deer Ear Gate. **Left,** the altar of Matsu's main shrine at Deer Ear Gate. **Above,** a devotee prays.

the house, and even the god of latrines, had to be remembered. The deities of streams and rivers were considered to be particularly dangerous and unpredictable. Apart from Confucianism, Daoism and Buddhism, there was also a working-class religion known as Daoist Buddhism.

China had been divided into numerous small states. Only after the Qin dynasty had won over its rivals in 221 BC did the first emperor over a united China come to power. At the time, there were a number of schools of philosophical thought. Only Confucianism and Daoism gained wide acceptance.

Daoism: Central concepts of Daoism are the *dao*, which basically means way or path,

were opposed to feudal society, yet they did not fight actively for a new social structure, preferring instead to live in a pre-feudalistic tribal society.

Laozi, it is said, was born in a village in the province of Henan in 604 BC, the son of a distinguished family. For a time, he held the office of archivist in Luoyang, which was then the capital. But he later retreated into solitude and died in his village in 517. According to a famous legend, he wanted to leave China on a black ox when he foresaw the decline of the empire.

Experts today are still arguing about Laozi's historical existence. Since the second century AD, many legends have been told about

but it also has a second meaning of method and principle; the other concept is *wuwei*, which is sometimes simply defined as passivity, or "swimming with the stream". The concept of *de* (virtue) is closely linked to this, not in the sense of moral honesty, but as a virtue that manifests itself in daily life when dao is put into practice. The course of events in the world is determined by the forces *yang* and *yin*. The masculine, brightness, activity and heaven are considered to be yang forces; the feminine, weak, dark and passive elements are seen as yin forces.

Laozi was the founder of Daoism. He lived at a time of crises and upheavals. The Daoists

the figure of Laozi. One of them, for instance, says that he was conceived by a beam of light, and that his mother was pregnant with him for 72 years and then gave birth to him through her left armpit. His hair was white when he was born; he prolonged his life with magic.

The classic work of Daoism is the *Daodejing*. It now seems certain that this work was not written by a single author. The earliest, and also most significant, followers of Laozi were Liezi and Zhuangzi. Liezi (fifth century BC) was particularly concerned with the relativity of experiences, and he strived to comprehend the dao with the help of meditation. Zhuangzi (fourth century BC) is especially famous for his poetic allegories.

The ordinary people were not particularly attracted by the abstract concepts and metaphysical reflections of Daoism. Even at the beginning of the Han period (206 BC–AD 220), there were signs of both a popular and religious Daoism. As Buddhism also became more and more popular, it borrowed ideas from Daoism, and vice versa, to the point where one might speak of a fusion between the two.

The Daoists and Buddhists both believed that the great paradise was in the far west of China, hence the name, Western Paradise. It was believed to be governed by the queen mother of the West (Xiwangmu) and her husband, the royal count of the East (Dongwanggong). Without making any changes to it, the Daoists also took over the idea of hell from Buddhism.

Religious Daoism developed in various directions and into different schools. The ascetics retreated to the mountains and devoted all their time to meditation, or else they lived in monasteries. In the Daoist world, priests had important functions as medicine men and interpreters of oracles. They carried out exorcism and funeral rites, and read mass for the dead or for sacrificial offerings.

Historical and legendary figures were added to the Daoist pantheon. At the head were the Three Commendables. The highest of the three deities, the heavenly god, is identical to the Jade Emperor, worshipped by the common people. There is hardly a temple without Shouxinggong (the god of longevity), a friendly-looking old man with a long white beard and an extremely elongated, bald head. There are also the god of wealth (Caishen), the god of fire (Huoshen), the kitchen god (Zaoshen), the god of literature (Wendi), the god of medicine (Huatou) and others. Only the Eight Immortals are truly popular and well-known. Some of them are derived from historical personalities, some are fanciful figures. They are believed to have the ability to make themselves invisible, bring the dead back to life, and do other miraculous deeds.

Left, one of the ubiquitous old temples in the Penghu (Pescadores) Islands. **Above**, pig and pineapple meal for the spirits that roam during the Feast of the Hungry Ghosts.

Buddhism: The Chinese initially encountered Buddhism at the beginning of the first century, when merchants and monks came to China over the Silk Road.

The type of Buddhism that is prevalent in China today is the *Mahayana* (Great Wheel), which – as opposed to *Hinayana* (Small Wheel) – promises all creatures redemption through the so-called *bodhisattva* (redemption deities). There were two aspects that were particularly attractive to the Chinese: the teachings of *karma* provided a better explanation for individual misfortune, and there was a hopeful promise for existence after death. Nevertheless, there was considerable opposition to Buddhism, which con-

trasted sharply with Confucian ethics and ancestor worship.

At the time of the Three Kingdoms (AD 220–280), the religion spread in each of the three states. The trading towns along the Silk Road as far east as Luoyang became centers of the new religion. After tribes of foreign origin had founded states in the north, and the gentry from the north had sought refuge in the eastern Jin dynasty (317–420), Buddhism developed along very different lines in the north and south of China for about two centuries. During the rule of Emperor Wudi (502–549), rejection and hostility towards Buddhism spread among Confucians. And during the relatively short-lived northern Zhou dynasty (557–581), Buddhism was officially banned for three years.

Buddhism was most influential in Chinese history during the Tang dynasty (618–907). Several emperors officially supported the religion; the Tang empress Wu Zetian, in particular, surrounded herself with Buddhist advisors. During the years 842 to 845, however, Chinese Buddhists also experienced the most severe persecutions in their entire history: a total of 40,000 temples and monasteries were destroyed, and Buddhism was blamed for the economic decline and moral decay of the dynasty. In the course of time, 10 Chinese schools of Buddhism emerged,

eight of which were essentially philosophical ones that did not influence popular religion. Only two schools have remained influential through today: Chan (school of meditation or Zen Buddhism) and Pure Land (Amitabha-Buddhism). The masters of Chan considered meditation to be the only path to true knowledge.

Since the seventh century, the ascetic Bodhisattva has been a popular female figure in China. She is known as Kuanyin (Guanyin), a motherly goddess of mercy who represents a central and compassionate deity for the ordinary people. Kuanyin means "the one who listens to complaints".

In Chinese Buddhism, the centre of religious attention is the Sakyamuni Buddha, the founder of Buddhism who was forced into the background in the sixth century by the Maitreya Buddha (who was called Milefo in China, or redeemer of the world). In Chinese monasteries, Sakyamuni greets the faithful as a laughing Buddha in the entrance hall. Since the fourteenth century, the Amitabha school had dominated the life and culture of the Chinese people.

The most influential Buddhist school was the so-called School of Meditation (Chan in China, Zen in Japan), which developed under the Tang dynasty. It preached redemption through buddhahood, which anyone is able to reach. It despised knowledge gained from books or dogmas, as well as rites. Liberating shocks or guided meditation are used in order to lead disciples towards the experience of enlightenment. Other techniques used to achieve final insights were long hikes and physical work. The most important method was a dialogue with the master, who asked subtle and paradoxical questions, to which he expected equally paradoxical answers.

In 1949, the year the People's Republic of China was founded, there were approximately 500,000 Buddhist monks and nuns, and 50,000 temples and monasteries. A number of well-known Buddhist temples were classified as historical monuments.

By the beginning of the Cultural Revolution in 1966, it seemed as if the Red Guards were intent on completely eradicating Buddhism. The autonomous Tibet was hard-hit by these excesses. Only a few important monasteries and cultural objects could be protected, and completely or only partly preserved. Today, there are Buddhists among the Han Chinese, the Mongols, Tibetans, Manchus, Tu, Qiang and Dai (Hinayana Buddhists) peoples.

In the seventh century AD, another type of Buddhism, called Tantric Buddhism or Lamaism, was introduced into Tibet from India. With the influence of the monk Padmasambhava, it replaced the indigenous Bon religion, while at the same time taking over some of the elements of this naturalist religion. The monasteries in Tibet developed into centers of intellectual and worldly power, yet there were recurring arguments. Only the reformer Tsongkhapa (1357–1419) succeeded in rectifying chaotic conditions. He founded the sect of virtue (Gelugpa), which declared absolute celibacy to be a condition and reintroduced strict rules of order. Because the followers of this sect wear yellow caps, this order came to be known as Yellow Hat Buddhism.

Tsongkhapa had predicted to two of his disciples that they would be reborn as heads of the church. He had therewith anticipated the continuous transfer of powerful positions within the church – for instance, the position of the Dalai Lama and the Panchen Lama. The Dalai Lama represents the incarnation of the Bodhisattva of mercy (Avalokiteshvara), who is also worshipped as the

apart from the Buddhist deities, there are figures from the Brahman and Hindu world of gods and the old Bon religion. Magic, repetitive prayers, movements, formulae, symbols and sacrificial rituals are all means for achieving redemption.

Popular religion: Chinese folk religion is a blend of practices and beliefs that have developed out of animism, ancestor worship, Confucianism, Daoism, Buddhism and various folk beliefs. In Taiwan, these forms of worship are generally similar to those still practiced by Chinese elsewhere in Asia. But despite the common thread that runs through traditional beliefs and rituals, and the fact that the island is comparatively small with

patron god of Tibet. The Panchen Lama is higher in the hierarchy of the gods and is the embodiment of Buddha Amitabha. The present 14th Dalai Lama, who was enthroned in 1940, fled to India after an uprising in 1959 and has been living in exile since then. The Panchen Lama died in Beijing in January 1989, at the age of 50, after he came to an understanding with the Chinese authorities following the uprising.

In Lamaism, a complex pantheon exists;

Left, urns of ashes are marked by photographs of the dead in Taiwan. **Above**, a medium enters a trance during a temple puppet show, Taipei.

good communications, local practices in Taiwan differ considerably from region to region, even within a few kilometers from one another.

Although Taiwan has separate Buddhist, Daoist and Confucian temples, the common person blends the practices of all three with a measure of superstition and ancestor worship. To further confuse matters, peasant devotees refer to this religious blending by the umbrella term Buddhism, even as they regularly visit local folk-religion temples to worship heroes and deities unknown to Buddhism. Indeed, there is little concern for strict dogmatism in folk religion.

Most of the time, whether a temple is busy or not, incense is burned, and the reservoirs of the temple's oil lamps are constantly topped off to the tolling of a bell, providing devotees with a flame to light their paper offerings. Larger temples are almost always bustling with devotees presenting offerings of incense to the deities, or seeking advice through the use of divining blocks or sticks.

Religious solemnity is not a quality of temples, which are often retreats from the heat and where women and the elderly meet and chat with acquaintances, relax, or play cards. Some village temples even double as schools, stores and recreation centers.

Because the supernatural and human

worlds coexist in the popular folk religion of Taiwan, temples represent the place where the two worlds can meet and communicate, as folk-religion temples are the residences of the deities. The living devotees provide the resident deities with incense, oil and food offerings; in exchange, they receive advice and protection against demonic influences responsible for such earthly sorrows as plagues, disasters and illnesses.

Any number of requests might be put to a deity. Devotees may ask for something as minor as assistance for a child in passing a school examination, or as dire as a cure for a terminally-ill family member. An unem-

ployed man might ask for a job, a pregnant woman may request an easy delivery. These problems can be put to "specialists" such as the goddess of fertility, or to "general practitioners", who can hear any requests. Although devotees do not always leave the altar satisfied, most do feel renewed hope and comfort. Even Chinese who are skeptical about the gods' powers perfunctorily carry out rituals, just to stay on the safe side.

Temples: Taiwan's temples were originally built in the eighteenth and nineteenth centuries by craftsmen. They range in size from small shrines containing one or two images or tablets to large establishments with several main halls flanked by minor ones, each holding separate altars and murals. As a rule, a temple is named after the chief deity on the main altar. Even if the temple has a literary label or is home to a score of other gods, the locals still usually refer to it by the name of its principal deity.

Insight into Chinese folk religion can be gleaned from the architecture and decor of the temple buildings themselves. One important element is the temple roof, of ornate design and skilled craftsmanship. Indeed, temple roofs are alive with images of deities, immortals, legendary heroes and mythological animals, all of which serve to attract good fortune – and repel evil from the temple and surrounding community.

The center right of a temple usually is crowned with one of four symbols: a pagoda, which represents a staircase to heaven; a flaming pearl, which symbolizes the beneficial *yang* spirit; the sun, usually flanked by two dragons; a magic gourd, which is said to capture and trap evil spirits; or else the three Star Gods of Longevity, Wealth and Posterity. These roof symbols usually reflect the role of the temple's main deity. Often one of these symbols tops the main gate, while another crowns the main hall.

Below this central and symbolic image are the fantastic and often gaudy assortment of figures associated with Chinese temples. The eaves slope down, then rise again in sudden curves, with colorful dragons, phoenixes, fish and flowers flying from the tips. The phoenix, a mythical bird said to appear only in times of extreme peace and prosperity, and the dragon, symbol of strength, wisdom and good luck, are the two most auspicious symbols in Chinese mythology.

These exterior features are, at first glimpse, very much the same in Buddhist and folk-religion temples. Inside, however, the differences are obvious. Buddhist temples and monasteries, in general, contain few images, with one to three significant gilded Buddhas on a main altar. Confucian temples, severe by comparison, do not contain any images. (The image of Confucius can be found on one or two of the altars of a few folk-religion temples, however.)

Once drab with age and lack of maintenance, many of these old temples have been renovated in recent years. In some cases, their colorful new ornamentation has transformed them into exotic curiosities that may

painted on the outside faces of the main doors; these pairs can vary from ferocious generals to more benign-looking military and civil mandarins, or even young scholars.

Altars: The main altar of a typical folk-religion temple bears the image of its major deity, attended by images of aides, officials or servants. Fronting the principal deity is a smaller image of the same god; this miniature is taken from the temple occasionally to bless devotees as they stand in their home doorways, or is carried during festivals to other neighboring temples.

In addition to the main altar, most temples also have two secondary altars flanking the main one; in some larger temples, there are

appear garish to the Western eye. Modern folk-religion temples have also been built, especially in central and southern Taiwan. These are invariably large and costly buildings, with only one or two images.

The interior decoration of folk-religion temples varies considerably. Many of them contain fascinating murals depicting scenes from Chinese mythology and history. Pillars and balustrades may be intricately-carved works of art. Most temples have guardians

Left, Lu Tungpin, the main deity on secondary altar, Chinan Temple. <u>Above</u>, carrying an image of Matsu, the sea goddess, Peikang.

further altars along the side walls. Beneath the main altar, at ground level, are two forms of small altar. One contains a tablet dedicated to the tutelary or protective spirit of the temple itself; the other contains stone or wooden "white tigers" – the bringers or destroyers of luck. A common offering for these tigers is a slab of fatty pork.

There are always five items on the table before a temple's main altar. A large incense pot is flanked by two decorative vases and two candlesticks. The incense pot itself is a primary religious object; in some temples, it is regarded as the most sacred. It is filled with ash accumulated by years of worship, and is the repository for the spirit of the venerated Jade Emperor. When a new temple is constructed, ash is taken from an existing temple and placed in the incense pot of the new temple. In some temples, the main incense pot is situated just to the outside of the main entrance; it is here that devotees begin their round of prayers and offerings. They place one or three sticks of incense in each pot throughout the temple, depending upon the seniority of the concerned deity.

Offerings: In addition to incense, offerings include food, drink, oil and objects made of paper. The type of food provided depends upon the season, the appetite of the particular deity, and the pocketbook of the devotee. Food is normally left at the temple only long enough for the deity to partake of its aroma, a period often defined as the length of time it takes for an incense stick to burn down. Afterwards, the food is taken home to the dinner table of the devotee and family. Leftovers not retrieved are later "disposed of" by the temple keepers. In some temples, only fruit and vegetables are offered to the gods. In season, boxes of mooncakes – baked pastries stuffed with sweet bean paste – are placed on temple altars. Bowls of cold, cooked rice are often left before minor deities, including underworld gods. Tea or wine, in rows of three or five small cups, is occasionally offered. Nothing is ever presented in groups of four, the number of death.

Another form of offering is paper money, tied in bundles and placed under the image or on the altar table. This so-called hell money represents either large sums of cash drawn on the Bank of the Underworld, or else lumps of fake gold or silver taels, the currency used in Chinese imperial times.

In addition to the gods, ancestors are also commonly at the receiving end of offerings and tokens of respect in temples. Traditionally, ancestral tablets were kept in family homes, and respects were paid at a living-room altar. These tablets bear the ancestors' names and photographs, and it is important that they be given regular offerings, lest they become hungry ghosts. Increasingly, however, families have paid temples to house the ancestral tablets on a special altar and assume the responsibility for offerings and prayers, especially if there is a possibility of neglect at home.

According to traditional thinking, upon death a soul is hastened through the various courts and punishments of purgatory in order to be reborn again. Also, there is the belief that the underworld is remarkably similar to the human world, and that its inhabitants require food, money, clothes and a house. Thus, when someone dies, relatives do their best to see that the spirit of the deceased enters the underworld in comfort. Food offerings give symbolic sustenance, and hell money and paper artifacts represent houses, cars, clothes and often servants. These substitutes are transported to the underworld by burning. The practice serves the same function as making offerings to ancestral tablets, and failure to care for the spirit of a deceased family member sets another hungry ghost loose in the world.

Once every year, for 15 days in the seventh lunar month (in August or September), the needs of these ghosts are met in the Festival of the Hungry Ghosts.

At this time, hungry souls are released from the underworld to roam the human world in search of sustenance. Families take steps to propitiate these spirits. Fearing the depravations this rampaging band of ghosts might inflict, they burn paper money and leave food on the edges of streets just outside their homes.

Most towns also hold a large parade during this time, with images of the local tutelary god and his two generals carried around the streets, on patrol to monitor the ghosts' behavior. At the end of the 15-day festival, local temples hold banquets for the ghosts. Temporarily appeased and gratified, the spirits return to the underworld for another year.

Catalogue of deities: A huge pantheon of gods and goddesses fills traditional Chinese religion, and the origins and legends that surround these deities go deep into Chinese history. Most are the heroes and notables of Chinese myth, legend and history, deified either by imperial order or popular choice (in a fashion not unlike the saints of Christianity). Some of these deities are so well-known that their images are found in many or most temples; others are unique to a single temple. Some communities have cult followings, which developed around a particular historical figure believed to have protected or guided the town, or to have worked a miracle there.

Buddhist image on tapestry, Qing dynasty.

IMPORTANT DEITIES

Together, Daoism and Buddhism offer a rich pantheon of deities. The two deities most frequently seen on altars in Taiwan's temples are Kuanyin (in pinyin, Guanyin) and Kuan Kung. **Kuanyin**, regarded by the Chinese as the goddess of mercy, has evolved over the centuries from its prototype, Avalokitesvara, an Indian bodhisattva who foreswore nirvana in order to save mortals.

Kuanyin is a shortened form of a name that means One Who Sees and Hears the Cry From the Human World. Worshipped especially by women, this goddess comforts the troubled, the sick, the lost, the senile and the unfortunate.

Her popularity has grown such through the centuries that she is now also regarded as the protector of seafarers, farmers and travelers. She cares for souls in the underworld, and is invoked during post-burial rituals to free the soul of the deceased from the torments of purgatory.

No other figure in the Chinese pantheon appears in a greater variety of images. Kuanyin's standard image depicts her as a barefoot woman carrying a small upturned vase of holy dew. She may be seated on an elephant, standing on a fish, nursing a baby, holding a basket, having six arms or a thousand, and one head or eight, one atop the next. Her bare feet are the consistent quality. On public altars, Kuanyin is frequently flanked by two aides: a barefoot, shirtless youth

with his hands clasped in prayer, and a maid demurely holding her hands together inside her sleeves. Her principal feast occurs yearly on the nineteenth day of the second lunar month.

Kuan Kung is the second-most popular of deities in Taiwan. A historical soldier of the third century, he fought with two sworn companions to try to save a disintegrating dynasty. When captured by the enemy in 220, he refused an offer to defect and so was executed by decapitation, thus proving his loyalty. The heroes' courage has been chronicled in one of China's most famous novels, *Romance of the Three Kingdoms.*

Today, Kuan Kung is the patron deity of such disciplined groups as soldiers and the police, and of merchants and business people, but he is often incorrectly referred to as the god of war. In Buddhist temples, he is one of the two guardians on the main altar. Also known as Kuan Ti, his image is easily recognized by the severe puce or red face. Often he is accompanied by his two cohorts – Chou Tsang, a tall, black-faced sword bearer, and Kuan Ping, his scholarly adopted son. Kuan Kung may be standing or seated, astride a horse or holding his black beard in one hand and a book in the other. His festival is held on the thirteenth day of the fifth lunar month.

Another important deity in Taiwan, and China, is **Yu Huang Shang Ti**, the **Jade Emperor**. Also known as Tien Kung, he is the supreme deity of folk religion. His rule was traditionally conceived of as equal to that of the reigning emperor of China. His concern is meting out justice to men through his subordinate deities. He is ultimately responsible for the deification of other gods, or for their dismissal from the pantheon.

On the Jade Emperor's birthday (the ninth day of the first lunar month), special sacrifices of pork, chicken, duck and occasionally goat are placed before his image. Although the emperor himself is considered a vegetarian, he is believed to feast with meat-eating friends. The emperor is usually depicted with two servants who hold fans above his head. In a few temples, he is flanked by civil and military aides. Images of the Jade Emperor normally show him seated in imperial robes, his flat-topped crown notable for the short strings of pearls that dangle from the front. He holds a short, flat tablet in both hands before his chest. Historically, he did not come into prominence until the ninth century, considered late by Chinese historical standards.

San Kuan Ta Ti, or the Three Great Rulers, rule Heaven, Earth and the Waters, and are regarded as second only to the Jade Emperor in the pantheon's hierarchy (which bears important similarity to the imperial bureaucratic structure).

Devotees look at the San Kuan to deliver them from evil and calamity. Originally worshipped throughout China, they are the main deities at about 60 temples in Taiwan, especially in Taoyuan and Hsinchu districts. They are depicted as a trio of identical images who sit side-by-side on thrones – three bearded mandarins with scholar's bonnets, each holding a tablet.

Matsu, also known as Tien Shang Sheng Mu or Tien Hou, is an exceedingly popular figure throughout Taiwan. Legend claims that she was the daughter of a ninth-century Fujian fisherman, Lin. One day, her father and two brothers were caught in a typhoon at sea. The girl, asleep at home, left her body during a dream and appeared from out of the clouds above the boat. She grasped her two brothers with her hands and her father with her teeth. Unfortunately, back at home, the mother kept asking the body of the sleeping girl what was happening. In

Huang Cheng, the city god appointed by the Jade Emperor to protect a specific town and its inhabitants, is the final judge on what should be recorded in the report on each soul of those who die within his parish. He also acts as a link between humanity and the higher gods. In some locales, there may be two or even three city-god temples – one each for the city, the county and the prefecture. In some city-god temples, a large abacus is suspended from a ceiling or wall with an inscription: Beyond human calculations. In other words, man's life is ordained by fate.

Kai Tai Sheng Wang, the Saintly King Who Settled Taiwan, is better known to history as **Koxinga**, a real emperor who fled to Taiwan. His image is approached by devotees for advice and guidance. A festival honoring Koxinga is held on the sixteenth day of the first lunar month.

desperation, the daughter answered – in doing so, she lost her father. The daughter of Lin died at the early age of 20, and some believe she was deified by the emperor of China. She became the patron deity of sailors, evolving into a goddess to whom any problem could be put. Her image is usually that of a seated dowager wearing a flat-topped crown. She normally holds a scepter in her right arm or a tablet before her chest.

There are about 385 temples in Taiwan in which Matsu is the principal deity. Among the most important are those at Lukang and Tainan.

Left, wooden image of the Jade Emperor, Kaohsiung. Above, Kuan Kung peers through light reflections, Tainan.

Fu Te Cheng Shen, the Earth God, protects the community. In return, all births, deaths and marriages must be reported to this god. Among his responsibilities are controlling ghosts and protecting crops from pests and disease. He rarely has a temple to himself, but in rural areas often resides in a small roadside shrine.

Tsao Chun (**Zaoshen**), the Kitchen God, sees and hears the family's domestic affairs. His likeness – on a cheap print or a tablet, rather than a wooden image – is found over the stove in most traditional Chinese homes. The week before the lunar new year, when he reports a family's activities of the past year directly to the Jade Emperor, he is given a proper and festive send-off by the family. ∎

Writing grew from the need to express ideas, and painting grew from the desire to represent forms. This was the intention and the purpose of nature and of the sages…
– from a 9th-century treatise on painting by Chang Yenyuan

A Chinese painting appears as it does because it was painted by a Chinese artist. He had special tools, a certain training, a somewhat predictable place in society, skill as a calligrapher, and particular philosophic and aesthetic assumptions.

The aesthetics of painting are part of the Chinese cosmogony. Indeed, the Chinese assign painting and the complimentary art of calligraphy an important place in the natural order of things. Painting fulfills culture, helps human relations, and explores the mysteries of the universe. Its value is equal to that of the classics of Confucius, and, like the rotation of the seasons, stems from nature. Ideally, it is not something handed down by tradition, although, over the centuries, Chinese art has, in fact, become constrained by specific schools and styles.

Chang described the origins of Chinese painting in almost mystical terms. "When the ancient rulers received the mandate to rule from heaven, inscriptions on tortoise-shells and drawings presented by dragons appeared… These events have been recorded in jade and gold albums. Fuxi obtained the hexagrams from the Yung River, which was the beginning of books and painting; Huangdi obtained (drawings) from the Wen and Lo rivers, and Xihuang and Zangjie, who had four eyes, looked up at the celestial phenomena and copied bird footprints and tortoise-shell markings, thus fixing the forms of written characters. Nature could not conceal its secrets, hence it rained millet. The evil spirits could not conceal their forms, therefore the ghosts wailed at night."

In short, Zangjie saw the forms of Chinese characters in nature and recorded them for

humanity's use. In contrast to Western lore, in which Adam and Eve acquired knowledge that resulted in guilt, the Chinese received their culture as a gift or won it through astuteness. The evil spirits that conquered Eden turn up losers in the Chinese tale.

In historical terms, the earliest Chinese characters were pictographic or ideographic. Indeed, they remain so today, although many characters are derived from these originals on a phonetic basis. The original forms of the characters are difficult to discern, as they

have evolved into new shapes over the centuries. But the striking fact about Chinese writing is that, as the script developed, the older forms were not cast off. Many were preserved and used as they are today. This structural evolution of Chinese symbols was essentially completed by the fifth century.

Almost without exception, the artist of early China was a calligrapher, and from a privileged class. Otherwise, he would never have had the endless hours of time needed to acquire skill with the *maubi,* the brush used to write characters. In fact, competence with the brush was a necessary reflection of an education in ancient China. If a young man (there were no women involved, though some were well-educated) sought to pass the civil service exam, the path to all posts in government, he might be judged as much for his writing skill as for his ability to produce the rote answers required by the examination.

Four treasures: The maubi combined a long, straight handle of wood or bamboo with a round tip that came to a point. It was soft, but firm and springy, and was probably made of rabbit, wolf or deer hair. Softer goat hairs were more often used by the painter than the calligrapher. The artist generally wrote on paper, which may have been invented as early as the second century AD. Lacking paper, he might have chosen silk for his canvas. Paper, however, provided an extremely sensitive surface that readily revealed the speed of the brush, the manner of its handling, and its charge of ink. Paper permitted no corrections.

The artist's ink came in the form of a dry stick made from lampblack mixed with glue. After adding a little water, the stick was rubbed into an inkstone. Although grinding the ink was a slow process, it was a part of the painting ritual – quieting and focusing the spirit before the art could commence.

These four treasures – maubi, paper, ink and inkstone, the tools of the calligrapher and painter – were the subject of much discussion and critique. The best brush would be made by famous craftsmen, with hairs from the pelt of an animal captured in the first weeks of March. The best inkstone would grind fine ink quickly and was "cold" enough to keep the fluid wet for long periods. It might come from a famous mountain miles away. The choicest inks were made from the smallest particles of smoke, gathered at the greatest distance from the burning pine wood of *tung* oil, then beaten thousands of times to improve their quality. The finest papers came from the best paper-makers; they had access to the cleanest water and washed all traces of impurity from the pulp.

The best of the four treasures were held in awe. But even basic, common tools were regarded with great respect. One Sui-dynasty calligrapher buried his used brushes in the earth with solemn ritual, a reflection of the reverence with which the painter-calligrapher approached his art.

The tools of the painter and calligrapher were essentially the same, as was their approach to painting and writing. The difference lay in the painter's use of color. Although the aesthetic role of color in Chinese painting never approached the development that occurred in the West, its symbolic role was important. Sze Mai-mai wrote in *The Way of Chinese Painting* that, in its use of color, painting "was akin to alchemy, for the simple range of colors in Chinese painting symbolized the Five Elements basic to the thought and practice of alchemy, and the methods of preparing colors resembled and perhaps derived from alchemical brewing and distillation."

Calligraphy: Brush handling, by contrast, was all-important, and there was never a period of Chinese painting or a particular style in which good brushwork was not regarded as critical.

Brush control reaches its finest in the subtle art of calligraphy. Here, all are lines and dots – naked, infinitely challenging. The Chinese have always regarded calligraphy as the highest of the arts. With its abstract aesthetic, it is certainly the purest. That is why a man could pass examinations on the strength of his calligraphy. Writing was regarded as a window on the soul.

Few examples of ancient calligraphy still exist. Most ancient inscriptions were rubbings taken from cast-metal vessels. The earliest examples of Chinese writing in Taipei's National Palace Museum are Shang-period oracle inscriptions, incised on tortoise shells or the scapulae of oxen. (The museum's collection of calligraphy is extensive, its richest examples dating from the Yuan, Ming and Qing dynasties.)

The earliest examples of work by famous calligraphers, on display at the museum, include the *Ping-fu tieh* (On Recovering from Illness), by Lu Chi, who lived from 261 to 303. Samples of post-Eastern Qin calligraphy are more common. Wang Hsi-chi, who lived during that dynasty, is regarded as the patriarch of the art of calligraphy.

The importance of calligraphic skills grew during the Tang dynasty. Famous officials who were also renowned calligraphers of that era included Yu Shin-nan, Yen Chen-ching and Liu Kung-chuan. Despite the ancient bars against the role of women in society, one of the preeminent calligraphers of the Tang dynasty was Wu Tsia-luan. She went to work writing everyday for 10 years in order to support her ailing husband. Her fame spread so widely that she became deified as an immortal, flying to the heavens on the back of a tiger.

The Song dynasty saw the rise of calligraphers carving on wood or stone, then making rubbings on paper and compiling their works as copy books, a practice that became a popular method of studying an artist's style. Even the short-lived Yuan dynasty produced several noted calligraphers. But the 300 years of the Ming dynasty produced numerous masters and masterpieces. The Qing dynasty introduced two distinctive styles of calligraphy, one that marked the era from 1796 to 1820, the other from 1851 to 1874.

individual's role in society. Both reflect, however, humanity's oneness with nature's larger harmony, the oneness of dao.

The Chinese universe was an ordered, harmonic whole. Perceiving this order, the Chinese sought to take their place within and participate in the natural order. Ritual was important because it involved actual participation, rather than just symbolic participation. As Sze Mai-mai noted: "Painting and every other phase of Chinese life continued to be governed by the value of the ritual approach. It is worth noting, therefore, that the original purpose of ritual was to order the life of the community in harmony with the forces of nature (dao), on which subsistence

Painter's dao: The most obvious facet of Chinese painting is its expressions of a life rooted in the *dao* – in nature. The concept of dao existed even before the formal teachings of the school of Daoism, and is a basic term of Chinese cosmology, expressive of the idea that all things have a common origin.

The Confucianists and Daoists differed more in their preoccupations than on their concept of dao. The Daoists were concerned with humanity's direct, mystical relationship with nature, the Confucianists with an

Quails Among the Chrysanthemums, by Song-dynasty artist, 1131.

and well-being depended. It was not only pious but expedient to perform regularly and properly the rituals of study, propitiation and celebration. These were acts of reverence. They were also literal attempts to bring heaven down to earth, for they were patterned on the rhythmic transformations in the skies and in nature, in the hope that a like order and harmony might prevail in society."

The painter's preoccupation with the dao occurred at both the ritual level of the Confucianist school and the mystical level of the Daoists. The Chinese painter was often a pillar of society, well-educated, with a responsible government position and considerable duties to his family. He was a man of the world. Yet, as an artist, he needed peace and quiet. Chinese literature and poetry abound with references to this conflict between the weight of responsible citizenship and the withdrawal to relative seclusion that marks the life of an artist. After retirement, the artist was able to devote much more time to Daoist philosophy.

As a system, Daoism was better suited to the individual effort of painting, as it focused on the relationship between the individual and nature – on the creative act itself, between the painter and his subject, and the magical link between the two – art.

The dao is not to be understood, it is to be cogitates and moves the brush without such intentions, reaches the art of painting. His hands will not get stiff; his heart will not grow cold. Without knowing how, he accomplishes it."

Daoist thinking had a profound effect, not only on what the artist painted, but also on how he painted. His spiritual stance while painting was as integral a part of the art as the tools. Process was all-important.

Influences: This approach had some bearing on latter-day European surrealists, who used the process they called automatism to give free rein to the unconscious. It is perhaps a measure of the limited success of these surrealists that their iconography came

appreciated. To tie it down is to lose it. It is not unknowable, but it cannot be explained. To know the dao is to be at one with it, to operate by its principles, or to allow them to operate through one.

Laozi's disciple, Zhuangzu, elaborated on such mysteries: "Dao has reality and evidence but no action or physical form. It may be transmitted but cannot be received. It may be obtained but cannot be seen."

Such concepts apply equally to the painter, as Chang Yenyuan later wrote: "He who deliberates and moves the brush intent upon making a picture, misses to a still greater extent the art of painting, while he who fairly directly from Sigmund Freud. With the Chinese painter, it is not a matter of iconography, but of process. The term *dao* can be interpreted as the way, itself connoting process. The painter was a vessel for, or collaborator with, the dao. And in tune with nature, he was the vehicle for its expression.

European surrealism had an extremely anarchic flavor. Freud maintained that creativity sprang from the sublimation of unconscious energies, of restraint exercised by the ego. The Chinese artist seeking oneness with the dao could hardly be considered an anarchist. Yet his road often shunned social convention, as Chuang-tzu so vividly described: "When Prince Yuan of Song was about to have a portrait painted, all official painters came, bowed, and at the royal command stood waiting, licking their brushes and mixing their ink. Half of them were outside the room. One official came later. He sauntered in without hurrying himself, bowed at the royal command and would not remain standing. Thereupon he was given lodging. The prince sent a man to see what he did; the painter would take off his clothes, squatting down barebacked to paint. The ruler said, 'He will do. He is a true painter.'" Ever since, "squatting down barebacked" has become an expression that refers to the free and unshackled state of a painter at work.

Song imperial painting academy were Ma Yuan and Hsia Kuei. Their styles, which became popular in Japan, are typically asymmetrical. All the landscape elements and human figures are placed to one corner, the empty remaining surfaces suggested an enveloping mist. Such masterpieces as Ma's *Springtime Promenade*, painted between 1190 and 1225, and Hsia's *Chatting With a Guest by the Pine Cliff*, which dates between 1180 and 1230, are typical examples.

Because of the short duration of the Yuan dynasty, the number of paintings produced was relatively small. One Yuan-era painting in the National Palace collection is the masterpiece *Autumn Colors on the Chiao and*

Chinese painting blossomed during the Tang dynasty (618–907). The figure and horse paintings of that period were particularly exquisite. Few of them, however, have survived the centuries. The National Palace Museum has 65 paintings in its collection that date from the Tang dynasty and earlier.

Flowers, birds and landscapes were the favorite subjects of artists who painted during the Five Dynasties and Song periods. Two of the greatest masters of the Southern

Autumn Colors on the Chiao and Hua Mountains, by the Yuan-dynasty master artist Chao Mengfu, 1295.

Hua Mountains, dated 1295. It was executed by the scholar-painter Chao Mengfu, a member of the Song imperial family, and who had a profound influence on later generations of calligraphers and painters. The painting is supposed to represent the landscape of his friend's ancestral home in Shandong province. But it is more a display of Chao's knowledge of antique styles than it is an illustration of geographical features. There is an exaggerated disproportion between the elements, and spatial inconsistencies characteristic of work produced during the Six Dynasties period (420–589). Such work marked a turning point in Chinese painting.

The Ming dynasty saw the revitalizing of traditional Chinese institutions, including painting, following nearly a century of foreign domination. A painting academy was formed by the Ming court, and artists were summoned to the court, commissioned to paint and even conferred official titles. Among the myriad notables were Wu Wei, an ardent Daoist who so fully comprehended the mysteries of the dao that he came to be regarded as an immortal; Wen Cheng-ming, who exceled at images of old trees; and Tung Chi-chang, one of the most important artists of the late Ming period.

Although the leaders of the last imperial dynasty, the Qing, were originally from

Dongbei (Manchuria), they held great respect for Chinese culture and adapted themselves to local forms and customs. Under the Manchu, officialdom remained open to the Han Chinese, and many important Qing painters held government office.

The Qing period saw the flourishing of the so-called Individualists, including Chu Ta, Dao Chi, Kung Hsien, Kun Tsan and Hung Jen. A Jesuit priest, Giuseppe Castiglione, who went to China as a missionary and was called to the imperial court, also became famous as a painter of figures, flowers, birds and horses. Lang Shih-ning, as the priest became known, blended European natural-

ism with Chinese composition and media. It is perhaps impossible to discuss, in general terms, what it is that gives a painting life. The effect is a gestalt, a total impression that comes from a moment of genius. But although the whole may defy analysis, it is possible to examine the parts.

Techniques: As has been noted, a Chinese painter was almost always a skilled calligrapher, a master of the subtleties of brushwork. And calligraphy is the supreme art of the line – of naked, unadorned and undisguised brushwork. The paintings of the Chinese, far more than those of other traditions, are essentially based on line-work. Their color is primarily symbolic and decorative. Tone is more important, but it plays a supporting role. It either fills the forms defined by lines or provides definition where lines would be too strong – in mist or in the far distance.

The strokes, by contrast, are so important that they have even been given labels. There are hemp-fiber strokes, big ax-cut strokes, lotus leaf-vein strokes, raveled-rope strokes and others. It is critical that every line, stroke or dot in a painting be alive and have a validity that plays a part, yet can be separated from the painting as a whole. Each swish of the brush can thus be judged on its own merits, and a painting is perfect in whole and in parts. This is quite unlike the West, where an individual mark contributes to a marvelous whole, but can scarcely be subjected to a meaningful appraisal in itself.

What is less obvious, but far more important in the sweep of history, is the debt of painting to calligraphy. The isolation of the strokes in any painting, with their self-contained beauty and the many special qualities of the calligraphic line, stand as evidence.

Living lines have always been central to the Chinese painter's art. His years of training as a calligrapher made it difficult for him to make marks that did not exhibit their own beauty. To capture the harmony of the parts brought the painter closer to achieving the harmony of the dao.

The subtle art of Chinese calligraphy remains obscure to those who cannot see that a dot may be full of life and that a line may burst with energy.

Left, modern artist paints in the old style at lotus pond. Right, *A Ferry Scene in Autumn* by Ming dynasty master Chiu Ying.

5 中華民國郵票
REPUBLIC OF CHINA
明仇英山水畫

明仇英山水畫
中華民國郵票 5
REPUBLIC OF CHINA

5 中華民國郵票
REPUBLIC OF CHINA
明仇英山水畫

明仇英山水畫
中華民國郵票 5
REPUBLIC OF CHINA

Porcelain: The Chinese invented porcelain sometime in the seventh century – a thousand years before the Europeans did. The history of Chinese ceramic artifacts, however, goes back to neolithic times. Along the Huang He (Yellow River) and Chang Jiang (Yangzi), 7,000- to 8,000-year-old ceramic vessels, red and even black clayware with comb and rope patterns, have been found. The Yangshao and Longshan cultures of the fifth to second millennium BC developed new types of vessels and a diversity of pat-

Sancai ceramics – ceramics with three-color glazes from the Tang dynasty – became world-famous. The colors were mostly strong green, yellow and brown. Sancai ceramics were also found among the tomb figurines of the Tang period in the shape of horses, camels, guardians in animal or human form, ladies of the court, and officials.

The Song-period celadons – ranging in color from pale or moss green, pale blue or pale grey to brown tones – were also technically excellent. As early as the Yuan period,

terns in red, black or brown. Quasi-human masks, stylized fish, and hard, thin-walled stoneware, with kaolin and lime feldspar glazes, were created. Later, light-grey stoneware with green glazes, known as *yue* ware – named after the kilns of the town of Yuezhou – were typical designs of the Han period. Even during the Tang dynasty, China was known in Europe and the Middle East as the home of porcelain.

The most widespread form of ancient Chinese porcelain was celadon – a product of a blending of iron oxide with the glaze that resulted, during firing, in the characteristic green tone of the porcelain.

a technique from Persia was used for underglaze painting in cobalt blue (commonly known as Ming porcelain). Some common themes seen throughout the subsequent Ming period were figures, landscapes and theatrical scenes. At the beginning of the Qing dynasty, blue-and-white porcelain attained its highest level of quality. Since the fourteenth century, Jingdezhen has been the center of porcelain manufacture, although today, relatively inexpensive porcelain can be bought throughout China. However, antique pieces are still hard to come by because the sale of articles predating the Opium Wars is prohibited by the Chinese government.

Jade: With its soft sheen and rich nuances of color, jade is China's most precious stone. Jade is not a precise mineralogical entity but rather comprises two minerals: jadeite and nephrite. The former is more valuable because of its translucence and hardness, as well as its rarity.

The Chinese have known jade since antiquity, but it became widely popular only in the eighteenth century. Colors vary from white to green, but there are also red, yellow and lavender jades. In China, a clear emerald-

The oldest jades so far discovered come from the neolithic Hemadu culture (about 5000 BC). The finds were presumably ritual objects. Circular disks called *bi,* given to the dead to take with them, were frequently found. Centuries later, the corpses of high-ranking officials were clothed in suits made of more than 2,000 thin slivers of jade sewn together with gold wire.

Since the eleventh century, the Jade Emperor has been revered as the superior godhead in Daoist popular religion. Today, the

green stone is valued most highly. According to ancient legend, *yu,* as the jewel is known, came from the holy mountains and was thought to be crystallized moonlight. In fact, jade came from along the Silk Road.

Nephrite is quite similar to jadeite, but not quite as hard and is more common. During the eighteenth century, nephrite was quarried in enormous quantities in the Kunlun mountains on the mainland. It comes in various shades of green (not the luminous green of jadeite), white, yellow and black.

Left, intricate carving in ivory. **Above left**, carving ivory. **Above right**, jade cup, Song dynasty, 1782.

ring disk – a symbol of heaven – is still worn as a talisman; jade bracelets are believed to protect against rheumatism in some regions of China.

In the jade-carving workshops of today, there are thought to be as many as 30 kinds of jade in use. Famous among the jade workshops on the mainland are those in Qingtian (Zhejiang province), Shoushan (Fujian province), and Luoyang (Hunan province).

Genuine jade always feels cool and cannot be scratched with a knife. Quality depends on the feel of the stone, its color, transparency, pattern and other factors. If in doubt, a reputable expert should be consulted.

Lacquerware: The oldest finds of lacquered objects date back to the fifth millennium BC. The glossy sheen of lacquerware is not only attractive to the eye but is also appealing to the touch.

The bark of the lacquer tree (*rhus vernici-flua*), which grows in central and southern China, exudes a milky sap when cut, which solidifies in moist air, dries and turns brown. This dry layer of lacquer is impervious to moisture, acid, and scratches, and is therefore ideal protection for materials such as wood or bamboo.

Bowls, tins, boxes, vases, and furniture made of various materials (wood, bamboo, wicker, leather, metal, clay, textiles, paper)

are coated with a skin of lacquer. A base coat is applied to the core material, followed by extremely thin layers of the finest lacquer that, after drying in dust-free moist air, are smoothed and polished.

In the dry lacquer method, the lacquer itself dictates the form: fabric or paper is saturated with lacquer and pressed into a wood or clay mold. After drying, the mold is removed and the piece coated with further layers of lacquer. Items were already being made in this way in the Han period.

During the Tang dynasty, large Buddhist sculptures were produced by the lacquer-ware process. If soot or vinegar-soaked iron filings are added to the lacquer, it will dry into a black color; cinnabar turns it red. The color combination of red and black, first thought to have been applied in the second century BC, is still considered a classic. In the Song and Yuan periods, simply-shaped monochromatic lacquerware was valued. During the Ming period, the manufacture of lacquered objects was further refined.

The carved lacquer technique, which began at the time of the Tang dynasty, reached its highest peak during the Ming and Qing periods. The core, often of wood or tin, is coated with mostly red layers of lacquer. When the outermost coat has dried, decorative carving is applied, with the knife penetrating generally to the lowest layer so that the design stands out from the background in relief. The most well-known lacquerware is the Beijing work, which goes back to the imperial courts of the Ming and Qing dynasties. Emperor Qianlong (1734–1795) had a special liking for carved lacquerware; he was even buried in a coffin magnificently carved using this technique.

Cloisonné: The cloisonné technique – used to create metal objects with enamel decor – reached China from Persia in the eighth century AD, was lost and then rediscovered in the thirteenth century. In the cloisonné technique, metal rods are soldered to the body of the metal object. These form the outlines of the ornamentation. The spaces between the rods are filled with enamel paste and fired in the kiln. Finally, metal surfaces not covered with enamel are gilded.

Ivory: As a craft material, ivory is as old as jade, and early pieces can be traced to as far back as 5000 BC. During the Bronze Age, wild elephants were not a rarity in northern China; some were tamed during the Shang dynasty. The old artist carvers regarded elephant tusks as a most desirable material. The once-large herds of elephants in the south of China thus shrank to a small remnant, and eventually ivory had to be imported. Ming dynasty carvings exemplified the excellent craft skills and superior taste; during Qing times, ivory carving was further refined.

Most countries today, seeking to reduce animal poaching, now ban the import of items carved from ivory.

Left, carved lacquer plate, 18th century. **Right**, carving in nephrite.

Westerners usually cringe when first encountering the somewhat shrill tones of traditional Chinese opera. Indeed, the tones are quite different and unexpected.

To the ears of aficionados, however, the high-pitched notes lend emotional strength to the song lyrics, and the prolonged wails accentuate the singers' moods. When added to the traditional accompaniment of drums, gongs, flutes and violins, the end result is an ancient sound so abstract it might have been concocted by an avant-garde composer of the twentieth century.

The music provides the beat and the backing for a visual spectacle of electric shades of painted faces, glittering rainbow of costumes, exquisite pantomime and impossible acrobatics. The unique blend of sound and spectacle that results is called *jingxi*, capital opera, or better known as Beijing opera.

Beijing opera was formally established in 1790, and in the city for which it is named. That was the year the most famous actors from all corners of the Chinese empire gathered in Beijing to present a special variety show for the emperor. The performance proved so successful that the artists remained in the capital city, combining their ancient individual disciplines of theater, music and acrobatics into the form of Beijing opera that continues today.

The first venue for these spectaculars were the tea houses of the capital city. With greater popularity and increased complexity of performances, the tea houses evolved into theaters. Yet the carnival atmosphere of the small tea houses persisted, and continues to do so even today.

Foreigners visiting an opera in Taiwan may be stunned to find that audiences eat, drink and gossip their way through the operas in tried-and-true fashion, only to fall silent during famous scenes and solo arias. It may seem rude to Western viewers, but when the Chinese attend an opera, they go intent on enjoying themselves. Since audiences in Taiwan and in other Chinese communities

know all the plots of the operas by heart – and all the performers by reputation – they know exactly when to pay undivided attention to the stage action and when to indulge in other pleasures.

Chinese opera has no equivalent in the West, and it bears only minor similarities to the European style of classical opera. Thematically, the stories play like high melodrama, with good guys and bad guys who are clearly defined by their costumes and face paint. The themes are drawn from popular

folklore, ancient legends and historical events, much as Greek mythology or the legends of King Arthur sifted down into Western music, dance, theater and opera.

It is in terms of technique, however, that Chinese opera emerges unique among the world's theatrical forms. The vehicles of expression blend singing, dancing, mime and acrobatics, and utilize sophisticated symbolism in costumes, makeup and stage props.

Each of the vehicles of Chinese opera is an art form in itself. The use of face paint, for instance, is divided into 16 major categories representing more than 500 distinctive styles. Despite the complexity and enormous array

Preceding pages: fearsome faces of Beijing opera. **Left,** delicate colors of the painted mask. **Right,** making up for the show.

of facial ornamentation, proper application of the paint imparts a character with a distinct identity. "The moment we see the face, we know exactly who he is and the nature of his character," says a devoted opera fan.

History credits the invention of the makeup techniques to Prince Lanling, who ruled over the northern Wei kingdom during the sixth century. As his own features were so effeminate, the prince designed a fierce face-mask to improve his appearance and his chances on the battlefield. The ruse worked wonders. Lanling easily defeated enemy forces that far outnumbered his own. His savage mask was later adapted for dramatic use during the ensuing Tang dynasty. To facilitate the ac-

elaborate stage sets. The few backdrops and props that are incorporated in a performance are put to ingenious uses.

Water-sleeves and props: One inventive prop that is actually part of a performer's costume is the water-sleeve, often used to mime emotion and imply environmental conditions. These long, white armlets of pure silk are attached to the standard sleeves of the costume and trail down to the floor when loose.

Although it is merely an extra length of cloth, the expressive power of the water-sleeve can be remarkable when flicked by expert wrists. To express surprise or shock, a performer simply throws up his arms. The sleeves fly backwards in an alarming man-

tors' movements and their ability to sing, the design was painted directly onto their faces.

Each color applied possesses its own basic properties: red is loyal, upright and straightforward; white denotes craft, cunning and resourcefulness, even a clown or a criminal; blue is vigorous, wild, brave and enterprising; yellow dominates an intelligent but somewhat reserved character; brown suggests strong character with stubborn temperament; green is reserved for ghosts, demons and everything evil; and gold is the exclusive color of gods and benevolent spirits.

The extensive use of pantomime in Chinese opera virtually eliminates the need for

ner. An actor wishing to convey embarrassment or shyness daintily holds one sleeve across the face, as if hiding behind it. Determination and bravery can be emphasized by flicking the sleeves quickly up around the wrists, then clasping the hands behind the back. The message is universally understood.

The range of symbolic gestures made possibly by the water-sleeve is endless. These complement other expressive gestures in mime. Performers dust themselves off to indicate that they have just returned from a long journey. They form the sleeves into a muff around the clasped hands as protection against the cold weather of a winter scene.

To cope with hot summer weather, the sleeves are flapped like a fan.

Simple devices like the water-sleeve, with its wide range of expression, make stage props generally unnecessary. The few that are used have obvious connotations.

Spears and swords come into play during battle and action scenes. The long, quivering peacock plumes attached to the headgear of some actors identify them as warriors. Ornate riding crops with silk tassels tell any tuned-in Chinese audience that the actors are riding horses. Black pennants carried swiftly across the stage symbolize a thunderstorm, but four long pennants held aloft on poles represent a regiment of troops. A character

is transformed into a mountain. Or it can be used as a throne. If an actor jumps off a chair, he has committed suicide by flinging himself into a well. After that, long strips of paper may be hung from just above his ears to indicate he has become a ghost.

With some basic grounding in the rich symbolism of the costumes, props, face paints and mime gestures, even a spectator who doesn't understand a word of Chinese may be able to follow much of the plot.

While neon-colored costumes and dazzling makeup can enthrall audiences for hours, the long intervals of song and dialogue can invariably induce bouts of boredom. But just as attention begins to drift, the

riding a chariot holds up two yellow banners horizontally about waist high, each painted with a wheel. An actor who appears bearing a banner with the character for *bao*, which means report, is a courier delivering an important message from afar.

Chinese opera also employs single props for a variety of uses. As simple an item as a chair is exactly what it appears to be when sat upon. But when placed upon a table, a chair

Left, the obligatory family dispute scene in a Chinese opera. Above, conspicuous painted masks are a distinguishing feature of all forms of Chinese opera.

performances are punctuated by rousing feats of athletics and prestidigitation. In fact, it is often difficult to distinguish the magic tricks from the acrobatics.

Chinese operas don't unfold on a stage. They leap, bound and bounce into action. Performers appear to have an uncanny knack for doing one midair somersault more than is humanly possible before they return to earth. Hands become feet and inverted stomachs become grotesque faces, as two or more acrobats link arms and legs to become one fantastic creature.

The most thrilling portions of Chinese opera are indisputably the battle scenes. They employ every form of martial art and acrobatic maneuver conceivable – and then some. Sabers, axes and fists fly through the air in a manner that would end in buckets of bloodletting amidst novices. The stars of Chinese opera can fling a sword high in the air – and somehow, quite miraculously, catch it in the razor-thin slit of its scabbard.

A famous maneuver of the most famous star of twentieth-century Beijing opera, Mei Lan-fang, was the celebrated "kite's turn". Mei, a consummate male actor who specialized in playing female roles, is remembered for his enduring performance as the fickle Yang Guifei in an opera called *The Drunken Concubine*. Yang Guifei was the favorite

consort of the emperor Xuanzong, of the Tang dynasty. In the play, Mei Lan-fang exquisitely portrayed the pampered concubine as she slipped ever deeper into a drunken stupor, culminating with the kite's turn. The maneuver began with Mei Lan-fang lifting – with his teeth – a cup of wine from a tray held by trembling eunuchs. He drained the cup dry and made a 180-degree turn. Then Mei arched over backwards and bent almost double to replace the cup on the tray, never once using his hands nor spilling a single drop of wine.

Mei is highly revered by Taiwan's opera companies and fans, and *The Drunken Con-*

cubine remains a favorite on the island. The emperor Xuanzong, who was eventually obliged by disgruntled troops to execute his beloved but bibulous concubine, was a great patron of the performing arts and has been consecrated as the patron saint of Chinese opera in Taiwan.

Traditionally, female roles in Chinese opera were performed by impersonators, like the incomparable Mei Lan-fang, but modern performances usually employ women as women. Yet the old impersonators perfected such stylized feminine gestures that aspiring actresses find themselves in the odd position of having to learn to imitate a man imitating a woman.

Aside from the introduction of women, Chinese opera continues to flourish in Taiwan in all the traditional splendor and classical pageantry of its form.

The route to becoming an accomplished performer is a grueling one. Most children attend classes in opera schools as early as age seven, and instruction requires at least eight years. The most noted training center in Taiwan is the Fuhsing Opera School, which offers full tuition for Beijing opera, but the school also requires students to take standard educational courses along with the rigorous operatic training.

Taiwan opera: In addition to Beijing opera, an offshoot simply called Taiwan opera has become popular on the island. Taiwan opera is usually performed outdoors on elevated stages in public markets. The shows incorporate sparkling, colorful costumes and elaborate backdrops.

The innovations in Taiwan opera range from the use of Taiwanese dialect, instead of the difficult Hubei dialect of Beijing opera, to disco-colored robes and Western makeup techniques. These changes have expanded the popularity of Chinese opera to the average person on the street.

Traditional Chinese puppet shows are also staged frequently throughout Taiwan, and are based on the themes, roles, music and costumes of Beijing opera. Before television had arrived in Taiwan, puppet shows were one of the primary forms of entertainment. As in opera, costumes and makeup indicate the type of character.

Left, a performer waits his turn in the wings of a Taiwan opera.

TAIWAN'S FILM FARE

Taiwan has long been a treasure house of talent that has entertained people through out Asia and many other parts of the world. Its movies, with their emphasis on spectacle and impossible feats of martial artistry, pack theaters every day. Its television dramas, which twist and turn through plots set in the imperial past and inimical present, command legions of devoted followers. Serious theater, modern dance and classical music have also become an increasingly important component of the island's contemporary repertoire.

Taiwan's long romance with the making of motion pictures dates back even before the Republic of China moved its Nationalist government to Taipei. The republic's first film, produced on the mainland while the Nationalists were in charge, was *The Orphan Who Saved His Grandfather*. It was first screened in 1922.

The film industry enjoyed a "golden age" during the 1930s and 1940s, as Shanghai became the Chinese equivalent of Hollywood. The years of political upheaval and war, however, slowed development in the industry until the move to Taiwan. In cooperation with the former British colony of Hong Kong – filmmakers from there preferred the natural locations and low costs of production in Taiwan – film-making entered a period of rehabilitation in 1952. The next five years saw the island's producers turning out new movies that were marketed in Singapore and Malaysia, as well as locally.

Initially, most of the local movies were dubbed in Amoy, the local dialect often called Taiwanese. The first 35mm color film produced in Taiwan was the 1957 production of *Liang Hung Yu*, the story of a heroine of the Song dynasty. The first private concern to begin turning out films in the national language of Mandarin was Kuo Lien Film Company, a joint venture of Taiwan and Hong Kong entrepreneurs. Their first offerings hinged on war themes and literary works. Later, they hit on a formula that was to be reckoned with throughout the world. Kuo Lien filled its films with action and eventually packed them with martial arts sequences. Soon the sequences were drawn out into entire films full of flying fists, kicking feet and swishing swords.

Taiwan's golden age of film-making began in 1967. The government, increasingly aware of the cultural and financial benefits of movie exports, put technical and monetary assistance behind the business. Import quotas for foreign films were raised as an incentive for increasing

production. Import taxes for overseas Chinese films were rebated to talented studios to encourage local productions. The Golden Horse Award was established. Like Hollywood's Oscars, it provides recognition to outstanding Mandarin films, actors, actresses and directors.

By the late 1970s, the studios of Taiwan, often working with production companies from Hong Kong, were prospering. The island produced more than 150 films each year. But in the last few years, Taiwan's film industry has suffered a tremendous setback on its own domestic market. In 1994, only 29 feature films were made in Taiwan.

Critics have warned that local audiences as well as the overseas faithful have begun to tire of the formula-action epics and soppy love stories that have been a staple of Taiwan directors

for decades. In the 1990s, nevertheless, some of Taiwan's films moved into the international limelight. At the 39th Asia-Pacific Film Festival in Sydney, in 1994, the film *Eat Drink Man Woman* won the best picture and best editing awards. And at the 51st Venice International Film Festival, *Vive l'Amour* took the Golden Lion for best picture.

Cartoons: If you enjoy watching cartoons, pay attention to the credits. Many of the current animated films – including Donald Duck and the Pink Panther, just to name two – include a credit to Cuckoo's Nest.

This is the brand name used by Wang Film Productions, of Taiwan, one of the biggest animation processing firms in the world. Cuckoo's Nest is now also producing its own distinctive Chinese cartoons. ∎

Right, workmen piece together massive movie poster in Taipei's West Gate.

It's three o'clock in the morning. From the darkened doors of a candle shop in the western district of Taipei, an ancient man emerges. He strides vigorously up to Round Hill Park, on the northern edge of the city, as he has for most of his more than 90 years.

There the old man begins the dance that wakes the dawn. His arms arch upward slowly in a giant circle that symbolically splits the primordial unity of the cosmos into *yin* and *yang*. He moves his hips, spine and limbs in a practiced harmony that animates the mystical ballet of *taiji*. With his circular movements synchronized to his abdominal breathing, he absorbs the potent yang energy that peaks between midnight and dawn.

The sun begins to rise. The old man, looking as spry as the new day, finishes with a regimen of *gongfu*. Back home, he sips the first of many cups of an herbal brew containing white ginseng and red jujube, sweetened with raw sugar to help maintain the level of vital energy that pulses through his legs, spine and nervous system. By the time Hung Wu-fan – head of a family world-renowned for its contribution to martial arts – begins breakfast each morning, all Taipei has come alive with lithe people jogging through the streets, stretching in the parks, shaking off the night's grip and egging their bodies into consciousness with an array of exercise. New Taipei Park, downtown, is a particularly popular spot for this impressive display of physical culture.

From the slow-motion flourishes of taiji and the graceful thrusts and parries of classical sword-fighting, to innovative fighting techniques and Chinese versions of aerobic dancing, spirited residents of Taipei display an impressive range of athletic abilities. It's in their blood.

Many of the movements performed in New Taipei Park hark back to that most noble of Chinese institutions, the martial arts. Contrary to popular misconception, the Chinese martial arts are collectively called *guoshu*, or national arts, not gongfu, which literally

translates as "time and energy spent on cultivating an art or skill". In fact, it can refer to any skill. A great calligrapher has good gongfu. So does a master chef, master lover or master fighter.

The secrets of the martial arts have been handed down from master to disciple in an unbroken tradition reaching across tens of centuries. Many great masters joined the exodus to the island of Taiwan in 1949, bringing their secrets and skills with them. Here, they have trained a new generation of

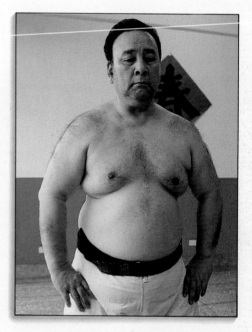

adepts. Some of those old masters still appear among the teachers who lead exercise groups in New Taipei Park.

The dragon awakens: Two of the greats who came from the mainland were Chang Chun-feng and Chen Pan-ling. Hung Wu-fan welcomed these homeless and destitute masters to his wealthy household, fed them and lavished gifts upon them. In gratitude, Chang Chun-feng began to school Hung's five sons in the ways of the ancients. Subsequently, Cheng let the Hung family in on the secrets of his mastery of *shaolin* and taiji.

Among Hung's five sons, the two masters discovered a sleeping dragon, someone with enormous talent not yet fully developed. Under the tutelage of Cheng, Chang and 15 other renowned masters, the sleeping dragon awoke. Hung Yi-hsiang today is considered one of the greatest living masters of the ancient arts.

Hung Yi-hsiang defies the typical image of a gongfu master. He is neither the taut old man with flowing robes and knee-length white beard, nor the brash young fighter of Bruce Lee ilk. Master Hung packs more than 90 kilograms (200 lbs) of powerful bulk into a compact 1.7-meter-tall frame. He looks more like a stevedore than a master of the martial, medical and fine arts. He wears baggy, nondescript clothing and rarely

in mortal combat. Thus, the Tiger Form, Mantis Form, Bear Form and other classical stances took their shape.

During the fourth century, the Indian pilgrim Bodhidharma, known to the Chinese as Tamo, introduced Buddhism to China and enhanced Chinese fighting forms by teaching the deep-breathing methods of yoga. Tamo also taught the Chinese that martial arts should be cultivated for spiritual development, not for superficial shows of force, and should be used exclusively for defense, never for offense. Tamo has been the patron saint ever since. His blend of external fighting forms, derived from animal postures, and internal breathing methods has been the

shaves. Hair grows over his chest, arms, shoulders and back, and he usually answers questions with perfunctory grunts rather than long-winded explanations.

But to watch him perform his taiji forms, or demonstrate the mesmerizing circles of *bakua*, is like watching a gentle wind stir willow branches. He breezes through steps that seem impossible. Each move is smooth and fluid, yet swift and sudden.

Eagle and snake: The Chinese originally developed fighting forms by imitating the stances of animals. In fact, martial lore tells that taiji was invented when a master fighter stumbled upon an eagle and a snake locked

model for all styles of Chinese martial arts.

These arts are based on the cosmic principals of yin and yang, and on the Five Elements of the cosmos: earth, water, metal, wood and fire. The most fundamental concept, a trait it shares with Chinese medical theories, is *qi* (pronounced *chee*), which translates as vital-energy or life-force. But it also means air and breath. Qi is an invisible element contained in air, food, water and every living thing on earth. Martial arts exercises like taiji cultivate qi through deep-breathing and direct it around the body with rhythmic motions.

People who deny the existence of anything

that cannot be seen and measured have trouble accepting the concept of qi, but it is the force that fuels Chinese life and the martial arts. Hung Yi-hsiang explained: "Without food we can live for two months, without water for two weeks, but without qi we would die in five minutes." Proper breathing is of central importance in all fighting forms and must be correctly cultivated before a student of the martial arts moves on into complex external movements. "Of all forms of exercise, breathing is best," noted Master Hung.

Soft and round: The essence of classical Chinese martial arts can be defined in two words: *rou* (softness) and *yüan* (roundness). By remaining soft and loose at all times, a person conserves vital energy while an opponent expends his by thrashing about. By employing round, circular movements, the master combatant deflects his opponent's direct linear attacks, and all his parries naturally flow the full circle to become counterattacks, and successful.

Softness and roundness are maintained and enhanced through rhythmic breathing. Breathing also permeates the body with qi during combat. Qi cannot flow properly through a hard tense body, and the hard linear movements glorified by the modern Chinese gongfu movies do not promote the circulation of qi. Hard styles like Japanese *karate*, Korean *taekwondo* and Chinese shaolin are better known in the West, but the soft rhythmic Chinese styles like taiji, *xingyi* and bagua are more traditional.

Hung Yi-hsiang's mastery over his own qi came to the forefront under his last and greatest teacher, Master Peng. Peng was a mainlander who had never accepted a single student after fleeing to Taiwan. But his attitude changed when he grew old. He realized he had to reveal his precious secrets before his death, or they would be lost to posterity. When word of his decision went out, scores of hopeful adepts rushed to his home in the central Taiwan city of Taichung to be interviewed for the honor.

Master Peng conducted his audiences in a stark, dark room lit by a single candle. The candle stood on a low table between himself and his visitors. One by one, the eager adepts filed in, spoke briefly with the master, then

left. Little did they know that they had been judged before uttering a word!

Only one man passed the test. He managed to enter the room, approach the master and pay his respects without once causing the candle flame to flicker. Here was a man in full control of his qi. Master Peng had found his disciple: Hung Yi-hsiang.

Master Hung not only took up the mantle of his great teachers, he has also developed his own system of martial arts. Hung called his school *tangshoutao*, the Way of the Hands of Tang. It blends the finest elements of xingyi, bakua, taiji and the more difficult shaolin. It takes its name from the so-called golden age of Chinese culture, the Tang

dynasty of the sixth to eighth centuries. It was also the formative age of Chinese gongfu. It is Hung's personal attempt to restore the Chinese martial arts to their authentic forms and traditions.

Tangshoutao is Chinese gongfu at its classical best – internal, subtle and deeply linked to Daoist philosophy.

Master Hung, like Tamo, believes that health and longevity are the true goals of martial arts. He says that self-defense techniques using martial arts can indeed increase longevity and promote health by protecting one from bandits and bullies, but he emphasizes that if one's internal powers of qi are strong and steady, the bullies will instinctively steer clear.

"The most accomplished martial artists are those who never have to fight. No one dares challenge them," Master Hung says. Quoting Tamo, he further advises the student, "Concentrate on the inner meaning, not the outer strength."

He also elaborates on the apparent contradiction that in softness there is strength. Hung notes that water eventually wears down the hardest rock, that yin is ultimately more potent than yang, and that when properly applied, "four ounces of strength can topple 1,000 pounds".

The most dedicated disciple of tangshoutao is Hung's second son, Hung Tze-han, who resembles a gongfu movie star. Ah-han, as friends call him, practices tangshoutao for long hours each day, and spends his spare time poring over ancient Daoist texts and martial-arts manuals. He even writes and edits scripts for television programs and movies with gongfu themes. Ah-han explains why.

"Chinese martial arts make very popular movie themes these days, but most scriptwriters know nothing whatsoever about the subject. Consequently, the public gets a distorted view of Chinese gongfu. By writing some of the scripts myself, and editing others, I try to help correct many common misconceptions held by the public."

Concrete proof: So what of the explosive war-whooping, high-kicking acrobatics of famous stars like Jackie Chan and the late Bruce Lee? They do flourish, but masters like Hung take a dim view of such sport. Hung Yi-hsiang acknowledges that karate can enable one to smash bricks, and to break boards with bare hands and feet, and that taekwondo can protect a person from bullies. But he warns that these forms of combat can also bring a premature end to a man's martial arts career.

The popular aberrations in traditional forms of modern arts did not appear in China until the seventeenth century, when the militant Manchu attacked the effete Ming dynasty. Patriotic Ming loyalists needed to turn out trained fighters as fast as possible, so they eschewed the "soft" Chinese styles that required decades of training. Classical forms were abbreviated and hardened, and training was reduced to three years. That's all it takes for some devoted adepts to become skilled in karate or shaolin. Master Hung says that few karate or taekwondo masters ever live to a ripe old age. And if they do, they are so stiff from a lifetime of beating their bodies against bricks and board they can barely move. However, the soft internal forms taught by tutors like Hung steadily increase stores of vital-energy, and also gradually improve the tone of muscles, joints and tendons, keeping them pliant and supple.

Hung has been preaching the superiority of soft forms for decades. But his warnings have only begun to be taken seriously in recent years, as scores of fellow artists from opposing schools have hobbled into his studios from all over Asia, seeking to work themselves back into physical and spiritual shape using Hung's soft exercises and abdominal breathing techniques.

Still, given the challenge, Master Hung graphically demonstrates the truths of the Dao and the sudden explosions of power that his theories and training enable him to summon at will. Once challenged by a Japanese artist to prove his might, at a tournament in Taipei in the late 1960s, the usually modest Hung acquiesced to save face. With typical Japanese fondness for the drama of crushing boards and bricks, the man dared Master Hung to smash three solid cement cinderblocks with a single blow, a feat he claimed could not be done.

The blocks were stacked flush against each other. They were placed on a solid flat surface rather than positioned up on blocks to provide space beneath, in the usual manner. Gathering and focusing his qi within, Hung silently mustered intense concentration. Then he raised his fist high above his head and brought it down with a single devastating blow. He didn't break the cinder blocks. He shattered them. Debris flew in all directions.

The feat was recorded on film. A replay showed that, at the moment of impact, every hair on Master Hung's right arm and shoulder was standing erect. That phenomenon was qi running down his arm, he later explained. His reaction to performing the impossible task?

"Smashing bricks and boards is nothing. Only amateurs are impressed by that!"

Performers strike a threatening posture during filming of a martial arts movie.

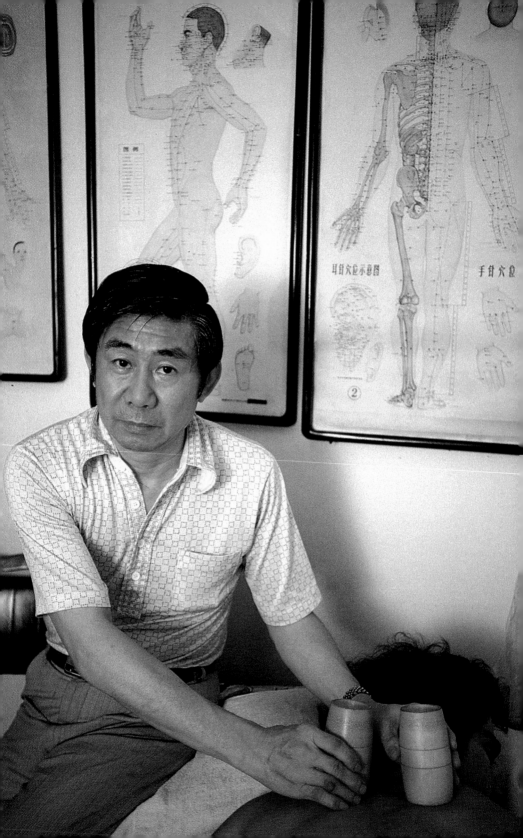

Consider the case of the curious goatherd, who one day noticed that several of his billy goats were behaving in an unusually randy manner, mounting the nearest females repeatedly in remarkably brief spans of time. Concerned by their amorous behavior, perhaps even a bit envious of their prowess, the goatherd, in time-honored scientific tradition, kept careful watch on his horny herd for a few weeks. He soon detected a pattern. Whenever a billy goat ate from a particular patch of weeds, the goat's promiscuous proclivities peaked.

Before long, Chinese herbalists had determined what goats had long known: that a plant of the *aceranthus sagittatum* family was one of the most potent male aphrodisiacs in their catalogue of confections. So they called the herb *yin-yang-huo* – horny goat weed is the best translation possible.

Like the martial arts, China's medical arts have come a long way from prehistoric fable to twentieth-century fact. The goat story is trite, but true.

Many of China's most efficacious herbal remedies were gradually discovered in precisely that manner. If a dog nibbled on certain weeds that induced vomiting, the curious Chinese experimented with the emetic properties of those weeds. Centuries of such observations and experimentation have provided Chinese medicine with the world's most comprehensive pharmacopoeia of herbal remedies.

From the open-faced fronts of garishly lit emporiums in Taipei to dim, closet-sized shops in the back alleys of small Taiwan towns, herbal doctors and dealers do a brisk business providing ancient remedies to contemporary customers.

Historians have traced the beginnings of herbal medicine to Shen Nung, the legendary emperor known as the Divine Farmer for his teaching of agricultural techniques, around 3500 BC. "Shen Nung tasted the myriad herbs, and so the art of medicine was born," proclaimed a Han-dynasty historian. References to various diseases and their

A doctor administers traditional Chinese medical treatment with suction cups.

herbal remedies first appeared on Shang dynasty oracle bones, circa 1500 BC, that were unearthed this century in China. Their discovery proved that medicine was a formal branch of study in China as long as 3,500 years ago. Later, books on medicine were among the few tomes spared from destruction during the infamous burning of books by Qin Shi Huangdi, in 220 BC.

The first volume that summarized and categorized the cumulative knowledge of disease and herbal cures in China appeared during the Han dynasty, in the second century BC. *The Yellow Emperor's Classic of Internal Medicine* contained the world's first scientific classification of medicinal plants, and is still used by Chinese physicians and scholars today.

The quintessential herbal doctor Sun Ssu-mo appeared on the scene 800 years later, during the Tang dynasty. He established a pattern of practice still followed by Chinese physicians today. "When people come in for treatment, one does not inquire about their station in life or their wealth. Rich and poor, old and young, high and low are all alike in the clinic," Sun wrote.

Three emperors, all of whom he outlived, invited Sun to be their personal physician. He declined, preferring to pursue his clinical practice among the commoners. Previously only the high and mighty had access to professional medical care, but Sun applied the Confucian virtue of *ren*, or benevolence, to his trade. He established the great tradition of *renshu renhsin* (benevolent art, benevolent heart) that has guided Chinese physicians ever since.

Sun Ssu-mo was also medical history's first dietary therapist. In his famous study *Precious Recipes*, he wrote, "A truly good physician first finds out the cause of the illness, and having found that, he first tries to cure it by food. Only when food fails does he prescribe medication."

In fact, Sun diagnosed the vitamin-deficiency disease beriberi 1,000 years before European doctors identified it in 1642. Sun prescribed a strict dietary remedy that sounds remarkably modern: calf and lamb's liver (rich in vitamins A and B), wheat germ, almonds, wild pepper and other vitamin-packed edibles.

Another milestone in the history of Chinese herbal medicine was the publication of *Ben Tsao Gang Mu* in the sixteenth century. Known to the West as *Treasures of Chinese Medicine*, this authoritative pharmacopoeia was compiled over a period of nearly three decades, through research and study by the physician Li Shin-chen.

He scientifically classified and analyzed 1,892 entries, including drugs that were derived from plants, animals and minerals. The book became popular in Western medical circles during the 1700s and 1800s, and was used by Charles Darwin in the development

fragmented into specialized branches, Chinese medicine remains syncretic. The various combinations of therapies from different fields in yangsheng must be mastered by every Chinese physician.

In fact, prior to the twentieth century, most Chinese families retained family doctors much as modern corporations retain lawyers. The doctor was paid a set monthly fee and made regular rounds to dispense herbal remedies and medical advice specifically tailored to the individual needs of each family member.

When a member of the family fell seriously ill, the doctor was held fully responsible for failing to foresee and prevent the

of his famous system for classifying the various species in nature.

The theory and practice of traditional Chinese medicine takes an approach to disease and therapy that is diametrically different from Western ways. The Chinese prefer preventive techniques; the West concentrates on cures. The Chinese regard medicine as an integral part of a comprehensive system of health and longevity called *yangsheng*, which means "to nurture life". The system includes proper diet, regular exercise, regulated sex and deep breathing, as well as medicinal therapies and treatments. Unlike Western medicine, which has become increasingly

problem. Payments were stopped. Only when he cured the patient at his own expense did his normal fee resume. The system stressed the importance of preventive care. It also served as a powerful deterrent to malpractice, as doctors profited by keeping their patients healthy and happy rather than sick and dependent.

Modern families in Taiwan and in other Chinese communities can no longer afford to keep a physician on the payroll, but the precept of prevention prevails. The Chinese trace and treat root causes of weakness and disease rather than their superficial symptoms. The physician draws a medical picture that encompasses everything from the weather and season to a patient's dietary and sexual habits. And true causes are often found far from the symptoms.

For instance, Chinese medicine traditionally traces eye problems to various liver disorders. Such symptomatic connections are rarely established in the West, where the eyes and the liver are treated by two specialists separated by chasms of medical and ophthalmological training.

The Chinese method of probing everywhere for possible causes of disease sometimes raises Western eyebrows. One American woman introduced to a Taipei doctor returned from his clinic rather flustered. "He

using herbs, acupuncture and other methods to "clear energy stagnation, suppress energy excess, tonify energy deficiency, warm up cold energy, cool down hot energy". By reestablishing the optimum internal balance of vital energies and restoring harmony among the body's vital organs, a physician can keep his patient healthy.

Herbal therapy encompasses more than 2,000 organic medicines listed in the Chinese pharmacopoeia, but only about 100 are commonly used to treat people. The rest are reserved for only the rarest conditions. Many common ingredients of the herbal pharmacy are standard ingredients of Western kitchens: cinnamon, ginger, licorice, rhubarb,

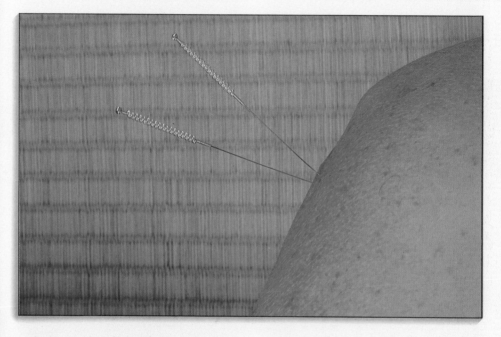

asked me such embarrassing questions!" she said. Everything from diet to bowel movements and sexual habits helps in the Chinese physician's diagnosis.

The theoretical foundations of Chinese medical arts, like those of the martial arts, are rooted in the cosmic theories of *yin* and *yang*, the Five Elements (earth, water, metal, wood, fire), and the concept of *qi,* or vital energy. Essentially, Chinese doctors manipulate a patient's internal balance of vital energies by

nutmeg, orange peel and other spices and condiments. Herbal prescriptions routinely contain at least a half-dozen ingredients, some added simply to counteract the side-effects of more potent additives.

The old adage "fight poison with poison" originated in this branch of Chinese medicine. Some of humanity's most virulent ailments are fought with such potent toxins as jimsonweed *(Datura stramonium)*, centipedes, scorpion tails and mercury.

Herbal prescriptions come in a variety of forms. There are pills formed by blending finely-powdered herbs with honey, brews made by boiling and reducing ingredients in

Left, *A Village Doctor Using Acupuncture*, painted by Li Tang during the Song dynasty. **Above**, the fine points of modern acupuncture.

water, powders dissolved in juice or water, pastes for external plasters, medicinal wines distilled from herbs steeped in strong spirits for a year or more, serums fermented from herbs using flour and water, and refined concentrates extracted from raw and dried herbs using modern technology.

Acupuncture is probably the most widely used of Chinese therapies in the West. Acupuncturists stick fine steel needles into "vital points" along the body's "vital-energy" network. More than 800 such points have been identified, but only about 50 major spots are used in common practice.

The insertion of a needle in each point produces a specific therapeutic effect on a puncture, but is applied with deep finger pressure rather than needles.

Massage, called *tui-na* (push and rub), is applied to joints, tendons, ligaments and nerve centers, as well as to vital-points and meridians. With regular application, tui-na can be effective in relieving and gradually eliminating arthritis, rheumatism, sciatica, slipped discs, nerve paralysis and energy stagnation and dissipation.

Skin-scraping involves the use of a blunt spoon or coin, dipped in wine or salt water, and rubbed repeatedly across vital-points on a patient's skin, usually on the neck or back, until a red welt appears. In cases of heat stroke, colds, fever, colic and painful joints,

specific organ, gland, nerve or other body part. The points are connected to the internal organs and glands by energy channels called meridians. While many of the secrets of acupuncture still mystify physicians in the West today, they acknowledge that it can be effective in treating certain ailments.

Acupuncture has also proven to be effective as a local and general anesthetic. In recent years, patients have undergone painless appendectomies, major operations and even open-heart surgery while remaining alert and wide awake under acupuncture anesthesia. In most ways, acupressure utilizes the same points and principles as acu-

the practice draws out what Chinese physicians call "heat energy", releasing it through the skin and hopefully eliminating the cause of the problem.

Blood-letting requires a sharp, thick needle with a triangular point that is used to prick open the skin at a vital-point related to the diseased organ. The release of blood induces "evil qi" and heat energy to travel along the meridians and escape through the open point.

Suction cups made from bamboo or glass are briefly flamed with a burning wad of alcohol-soaked cotton to create a vacuum, then pressed over a vital-point, usually along the spine. They stick tightly to the flesh by suction. Skin and flesh balloon into the cup, drawing out evil energies by pressure. The method has been found very effective in the treatment of arthritis, rheumatism, bruises, abscesses, and any ailments related to excessive exposure to wind or dampness.

Moxibustion is the term for a treatment in which a burning stick of *moxa,* made from wormwood and resembling a thick cigar, is held directly over the skin at particular vital-points. The herbal energy radiates from the glowing tip into the vital-point and transmits therapeutic benefits along the meridian network to the diseased organ.

As bizarre as bloodletting, moxibustion and other Chinese medical treatments may

sound, all are utilized with apparent success in Taiwan. For many common ailments, the Chinese approach puts faith in natural, organic curatives. However, Chinese medicine does not dispute the superiority of Western medicine in the treatment of acute traumatic ailments, injuries and emergency cases.

In fact, physicians in Taiwan now blend Chinese theories and Western technology, and Chinese therapy and Western diagnosis. Today, centuries-old practices are combined with high technology.

Left, herbal medicine shop in Lukang. **Above**, herbalist displays his cure-alls.

Because of these modern developments, Chinese medicine is not a dying relic from ancient times. The combination of old and new has formed a comprehensive system of medical care called the New Medicine. Eastern physicians use X-rays, blood and urine analysis, electrocardiograms, biochemical labs and other technology to improve their diagnostic methods, while at the same time relying on ancient, time-tested Chinese methods of treatment for common ills.

Intrinsic to the prevention of illness is a correct diet, but not as one in the West might think. The concern is not with calories and cholesterol, but rather with how foods and drinks encourage or dissipate moods, for lack of a better word, within the body.

For the traveler who has long suffered from nagging backache, persistent rheumatism, chronic fatigue, throbbing shoulder, "trick" knee, indigestion or other problems, a visit to the right physician during a trip to Taiwan may hold unexpected benefits. Bona fide stories of satisfied customers from abroad are common.

Should you travel to Taiwan in hope of some traditional Chinese treatment, your chances are good to find a specialist just for your problem. Nevertheless, Western medicine is more commonly practiced in Taiwan than traditional medicine, which is also true in mainland China. In the mid 1990s, there were 2,895 licensed doctors of Chinese medicine and about 1,900 hospitals and clinics using traditional treatments. There is, in Taiwan, one doctor of Chinese medicine for every 8,000 people, but one doctor of Western medicine for every 1,000 persons.

Herbal medicines are produced by about 250 manufacturers, and then distributed by more than 8,850 licensed herbal dealers. Even several large Western-style hospitals have their own departments for the use of traditional Chinese treatments.

Traditional Chinese treatment is covered by Taiwan's national health insurance program, which began in 1995. Before then, only 59 percent of Taiwan's total population was covered, and under 13 different public health insurance plans. Now, under the new law, participation is mandatory for all people. Rapid industrialization and urbanization have highlighted the need for better health care and medical services – whether Western or traditional Chinese – for all Taiwanese.

"Chirfan le may yo?" This common Chinese greeting, heard often in Taiwan, translates into "Have you eaten yet?" Yet it is, in fact, a greeting, much like "Hi, how are you?" The phrase carries the implicit cultural assumption that anyone who has eaten recently must be feeling fine. Anyone who is hungry, and says so in response to the greeting, will without hesitation be offered something to eat before the business at hand proceeds.

The preparation and eating of food is a primary preoccupation of the Chinese. Indeed, the typical Chinese considers the quality and quantity of daily meals as a measure of the overall quality and success of life.

Even the dead must be fed properly, believe the Chinese. Most of Taiwan's families still maintain ancestral altars in their homes, where twice each month they make lavish offerings of the best goods they can afford. After the spirits have descended and gleaned the "essence" of these succulent dishes, the living descendants eat the leftovers.

Most Westerners are well aware of the vast variety in Chinese cuisine, but few are prepared for the moment when they open an encyclopedic Chinese menu. More often than not, they'll fall back into ordering familiar dishes such as sweet-and-sour pork, chow mein and chop suey. Such meals are poor substitutes for the real thing.

In fact, chop suey is an American invention that few self-respecting Chinese would order, let alone eat. It dates back to the California gold rush days, in the mid nineteenth century, when American miners wandered into coolie camps for a bite to eat. Unwilling to share tables with Chinese laborers, they waited for the second seating, as it were. The cooks simply gathered the leftovers from Chinese customers, *chop-chopped* them until they were all *suey* (shredded), and served the resulting mess over rice to the unsuspecting Anglos, who loved it.

Even the obligatory fortune cookie served at Chinese restaurants in the West is an item

Preceding pages: midnight snacks and antics at the Shihlin night market. **Left,** a Taipei Hilton chef fashions flowers from fruit. **Above,** filled dumplings.

that never turns up on the tables of restaurants in Taipei, Hong Kong or Singapore. It was invented by a clever Chinese grocer in his San Francisco attic.

Preparing, ordering and eating authentic Chinese cuisine is an art requiring practice. And Taipei, with its reputation as one of the world's great Chinese culinary centers, is a perfect place in which to develop expertise.

Northern cuisine: Debate continues to rage among connoisseurs as to the proper classification of China's many regional styles of

cooking. Nine distinct styles are officially recognized by Chinese chefs; they can be further subdivided into regions based upon commonly shared geographic, historical, climatic and cultural factors.

The Northern school takes in the Beijing and Shandong cuisines. They are distinguishable by a staple base derived from wheat, rather than rice, including a wide variety of noodles, steamed buns, baked breads, stuffed dumplings and pancakes. Northern food generally appeals to Western palates, as it is heartier and more filling than other forms of Chinese food, and because it incorporates relatively conventional seasonings and ingredients. The Mongol and Muslim influence in northern China has made lamb a favorite meat of that region. The Northerners shy away from too much spice, like chillies and other pungent ingredients, but they love garlic, onions and the smoky saltiness of soy sauce. Beijing food is not greasy, because very little oil is used, but it is a little more salty than other Chinese cuisines.

Popular Northern selections include Peking Duck, mountain celery in mustard sauce, shredded lamb sauteed with scallions, baked-bean curd, steamed vegetarian dumplings and braised beef. The proper way to eat the delicious Peking Duck is to place slices of meat or crispy skin on a thin pancake, add scallions or leeks, and some of the soybean paste, and roll it up, eating with the fingers.

Cantonese: The southern school of cuisine is based on the culinary traditions of Guangzhou (Canton), which uses rice as the main staple. An abundance of rainfall, vegetation and wildlife blesses the regions around Guangzhou, producing a cornucopia of ingredients that please the eye as well as the palate. Cantonese cuisine is very rich in variety, and quite colorful. Cantonese chefs demand fresh ingredients and strive to retain the unique flavor and texture of each one. Most of the food is only lightly cooked.

The most ubiquitous and original of Guangzhou's specialties are *dim sum* (the word means snack), which are tasty dumplings stuffed with prawns, beef, pork and other surprises. Dim sum is often eaten as a meal in itself, usually as breakfast or lunch. While other regions of China also produce dumplings and such snacks, the southern Cantonese style surpasses all in variety and delicacy. Dim sum isn't ordered from a menu. Rather, trolleys laden with steaming dim sum of every shape and flavor are wheeled through dining rooms. Point and eat.

Other renowned Cantonese dishes include roast duck, barbecued pork, poached chicken with scallion oil, roast suckling pig, roasted pigeon, and steamed fish and greens with oyster sauce. Among the finest and most expensive Cantonese dishes are sharks' fin soup and boiled abalone. Hong Kong takes honors for Cantonese cuisine, but Taipei has its share of fine Southern-style eateries.

Eastern and Western cuisines: China's eastern school of cooking evolved in the fertile basin of the lower Chang Jiang (Yangzi River) and along the mainland's eastern seaboard. It usually refers to the cuisines of Zhejiang, Fujian and Jiangsu. Seafood, freshwater fish and mollusks are the stars of the menu; spices and sauces are rich and slightly sweet, and are sparingly applied.

Since most of Taiwan's mainland immigrants hail from the Fujian coast and Shanghai, the eastern school of Chinese cuisine is well-represented in the big towns. Favorite dishes include the incomparable West Lake vinegar fish, river eel sauteed with tender leeks, fried jumbo prawns, braised pork haunch and sauteed sweet-pea shoots.

The trendiest type of Chinese cooking throughout the world today is the western

school. It includes the meals of Sichuan (Szechuan) and Hunan, with their red chilies, fresh ginger root, garlic, scallions, and pungently-fermented sauces. The flavors are strong and spicy, but not necessarily red-hot, like many of Southeast Asia's cuisines. Traditional Chinese medical theories contend that garlic and ginger have remarkable antiseptic and cleansing properties, and that they drive excess dampness from the human system. That may explain the great popularity of Sichuan cooking in humid Taipei. Indeed, Sichuan cooking is the single most prevalent style of regional Chinese cooking in Taipei.

Memorable delights of Hunan cuisine include beggar's chicken, honey ham, steamed minced pigeon in bamboo cups, steamed whole pomfret, and frog legs in hot chili sauce. Hunan food is known for its generous use of oils, so expect dishes that are not only spicy and oily, but sour, sweet and salty.

Local style: Several major restaurants, and most night markets, feature Taiwan's local brand of cuisine, which rarely matches the exquisite flavors and classical presentations of mainland China's great styles. Instead, it is a simple, rustic cuisine that makes the best use of the available ingredients. And most abundant is everything from the ocean. When it comes to preparing fresh shellfish or whole fish, Taiwan's chefs shine brightly. They

like all their cultural pursuits – follows a kind of philosophical recipe, with physical and mental well-being as the prime ingredients. During the Tang dynasty (AD 618–907), Chinese herbal pharmacologists, not cooks or gourmands, determined what could or could not be eaten. They decided when food should be consumed and in what quantities and combinations it should be prepared. An elaborate system of food pharmacology developed, based on the cosmic theories of *yin* and *yang* and the Five Elements.

The Tang physicians and pharmacologists divided all foods into three major categories, based upon their physiological effects. Yang, or hot foods, stimulate the body and deplete

blend Chinese, Japanese and local influences in a manner that adds new dimensions to seafood. Try mussels, oysters, prawns, pomfret, fresh sashimi, squid and other seafood. Try, too, the baby abalone on the half-shell, poached shrimp, deep-fried shrimp rolls, steamed crab and grilled teriyaki eel.

After seafood, chicken is the most popular meat in Taiwan. In given the chance, order black chicken, which has a very special taste.

Philosophical menu: What the Chinese eat, why they eat it, and the way they prepare it –

Left, fresh poultry at a Taipei fast-food stall.
Above, family-style Taiwanese dining, Taipei.

its energies. Yin, or cool foods, calm and nourish the system. Neutral foods combined, in perfect balance, the best features of yin and yang. Thus, the ancient Chinese dieticians recommended that people eat whole barley, rather than milled barley, to benefit from the heating yang effects of the meal and the cooling yin effects of the bran. They warned people not to eat leeks at the same time as beef or honey. Most importantly, Chinese culinary experts insisted on maintaining optimum balance in each and every dish, as well as in the overall meal.

In many ways, recipes handed down through the centuries are actually medicinal prescriptions of health. The ingredients and the seasonings used in various dishes were selected to balance the body's vital energies. The hot yang foods are balanced with cool yin items. Crispy, deep-fried items are alternated with moist, steamed dishes. Meats complement vegetables. Winter banquets include "warming" specialties cooked with lamb, eel, ginger, chicken, chilies and such, while sumptuous summer feasts would favor cabbage, asparagus, spinach, seafood, turnips and other "cooling" dishes.

Ordering a Chinese meal: When entering a Chinese restaurant in Taiwan or elsewhere, avoid the pitfalls that await the average foreigner. If you don't get the same menu as ate one in the chaos and glare of a Chinese restaurant is doomed to failure. The more people in your party, the better. Chinese meals are meant to be festive, often boisterous, occasions.

In the event you find yourself alone and in need of a quick meal, Taiwan also offers the traditional Chinese version of fast-food. These "one-bowl" meals are the mainstays of any Chinese night market. But quick meals are also available on the ground floors of the large department stores, where you can select your meal from many different eateries. If you don't speak Chinese, just point to the ingredients you want in your bowl of rice or noodles. (If you go for lunch, do so at 11.45am

Chinese patrons, talk to a waiter who speaks your language. Pointedly inquire about the freshest items available that day and find out about the house specialties. That process will automatically identify you as one who knows his Chinese food and should help prevent the chefs from serving you watered-down versions of their fiery creations.

The general rule of thumb for ordering from any school of Chinese cooking is to select one main dish for each person in the group, several appetizers, a soup and fresh fruit for dessert.

The quiet, candle-lit dinner for two is strictly a Western tradition. Any attempt to recre- or earlier. Exactly at 12 noon, all spaces are overflooded with hungry folks.)

For starters, there is *huifan*, which consists of a large bowl of rice covered with a choice of fish, meats, gizzards, prawns, squid or the like, a savory sauce, and a side bowl of soup. China's famous *niuroumien* consists of a large bowl of fresh noodles in rich beef broth, covered with chunks of braised beef, green vegetables and condiments.

And if the craving for an occasional taste of Western food strikes your palate, Taipei also offers a wide variety of restaurants specializing in European or American meals.

No Chinese banquet is complete without

beverages, preferably alcoholic. The Chinese never drink on empty stomachs. Dispensing with the formalities of pre-dinner cocktails, they start drinking with appetizers of *jiou-tsai* (liquor-food) and continue long after dessert has been served. While Chinese pharmacologists consider the overall act of eating a cooling yin activity, drinking warms one with its yang property. In combination, balance is attained.

Rapture of drinking: The Chinese first began fermenting grains to produce alcohol during the reign of Yü the Great, about 2200 BC. A careless cook set some rice to soak in a covered rock, then promptly forgot about it. Several days later, the cook noticed a powerful aroma coming from the kettle. He tasted it, found the flavor and aftereffects to his liking, and soon he and his kitchen mates were crocked. The tale undoubtedly comes down through history from the unfortunate master of the house, who went hungry that evening.

On a more convincing note, the most ancient of all artifacts that have been unearthed in China are exquisitely-cast bronze drinking vessels, dating from the Shang dynasty, around 1,500 BC. Even that paragon of moderation, Confucius, took a tolerant view towards drinking. "There is no limit to drinking, as long as one does not become disorderly," he said.

But Confucius' Golden Mean of Drinking often fell on deaf ears. China's long history tells of many "drunken dragons". Most were famous poets and scholars renowned for possessing the capacity of an ocean and the ability to down one hundred cups at a sitting. China's most famous drunken dragon was the great poet Li Bai (699–762), sometimes known as Li Po. In fact, Li Bai is said to have died a poetically ironic death. Drunken and floating in a boat on a lotus pond, Li Bai reached to embrace the image of the moon on the water, fell overboard and drowned. Before, however, he praised wine as the key to the sublime in an immortal couplet:

The rapture of drinking
and wine's dizzy joy,
No sober man deserves to enjoy.

China has produced a variety of fermented wines and distilled spirits for centuries. Most are still available in Taiwan. The most pop-

ular dinner beverage is Shaohsing wine, a smoky brew fermented from rice. Dried plums are steeped in the wine, which is served piping hot. The best grade is a fragrant, amber vintage called *huadiao*.

Shaohsing wine effectively cleanses the taste buds of lingering oils and spices. It measures in at less than 40-proof, making it another popular toasting potion. The late James Wei, Taipei's master gourmet and consummate banqueter, insisted that hot Shaohsing is the only appropriate beverage for a Chinese meal. His advice – perhaps one should say, instruction – invokes the authority of Confucius himself: "You must drink Shaohsing at blood temperature. When cold,

reject! Drink with full heart and open throat. Remember, also, that while Confucius, a diner of moderation, argued that the meat a man ate should not be enough to make his breath smell of meat rather than rice, he imposed no limit on wine consumption…"

Maotai is a potent spirit distilled from sorghum and used mainly for the venerable Chinese custom of toasting. For serious drinkers, Kaoliang and Bai-Gar are also made from sorghum, but repeatedly distilled until they reach 150-proof.

The subtle flavor of bamboo sparks a light green spirit called Chu Yehching; five varieties of Chinese medicinal herbs add an extra

Left, *yin* and *yang* dishes of desserts and snacks.
Above, nightspots offering drinks and karaoke.

punch of yang energy to a dark viscous liquor called Wu Jiapi. But the overwhelming choice of people who eat Chinese in Taiwan, or anywhere in the Far East, is chilled beer. Although it is a Western import, the adaptable Chinese have found that beer is the perfect beverage for their cuisine. Its carbonation clears the palate and throat of residual oils and flavors between courses, permitting each dish to be savored for its own unique flavors. In addition, beer is brewed from grains, providing an alternate form of cereal – the staple so important to the Chinese diet. Beer promotes digestion, has few rivals as a thirst-quencher, and permits frequent toasting without the threat of excessive intoxication.

Taiwan produces its own brand of brew, simply called Taiwan Beer. It has received several international awards and is consumed by the island's sybaritic populace in immeasurable quantities.

Ceremonial etiquette: The catalyst for drinking at Chinese banquet is the time-honored tradition of the toast. Rarely do diners raise their glasses to their lips alone. The host customarily starts the bottles tumbling by toasting his guests or the occasion, *Gan-bei!* (Bottoms up!). He will cup the glass with both hands for courtesy, raising it high in the direction of the guest of honor.

From then on, anyone may toast anyone else at anytime, and for any reason. Even a tasty dish or clever comment may be used as an excuse for a rapturous round of toasts. The prose tends to wax more eloquent as the meal and the drinking progress. It is rude not to respond to the toast, but it is acceptable to resort to a glass of tea or juice instead of alcohol. At some parties, toasting continues until there is no one left still able to raise a glass off the table.

Semantics of Chinese tea: Tea is an intrinsic part of Chinese culture. Subtly fragrant yet physically fortifying, delicate but bracing, aesthetic while medically beneficial, tea reflects the harmony that is such an important part of the Chinese mind.

Good Chinese tea, taken after a heavy meal, promotes digestion and stimulates the mind – a blend of physical and spiritual benefits that has made tea the most popular beverage in Asia.

The Chinese never add milk and sugar to tea, preferring to savor the subtle bouquet and unique flavor without distraction or interference. That's why the quality and vintage of the tea leaf are so important to Chinese connoisseurs, who approach tea much as Westerners approach wine. They take several probing sniffs and sips so as to identify the type and origin of the leaf. Some may pay small fortunes for a few ounces of fine vintage tea leaves.

Like most of Asia, Taiwan offers three types of tea leaves. Those used for green tea are steamed immediately after picking, arresting bacterial growth. Then they are rolled by hand to squeeze out excess moisture and to release flavor enzymes. The leaves are finally dried and packed. When brewed, they turn a light green color, with a flavor that is delicate and somewhat tangy.

Green teas are rich in vitamin C. Experts contend that they stimulate the spirit better than any other blend, claiming that it improves their abilities to think and meditate for prolonged periods without fatigue.

Oolong, or black-dragon tea, is fermented to varying degrees after picking; the fermentation is then stopped by roasting of the leaves, which accounts for the darker color and more robust flavor. The taste is somewhat fruity, with a bouquet that has a spicy hint. In Taiwan, oolong is considered the top blend, and Tung-Ting oolong ranks as the best of the crop. This prized variety, grown on Tung-Ting mountain in Taiwan's central range, is renowned throughout the world for its fragrance and body.

The third type of leaf produced in Taiwan is black tea, inexplicably known to the Chinese as red tea. It is, in fact, more commonly drunk in the West than by the Chinese. Black teas are fully fermented, giving them a very dark color and strong taste when brewed. They lack the subtle bouquet and delicate balance of flavors that the Chinese prefer. Black teas are often used to make specialty blends, mixed with dried fruits like lichee or orange peel, with fragrant additions such as jasmine blossoms or spice – or simply with other varieties of tea.

In Taipei, the old-fashion way of drinking tea can be tried at several traditional tea houses, including Luyu Tea Center, Hengyang Road, and Wisteria Tea House, Hsinsheng South Road.

Style graces Chinese cuisine at a banquet in the cavernous ballroom of Taipei's Grand Hotel.

Among the most curious components of the anabatic skyline of Taiwan towns are the big, brightly colored balloons that bob above the rooftops. Moored to new construction projects, the balloons serve as beacons that beckon buyers to the city's newest condominium complexes, or curious people to a new "mousetrap".

In 1972, the Taipei Hilton was the tallest building in town, looming like a lighthouse over a sea of squat dwellings and tiled roofs. Today, the Hilton is barely discernible in the

forest of new skyscrapers that has sprouted during the building boom of the last decade. And it looks dwarfed now in comparison with the 245-meter-high (800-ft) Shin Kong Tower some steps away.

The average person enjoys a level of living well above that of most of the world. It is estimated that 99.7 percent of Taiwan's homes have electricity, and that there are more than 100 televisions for every 100 homes on the island. Taiwan's standard of living is higher than that of every other Asian country except Japan. And, in at least two respects, the people of Taiwan live better than the Japanese: they enjoy considerably

greater average living space, and they consume more calories of food a day, making Taiwanese the best-fed people between Tel Aviv and Tokyo. (The government is concerned that Taiwanese spend enough money in restaurants each year to finance the construction of two full-length, north-south expressways from Keelung to Kaohsiung.)

The prescription for the island's economic health is foreign trade. In the mid 1990s, total world trade with Taiwan reached US$180 billion. Despite political differences, America remains Taiwan's largest trading partner.

Trade has been Taiwan's biggest business since Chinese and Western merchants first discovered the island's wealth of resources. During the 1700s and 1800s, its major exports included sugar, coal, rice, tea, lumber and tobacco. But the most lucrative product was camphor, which flourished in Taiwan's dense mountain forests. Today, several thousand manufacturers export products.

While foreign trade has been Taiwan's principal money-maker, agriculture historically has been the primary occupation of its people. Taiwan's ten largest crops by value are rice, betel nuts, sugar cane, corn, tea, grapes, mangoes, watermelons, peanuts and pears. Each day, ships and cargo jets take containers of fresh fruits and vegetables to markets throughout the Far East.

Fishing is another traditional occupation that has contributed significantly to the island's prosperity. Fishermen haul in 1.5 million metric tons of seafood each year from the waters around Taiwan, which produces US$3.5 billion worth of fish annually. Most goes to local markets and restaurants. The frozen-food industry is highly developed, yet some of the seafood is shipped live for export. Each day, cargo jets lift off from Taipei bound for Tokyo, packed solid with wriggling live eels individually sealed in plastic bags of water. Taiwan has also been a pioneer in the field of "fish farming".

Yet the trading emphasis is rapidly changing. Modern industrial products are replacing agricultural products and natural resources as Taiwan's primary exports. For example, in 1960 sugar accounted for 43 percent of Taiwan's exports. By 1995, Taiwan had to import 60,000 metric tons of sugar to satisfy local demands.

The island's broad industrial base and foreign exchange reserves were cultivated during the 1950s and 1960s by emphasizing one major industry – textiles. With strong government support, Taiwan surpassed Japan and England as the world's major supplier of textile goods. Since the early 1970s, strict textile import quotas in Europe and the United States, and competition from labor-intensive neighbors like Korea and Indonesia, have put a dent in the textile industry.

The latest wave of economic progress has carried technology-intensive companies, like the electronics and computer industries, to greater significance over labor-intensive textile industries.

For the average resident of Taiwan, the per capita income in the mid 1990s was US$11,600. This is set to increase to US$15,000 by 2000. In Asia, only the people of Japan, Hong Kong and Singapore earn more. Taiwan's work force numbers about nine million. There is virtually no unemployment. The commercial and service sectors absorb 40 percent of the work force, and the manufacturing sectors about 28 percent. By comparison, the number of workers in agriculture and forestry has fallen to 11 percent of the total employed.

Laissez-faire, not to mention *savoir-faire*, can be credited for Taiwan's continuing economic successes. Virtually any citizen can open a shop, factory, restaurant or trading company simply by filling out the appropriate government forms and hanging a sign over the door. There is very little government interference or regulation in the free-wheeling business sphere. That has created a degree of chaos and fraud, but it has also prompted intense competition in the marketplace and has enabled the cream of the competitive crop to rise to the top of the system.

A century ago, Western traders believed that China formed a vast marketplace for Western-manufactured goods. Today, Chinese traders in Taiwan toast each other at banquets with a twist on that old phrase, "The American market is inexhaustible!"

Taiwan was long making bids to attract the fortune, fame and following that Hong Kong has enjoyed as East Asia's economic leader for more than 100 years. Banking laws were and are being reviewed to facilitate international transactions. The government also established three very successful export production zones (EPZ) at ports including Kaohsiung, Keelung and Taichung.

If Taiwan succeeds in luring some of the jittery Chinese fortunes and economic expertise of Hong Kong to its own shores, it will represent an economic coup of major proportions in the Far East.

The only possible stumbling block to continuing economic health for Taiwan is its overdependency on foreign trade. If the economies of the island's major trading partners suffer, as they do during recession years, Taiwan's may also suffer.

The island remains nearly self-sufficient in food production, even if seven percent of all imports are agricultural products (like wheat and sugar) and processed foods.

Left, a high-flying ham beckons buyers to a new apartment venture. **Above**, manufacturing electronic components.

With their bold handicrafts, stunning red-on-black ceremonial clothing, and vibrant dance and music, Taiwan's ethnic minorities have woven their own distinctive thread into the fabric of the island's population. More than 375,000 minorities, the remnants of nine main tribes, live in Taiwan, mostly in the remote valleys and along the rugged slopes of the central mountain range.

The nine tribes that prevail in Taiwan are the Ami, Atayal, Bunun, Paiwan, Puyuma, Rukai, Saisiyat, Tsao and Yami.

Inevitably, many minorities have been absorbed into the boom and urgency of Taiwan's commercial and industrial development. But some tribes still cling to the old ways, such as age-old techniques of slash-and-burn agriculture, moving on to virgin forests every few years. Their primary crops include millet for brewing liquor, sweet potatoes and taro. Cash crops such as wild mountain mushrooms, pears, peaches and plums – for the gourmet markets of the island – have also become a popular and lucrative form of income for some tribes.

Other minority groups still make their living by hunting for deer, bears, civet cats, wild boars and monkeys. Some of their take is sold to commercial markets, some used locally. Until the twentieth century, one of the most prized trophies of some tribal hunters was the human head. The Japanese stamped out that custom during their 50-year occupation of Taiwan. But the days of head-hunting are still recalled in the motif of a three-headed figure, which appears in the woodcarving and handicraft designs of some minority-group tribes.

Uncertain origins: The dispute surrounding the origin of Taiwan's minorities still heats up discussions in anthropological circles. The only point on which most scholars agree is that the tribes arrived on the island long before the Chinese, and have probably been here for about 10,000 years. Human artifacts of such antiquity have been found along the banks of the Peinan River, near Taitung.

The artifacts that were found may also help anthropologists pinpoint the original homelands of these peoples. Some schools of thought believe the tribes are proto-Malays, who migrated to Taiwan from the Malay peninsula and Indonesian archipelago. Another theory places their origins in Mongolia. A third theory is that the minorities represent the northernmost outpost of Polynesian culture, sailing here from the islands of the South Pacific. Given the diversity that exists even between individual tribes, some scholars have speculated that Taiwan's minorities probably have roots in all three regions.

All in all, minority-group society throughout Taiwan remains highly matriarchal. Women often tend the fields and orchards, while men stay home to care for the children and the housework.

The increasing exposure of the younger generation of minorities to Chinese and Western ways, through television and schooling, has begun to erode some of these traditions. Yet, the younger generation has remained on good terms with the more conservative, older tribal ways. There are signs of a renaissance of indigenous culture as the

Preceding pages: portrait of Lukai couple. **Left,** harvest dance of Lukai people, near Taitung. **Above,** Yami elder, Orchid Island.

young renew their understanding and appreciation of their roots.

The largest ethnic minority group is the Ami, which boasts more than 150,000 members. They populate the scenic mountains and valleys near Hualien, on the east coast. The Ami are mainly farmers; their annual harvest festival, held during the last weeks of July and early August, brings out the best of their traditional dance forms, music, costumes and customs. Travelers can observe Ami traditions at a cultural center in Hualien.

The minority group most accessible to Taipei visitors are the Atayal, who live in the lush valleys of Wulai, just an hour's drive away from the capital. Their proximity to

Taipei has changed their lives and driven them into the tacky tourism business.

A more authentic enclave of minorities are the Paiwan, who inhabit the mountains of eastern Pingtung, in the south. The snake-worshipping cult of the "hundred-pacer" still remains strong in Paiwan tradition. The hundred-pacer snake revered by the Paiwan and other minorities takes its name from its deadly abilities. The minorities say that victims of the snake drop dead before they can run 100 steps. Venerated as the spiritual elder of the tribe, the hundred-pacer is the embodiment of its ancestors. The snake's visage appears in abstract form on almost all arts and crafts.

The Paiwan, in particular, are master wood-carvers, making totems, doors, eaves, beams, smoking pipes and other masterpieces from the trees of Taiwan's alpine forests. They also weave, sculpt stone and fashion beadwork using ancient designs and techniques. The faithfulness of this tribe to its heritage has inspired Chinese anthropologists to research and record their ways.

Another culturally-interesting tribe, the Rukai, occupies a cluster of hamlets called Wutai, in lofty Pingtung country. The 200 households of the tribe engage primarily in agriculture. The buildings in the entire town are constructed from stone slabs that have been quarried in the surrounding mountains. The architecture of the dwellings resembles the piled slate homes that dot the Himalayan highlands of western China, northern India and Nepal.

The Rukai love remote, inaccessible cliff-side habitats – the higher, the better – and regard 10-hour treks to neighboring villages as simple strolls.

The strong attachment of the Rukai to their tribal traditions blossoms in the beautiful tunics and robes that they wear on special occasions. These garments are intricately embroidered in black and silver. Members of the tribes are also renowned throughout Taiwan for their athletic abilities, particularly archery and in marathon running.

One fascinating display of Rukai prowess occurs in their "swing contest", one of the most entertaining – if chauvinistic – rituals in Taiwan. Prospective brides mount an enormous swing, with their legs bound to prevent them from flailing. Then burly tribesmen in full ceremonial attire swing the ladies until they sail like kites to dizzying heights. Afterwards, the girls are carried from their swings and dropped into the arms of their most ardent admirers.

The Puyuma tribe shares traditions similar to those of the Rukai. They live mainly in the foothills of the central mountain range, near Taitung, and occasionally congregate on the city's outskirts for major festivals that include swing contests.

Another island tribe of note are the Bunun, of Tainan. They still practice a ritual form of night worship that remains essentially unchanged from ancient times – with two exceptions. Severed pig heads have replaced disembodied human heads as sacrificial offerings, and electricity has replaced torches for lighting. Another facet of the ritual is that many of the current participants are ethnic Chinese rather than part of the Bunun minority group. In fact, a large percentage of the tribe has abandoned its traditional form of worship for Christianity.

The ethnic group that has been least affected by Taiwan's headlong plunge into the twenty-first century are the Yami, who live on Orchid Island, off the southeast coast, and who are the only seafaring minority of Taiwan. For half a century during their occupation of Taiwan, the Japanese deliberately isolated Orchid Island as a living anthropological museum. Yami fishing boats, each hewn from a single giant tree, are beautiful vessels that glide over the waters of the southern Pacific.

Perhaps of particular interest to contemporary feminists are the marriage customs of the Yami. Women significantly outnumber the men of the island and have parlayed their numbers into a potent social force. Upon engagement, the male moves into the family home of the female for a one-month trial marriage – or, rather, a trial husband.

During that time, the prospective groom must constantly prove his prowess in hunting and fishing, exhibit his ability to design and build boats, and demonstrate other requisite skills.

If he fails the tests, he is sent packing in disgrace and another suitor is brought in for the bride's consideration. Even the man who successfully completes the trial period and wins the bride is expected to continually prove his worth to his wife and her family. Otherwise, the Yami woman may exercise her most prized right – the power unilaterally to divorce a husband at any time on any grounds and seek new more worthy mates.

Creativity: The remarkable vitality of these dwindling ethnic groups is best reflected in the creative arts.

The dazzling costumes of their ceremonial attire remains the most distinctive feature. They are usually woven by the women, who turn out bold primitive patterns for capes, shawls, shirts, vests, shoes and sandals. The

weaving of red on a black background is a dominant style, although motifs incorporate elements of the three regions from which anthropologists believe the tribes' ancestors may have come.

Minority creativity also finds expression in woodcarving, particularly tribal totems. The totems stress three motifs – faces, snakes and sex. Human heads and sexual organs are depicted with such bold strokes of the chisel that they turn out as abstractions, certainly still recognizable, but of highly-artistic sophistication.

In the performing arts, musicians and dancers move to the rhythms of nature. They perform their traditional steps with an agility

and enthusiasm that can infect spectators. In fact, many minorities have gone on to become popular contemporary singers and dancers. The participation of minorities in local and national politics is also increasing.

But there are, of course, many problems for Taiwan's ethnic minorities, as everywhere. The use of minority-group languages is declining, the overall educational level is lower amongst many tribes, and many minorities face acute social problems. On such a small land area, especially one that is as developed and as industrialized as Taiwan, it is surprising that these groups have retained any cultural identity at all.

Left, wooden carving of hunters capturing a wild boar, crafted by Paiwan artists of southern Taiwan. **Above**, a potential bride is lashed to a rope swing during harvest festivities near Taitung.

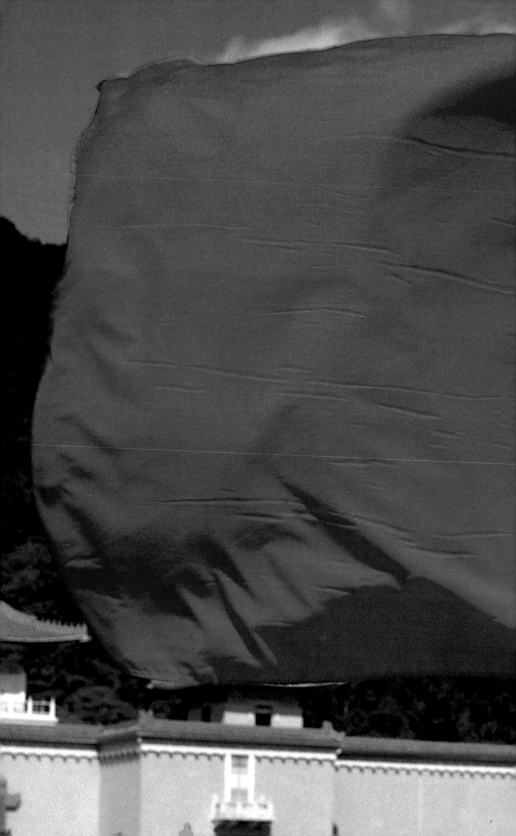

PLACES

An island is necessarily limited in its offerings, no matter how limitless its horizons. Islands typically offer neither grand expeditions nor journeys to the ends of the earth. Few small islands offer topographical diversity. Some islands – particularly those with a volcanic peak in the middle – offer nothing more than a circular road, around which one may drive and drive, again and again.

Taiwan defies these limitations. It is an island with a spectacular diversity in terrain and culture, not to mention a superb highway system that not only encircles the island, but also slithers through its interior mountains. For a reasonably small place, Taiwan reveals itself in an eclectic and resplendent fashion.

Northern Taiwan is the upper terminus of the Central Range that bisects long and narrow Taiwan. The north is of both flat land and foothills. Being so close to Taipei, the northern sights are, of course, sometimes crowded as city residents seek escape. The coastal route along the north shore, while lacking the tropical beaches of the south, skirts an unusually-sculpted sandstone seashore.

Taipei is, of course, Taiwan's largest city. Technically, it is considered by the Nationalist government as the provisional capital of the Republic of China, which the Nationalists say includes the mainland. In any case, it is a city of significant size and prosperity, with all of the cultural offerings and urban clutter of any city. (If there's one stop to be made in Taipei, it would be the National Palace Museum, with its immense collection of China's ancient past.)

Extensive expressways transit the island, and heading southwards can be as quick or as lazy as desired. Landscapes along the eastern coast are rustic and primal; down the west coast, both agricultural and industrial. The cities along the western coast of Taiwan – Taichung, Tainan, Kaohsiung – are a mix of ports, industry and history. Tainan is the Kyoto of Taiwan, in a modest way, while Kaohsiung is a distinctly industrial port city. Taichung falls somewhere in between.

Should a traveler choose the eastern seaboard, one finds little evidence of urbanization. Rather, it is a tempestuous shoreline of steep cliffs and crashing Pacific waves. Villages and towns along the coastal road – there are no cities – are pleasantly modest. Most notable of sights is Taroko Gorge, a fantastic marble chasm with an equally remarkable road sliced right through the marble.

Between the east and west coasts are the mountains of the Central Range, with numerous hot-spring resorts and honeymoon retreats such as Sun Moon Lake. (Romance knows no limits, even if surrounded by bus loads of tourists.) There are rambling bamboo forests and one of Asia's tallest mountains, Yu Shan, towering 3,952 meters (12,966 ft) above the Pacific.

Preceding pages: Taiwan's flag; fishing along the east coast; Ami harvest dance, Hualien; Taipei's National Concert Hall, with the Shin Kong Tower behind. Left, unusual southern coastline, Maopitou.

Taiwan

30 km / 19 mi

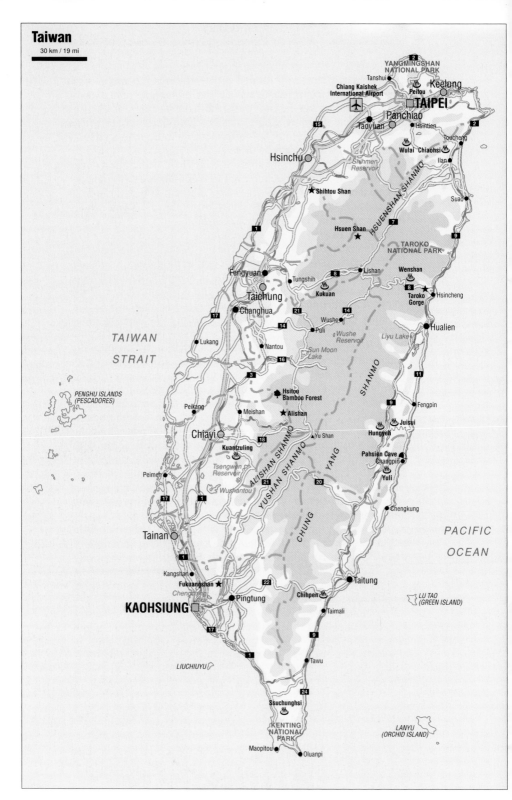

YANGMINGSHAN
NATIONAL PARK

Tanshui

Chiang Kaishek
International Airport

Peitou ♨ Keelung

TAIPEI

Panchiao

Taoyuan

Hsintien

Toucheng

Wulai ♨ Chiaohsi ♨

Hsinchu

Ilan

Shihmen
Reservoir

Suao

★ Shihtou Shan

HSUENSHAN SHANMO

TAROKO
NATIONAL PARK

★ Hsuen Shan

Fengyuan

Tungshih

Lishan

Wenshan ♨

Kukuan ♨

Taroko
Gorge ♨

Hsincheng

Taichung

Changhua

Wushe

Hualien

Wushe
Reservoir

Puli

Lukang

Nantou

Liyu Lake

TAIWAN

STRAIT

Sun Moon
Lake

SHANMO

PENGHU ISLANDS
(PESCADORES)

Fengpin

Hsitou ♨
Bamboo Forest

Peikang

Meishan

Juisui ♨

★ Alishan

Hungyeh ♨

Chiayi

Pahsien Cave ♨

Yu Shan

Changpin

Kuantzuling ♨

Yuli ♨

ALISHAN SHANMO

YUSHAN SHANMO

CHUNG

YANG

Tsengwen
Reservoir

Peimen

Chengkung

Wushantou

PACIFIC

Tainan

OCEAN

Kangshan

LU TAO
(GREEN ISLAND)

Fukuangshan ★

Taitung

Chengc...

Pingtung

Chihpen ♨

KAOHSIUNG

Taimali

LIUCHIUYU

Tawu

Ssuchunghsi ♨

LANYU
(ORCHID ISLAND)

KENTING
NATIONAL
PARK

Maopitou

Oluanpi

140

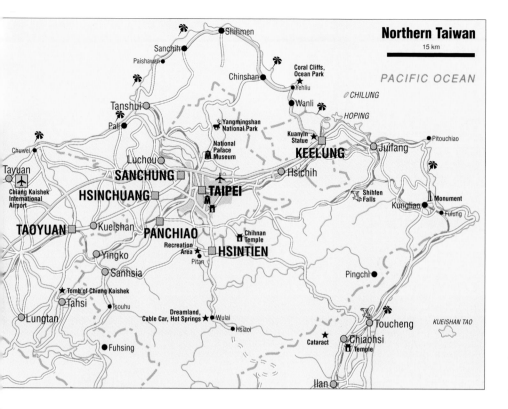

Northern Taiwan

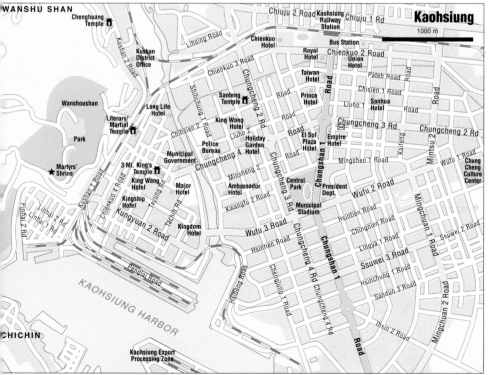

Kaohsiung

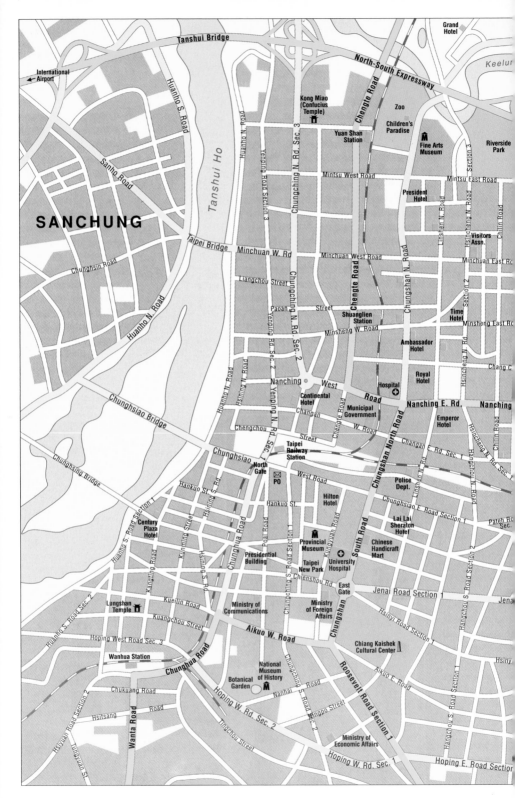

Tanshui Bridge

North-South Expressway

Keelu

Grand Hotel

International Airport

Huanho S. Road

Sanho Road

SANCHUNG

Chunghsin Road

Huanho N. Road

Tanshui Ho

Taipei Bridge

Huanho N. Road

Yenping Road Section 3

Chungching N. Rd. Sec. 3

Chengtie Road

Kong Miao (Confucius Temple)

Zoo

Children's Paradise

Yuan Shan Station

Fine Arts Museum

Section 3

Riverside Park

Mintsu West Road

Mintsu East Road

President Hotel

Visitors Assn.

Linsheng N. Road

Hsincheng N. Road

Chilin Road

Minchuan W. Rd

Minchuan West Road

Chengtie Road

Chungshan N. Road

Minchuan East Rd

Section 2

Liangchou Street

Chungching N. Rd. Sec. 2

Paoan Street

Street

Shuanglien Station

Time Hotel

Minsheng East Rd

Minsheng W. Road

Yenping Rd. Sec. 2

Ambassador Hotel

Hsincheng N. Rd.

Chang C

Nanching West Road

Continental Hotel

Chengtie Road

Hospital

Royal Hotel

Hsimin W. Road

Yenping N. Rd. Sec.

Municipal Government

Nanching E. Rd.

Nanching

Changan

Chungshan North Road

Emperor Hotel

Hsinchen N. Road

Chilin Road

Chengchou

Chengtie Road

W. Road

Changan E. Rd. Sec. 2

Hangchou N. Road

Chunghsiao

Street

Taipei Railway Station

North Gate

PO

West Road

Police Dept.

Linsheng N. Rd.

Chunghsiao Bridge

Hankuo St.

Hsimin S. Rd.

Chunghua Road

Hankuo St.

Hilton Hotel

Chunghsiao E. Road Section 1

Pateh Ro Sec.

Chunghsing Bridge

Century Plaza Hotel

Kunming Street

Hanko S. Road

Post Road

Provincial Museum

Kungyuan Road

South Road

Lai Lai Sheraton Hotel

Chinese Handicraft Mart

Hsinchu S. Road Section 2

Huanho S. Road Section 1

Kangting Road

Presidential Building

Chungching S. Road Section 1

Taipei New Park

University Hospital

Hsinyi Road Section 1

Jena

Lungshan Temple

Kueilin Road

Chienshou Rd.

East Gate

Jenai Road Section 1

Kuangchou Street

Ministry of Communications

Ministry of Foreign Affairs

Chungshan

Huanho S. Road Section 2

Hoping West Road Sec. 3

Aikuo W. Road

Hsinyi Road Section 1

Hsiny

Wanhua Station

Chunghua Road

Chiang Kaishek Cultural Center

Roosevelt Road Section 1

Chukuang Road

Botanical Garden

National Museum of History

Chungching S. Road Sec. 2

Aikuo E. Road

Hsinsiang Road

Wanta Road

Hoping W. Rd. Sec. 2

Nanhai Road

Mingpo Street

Hangchou S. Road Section 1

Tingchou Street

Ministry of Economic Affairs

Hoping W. Rd. Sec. 1

Hoping E. Road Section

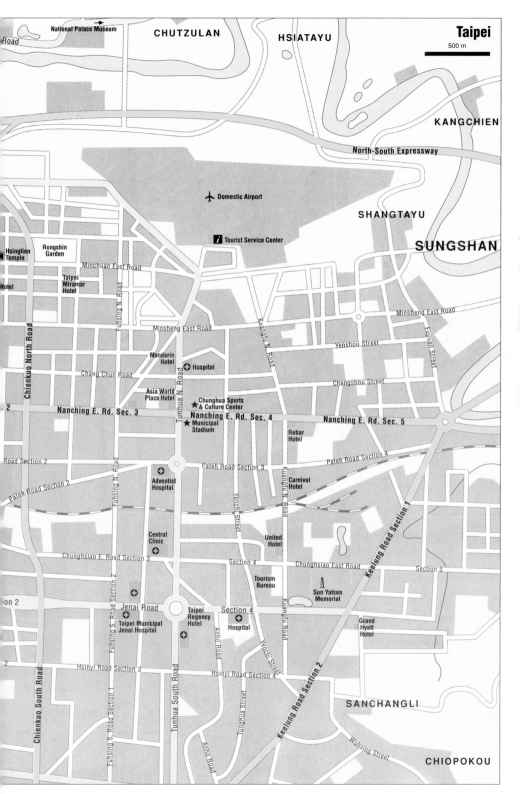

National Palace Museum

Road

CHUTZULAN

HSIATAYU

Taipei

500 m

KANGCHIEN

North-South Expressway

Domestic Airport

SHANGTAYU

Tourist Service Center

SUNGSHAN

Hsingtien Temple

Rongshin Garden

Hotel

Minchuan East Road

Taipei Miramar Hotel

Funsing N. Road

Chienkuo North Road

Minsheng East Road

Kuangfu N. Road

Minsheng East Road

Fuyuan Street

Yenshou Street

Mandarin Hotel

Hospital

Chang Chun Road

Tunhua N. Road

Changshou Street

Asia World Plaza Hotel

Chunghua Sports & Culture Center

Nanching E. Rd. Sec. 3

Nanching E. Rd. Sec. 4

Municipal Stadium

Nanching E. Rd. Sec. 5

2

Rebar Hotel

Road Section 2

Pateh Road Section 3

Pateh Road Section 4

Adventist Hospital

Pateh Road Section 2

Funsing N. Road

Yenchi Street

Kuangfu N. Road

Carnival Hotel

Keelung Road Section 1

Central Clinic

United Hotel

Chunghsiao E. Road Section 3

Section 4

Chunghsiao East Road

Section 5

ion 2

Jenai Road

Tourism Bureau

Sun Yatsen Memorial

Taipei Municipal Jenai Hospital

Taipei Regency Hotel

Section 4

Hospital

Kuangfu Road

Grand Hyatt Hotel

2

Funsing S. Road Section 2

Chienkuo South Road

Hsinyi Road Section 3

Anho Road

Hsinyi Road Section 4

Yenchi Street

Keelung Road Section 2

SANCHANGLI

Funsing S. Road Section 1

Tunhua South Road

Tunhua Street

Anho Road

Wuhsing Street

CHIOPOKOU

143

TAIPEI

When the leaders of the Republic of China established their government in northern Taiwan, in 1949, Taipei was no more than a sleepy country town, a moist blanket of rice fields and mud flats. Even in the mid 1960s, the city had few paved roads, and pedicabs were the primary means of public transportation.

The changes that forever altered the face of Taipei during the 1970s were truly dramatic. All the blessings and evils of modernization gripped the city in a frenzy of growth, which, for better or worse, continues today. The clatter of pedicabs has given way to the clunk of pile-drivers and the click of taxi meters. Tens of thousands of taxis, buses, private automobiles and lorries – and hundreds of thousands of motorcycles – clog the underpasses, overpasses, roundabouts and flyovers of modern roads and expressways. The drab, gray compartments of concrete that once characterized Taipei architecture now squat in the shadows of high-rise glass and metal.

The remarkable change that swept Taipei has also affected the city's three million residents. The utilitarian fashions of the 1950s were long ago put into mothballs in favor of the latest trends and designs from Paris, Hong Kong and New York. Youths patronize cafes that serve Starbucks coffee from Seattle, and dance in discos to the latest from Tokyo and London.

Yet this veneer of twentieth-century sophistication does not mask one implacable fact: Taipei remains one of the most staunchly traditional cities of Asia. For all its modern appointments, Taipei has not succumbed to the creeping Westernization that has woven itself into social fabric of Asian cities like Hong Kong and Singapore.

In their headlong lunge into the future, neither Taipei nor its people have left behind their heritage – the heart that keeps Taipei moving is unquestionably Chinese. And it is that unfaltering beat that makes Taipei endlessly fascinating for visitors.

Policy shifts: Taipei's stylish facade can be attributed, in part, to a pair of changes in governmental policy in the late 1970s. First, the government rescinded a long-standing ban on the construction of new hotels and other high-rises in Taiwan. Permits to build scores of skyscrapers were quickly issued. Hotels and office buildings mushroomed, and well-heeled residents donned the latest fashions to see and be seen in the new atrium lobbies, revolving bars and chic boutiques.

The second move that proved to be a catalyst for internationalism was a relaxation of restrictions on overseas travel. Prior to 1978, residents of Taiwan were prohibited from leaving the country, except to visit relatives, or for business or educational purposes. The change in policy permitted people to receive passports and exit visas purely for pleasure trips. Applications poured in faster than they could be processed. Many residents of Taipei had been saving for decades for the chance to taste foreign flavors firsthand. They flocked

Preceding
pages:
Martyrs'
Shrine. Left,
an unusually
empty side
street. Right,
offices near
West Gate.

to Tokyo, Manila, Singapore and Seoul. Some ventured as far as Europe and the United States. Along with new tastes in food, fashion and recreation, they brought back modern problems.

The new construction laws have resulted in some ill-conceived buildings, but most are, nonetheless, modern models of architectural aesthetics. In addition, nearly-continuous road construction has been unable to keep pace with the ever-increasing numbers of motor vehicles; there are now over a million motorcycles and scooters in Taipei, at least one per household. The resulting traffic congestion has made it difficult to enforce traffic codes. In order to cope with the chaos, drivers have coined an expression that accounts for their reckless road habits: "Fight to be first, fear to be last!"

Exhaust from the vehicles, combined with smoke from the industrial complexes that ring the city, has added another modern malaise to Taipei.

Even more problematic has been the constant flow of newcomers seeking their fortunes in the big city. Despite their earthly philosophy and appreciation of nature, the Chinese have traditionally favored city life to rural life, especially during healthy economic times. Taiwan's steady economic growth has attracted thousands from the countryside each month.

Yet for all its newly acquired ills, the underlying currents of traditional Chinese culture continue to make Taipei an attractive destination for travelers. Not unexpectedly, the greatest source of visitors to Taiwan annually are the overseas Chinese communities of the world. Taiwan also remains a magnet for Japanese, who have borrowed heavily from classical Chinese culture during the past 1,000 years. Overseas Chinese and foreigners alike find another irresistible facet to Taipei – its people. In the end, *ren chingwei* – the flavor of human feelings – leaves every visitor with thoughts of returning.

Administrative beginnings: Historically, Taipei's outskirts have attracted more interest than its center. When Koxinga drove the Dutch from Taiwan in 1661,

he appointed a general named Huang An to command army and naval forces stationed at Tanshui, at the mouth of the Tanshui River and northwest of modern Taipei. New farming methods were introduced along the river banks, and soldiers were sent to reclaim land.

Early in the eighteenth century, reclaimed lands were extended from Hsinchuang to the area of modern Wanhua, now the heart of old Taipei. Wanhua, then known as Mengchia, became a major port that reached its peak in the early 1850s, before port activity shifted to Tataocheng.

An emperor of the Qing dynasty was the first to designate the area as an administrative center, in 1875, when the district of Taipei Fu was established, at the site of modern Chengchung. At the same time, a five-kilometer (3-mi) protective perimeter was constructed around the city.

The Japanese furthered the area's administrative reputation when they took control of Taiwan in 1895. They changed Taipei Fu into Taipei Chou, then merged suburban areas into an administrative district known as Taipei Ting.

In 1920, 23 years after plans had been drawn, Taipei was formally recognized as a city. During the next dozen years, its population soared from 150,000 to 600,000 people; the area it occupied expanded from 20 to 70 square kilometers (7 to 25 sq mi).

Less than five years after China regained Taiwan from a defeated Japan, in 1945, Taipei was made the focus of government activities. It became a special municipality by decree in 1966, confirming it as Taiwan's political, cultural, economic and military center. The towns of Chingmei, Mucha, Neihu, Nanking, Peitou and Shihlin were incorporated into Taipei in 1968. In 1990, the former 16 districts of Taipei City were reorganized into 12 districts.

Into the city: Modern visitors to Taipei, like the settlers of old, experience the city's outskirts first. **Chiang Kaishek International Airport** (CKS) is located in Taoyuan, about 40 kilometers (25 mi) southwest of the capital. The airport's modern glass-and-concrete terminal is one of Asia's largest. Buses and taxis whisk new arrivals along the fast, clean North-South Highway, linking airport and points north to Taipei.

Taipei was once described as the ugly duckling of Asian cities. That impression took root during the 1960s from the city's drab buildings, dusty streets, open gutters and battered pedicabs. The modern look that Taipei has fostered during more recent times has all but erased its old reputation. Spacious six-lane boulevards shaded by islands of tropical trees have helped provide breathing space between the walls of new buildings. Indeed, Taipei differs little from other burgeoning modern Asian cities.

Taipei once had a notorious reputation among travelers and tour operators as a place of insufficient, inadequate hotel space. At the time, the government suspiciously viewed the hotel business as a "special industry" intimately connected with the pursuit of wine, women and song – a view that was perhaps a mental hangover from the infamous days of prewar Shanghai, the

Fortune teller, Snake Alley.

city of inspiration for Taipei's builders. It's all history now. The dearth of accommodations has given way to a glut of hotels that range from inexpensive establishments to posh palaces of Sybaritic comfort.

Street rambles: Wandering aimlessly through Taipei's streets (but take a card with your hotel's name, in Chinese, just in case) is a good way to familiarize oneself with the city and its people. It will uncover many surprises that could never be duplicated on guided tours around the main tourist attractions. Walking through Taipei, despite heat and dust, is perhaps better than being stuck in a taxi, surrounded by several hundred more cars, all fighting for space to move a little bit further. Helpful for getting a broad-brush impression of Taipei is a trip on the Metro's Mucha line, which runs high above the traffic.

Taipei is divided into northern and southern districts by Chunghsiao Road, site of the Taipei Railway Station. Chungshan North and Chungshan South roads slice the city into eastern and

western portions. Depending upon which side of this north–south axis a street lies, it is assigned either East or West. Very long main roads are divided into sections. Section 1 is near the city center, while Section 5 is quite a distance out. Addresses therefore provide at least a rough indication of where one must look on the map.

One would think that this classically Chinese grid layout would make it childishly easy to find one's way around the city. But problems are compounded for foreign visitors by the fact that few street signs use roman characters.

One of the city's easiest landmarks for orientation is the **Grand Hotel**. Located atop a ridge at the northern end of the city, this 530-room hotel looks somewhat like an ancient palace, built in the classical imperial style of old China. The massive multi-story new wing is crowned by the largest classical Chinese roof on earth.

The Grand Hotel is as good a spot as any to begin touring Taipei. East of the Grand Hotel about half a kilometer is the **Revolutionary Martyrs' Shrine**, on Peian Road. Open daily, the entire complex is built in the palace style of the Ming dynasty. Each structure attempts to reproduce a similar hall or pavilion in Beijing. Dedicated to the fallen heroes of China's wars, the arched portals of the main gate open onto a vast courtyard, past guest pavilions, drums and bell towers. Two gigantic brass-studded doors open onto the main shrine, where the names of the heroes are inscribed beside murals depicting their feats. The late Chiang Kaishek considered this a favorite retreat, frequently spending entire afternoons strolling through the grounds and halls. A changing of the guard occurs every hour.

Only a short taxi ride in the opposite direction, to the southwest of the Grand Hotel, is **Kong Miao**, the Confucius Temple, on Talung Street. A tranquil retreat compared to the city's other places of worship, absent are the throngs of worshippers supplicating their gods with prayer and offerings, the cacophony of gongs and drums, and the gaudy **Grand Hotel.**

idols. Absent, too, are images of Confucius. The tranquility is fitting – Confucius preached the virtues of peace and quiet. The architecture of the temple is subtle yet exquisite, and highlighted by magnificent roofs.

By contrast, the **Paoan Temple**, on Hami Street and next to the Confucian Temple, is a gaudy monument to traditional Chinese folk religion. This 250-year-old Daoist temple sports carved dragons writhing in solid rock on the main support columns, and an interior crowded with the images of many deities. Buddhist elements are also apparent in the architecture, in testimony to the syncretic nature of Chinese religion.

Another temple of note is **Hsingtien**, on Minchuan E. Road, Sec. 2, in the northeast quadrant of the city. Dedicated to the red-faced, black-bearded Kuan Kung, this Daoist temple is filled with worshippers day and night. On either side of the main prayer hall is a miniature garden alcove built around a tiny pond, examples of how the Chinese symbolically incorporate elements of nature into temple design and architecture.

Just south of the Grand Hotel is the **Taipei Fine Arts Museum**, with 24 galleries of modern art, and the **Lin An Tai Homestead**, an original 30-room family home of a wealthy merchant from the Qing-dynasty era and built in the 1820s. Designed for the very young lovers of Chinese history and culture – but adults will like it, too – is **Children's Paradise**, which includes a World of Yesterday and a World of Tomorrow.

Located in the eastern part of the city is an important memorial to Chiang Kaishek's mentor and the founder of the Republic of China, Dr. Sun Yatsen – the only common denominator between the rival Communist and Nationalist regimes, which both revere him as the founder of modern China. On Section 4 of Jenai Road and a long taxi ride away, the main building of the **Sun Yatsen Memorial** boasts a sweeping, gracefully-curved Chinese roof of glazed yellow tile. A six-meter-high (20-ft) bronze statue of Sun Yatsen graces the main lobby.

Golden window shopping.

In the suburb of Mucha, to the southeast of the city, is the municipal **zoo**. It is primarily of interest to Taiwan residents, although it does exhibit creatures indigenous to the island, such as the rare Formosan spotted deer. The best way to go there is via the Metro's Mucha line.

Downtown walkabout: The best place to begin a downtown walking tour is from the **Taipei Railway Station**. This is not just a station, but an impressive and spacious palace, with four floors below street level. Close to the railway station are the bus terminals.

Over the years, the downtown area has been remodeled at the same time as the construction of the new underground rail arteries. Many old buildings were removed, giving space to modern skyscrapers. One pride of Taipei is the 245-meter-tall (800-ft) **Shin Kong Tower**, just opposite the train station and overshadowing the Taipei Hilton. High-speed elevators shoot visitors upwards at 540 meters per minute (1,770 ft/min), topping out in 35 seconds at the observatory on the 49th floor (out of 51). A Taipei landmark since 1994, the tower's unobstructed view on clear days is a popular excursion. The inner wall of the observatory is adorned with old black-and-white lithographs depicting Taipei of yesteryear.

Tempting is shopping in one of the large shopping malls. But first consider the Chinese way of daily shopping. East towards the Tanshui River is the narrow and unique **Tihua Street**, perhaps Taipei's most important historical street and paralleling Yenping Road. In the mid 1800s, the first merchant established his business in this area; most of the houses are from the first decade of this century. Back then, goods arrived mainly by boat on the Tanshui River.

The construction is typical for early establishments in Taiwan: the structures look very small from the front, but extend quite a ways back. Here, the merchant's family lived, inventory was stored, and often products were manufactured. Today, an unbelievable variety of Chinese products are sold along Tihua Street, from dried lotus nuts to shark fins, from just-harvested herbals to shells and fresh fish.

The air is thick with incense at the small and unpretentious **Hsiahai Temple**, also on Tihua Street and home to Taipei's city deity and his disciples.

West from the railway station and opposite the **main post office** (which offers a good philatelic section) stands the ugly **North Gate**, one of the four remaining city gates. Located at the intersection of Chunghsiao and Chunghua roads, just before Chunghsiao crosses the river, the gate was erected in 1984, looking somewhat out of place amidst the tangle of expressway flyovers that are modern Taipei.

The area from Chunghua Road to the Tanshui River further west is called **Hsimenting**, a local shoppers' haven.

South of the train station stands the **Taiwan Provincial Museum**, eye-catching in its Greek Revival style on Hsiangyang Road. It is less fascinating than, say, the national museum, but it offers important displays of minority group handicrafts, clothes and artifacts. **Red is auspicious.**

Behind the museum is **Taipei New Park**, "newly" opened in 1907 and featuring ponds, pagodas and pavilions. The best time to walk the grounds of New Park is at dawn, when thousands of the city's residents stretch, dance, exercise and move through various forms of *taiji, shaolin* and other disciplines. Visitors are welcome to join in with the groups for an invigorating start to a day in Taipei. (Evenings, however, are best spent somewhere else by visitors.)

To the east of the New Park are most of the important government ministries and offices. From the park's southwestern end, it is only a short distance to the governmental center of Taiwan.

Most prominent is the **Presidential Building**, fronting an enormous plaza that is the site of the annual and colorful celebrations during the Double Tens: October 10, or National Day. The five-story complex, finished in 1919, has a central tower 60 meters (200 ft) high.

At the south end of Chungshan Road is the impressive **East Gate**, the biggest of the original five gates of the nine-teenth-century city wall. In 1966, it was renovated and underwent considerable ornate embellishment on its once-very-simple facade.

A massive monument to the late president, the **Chiang Kaishek Cultural Center** is located at Chungshan South Road, close to the East Gate. Dedicated in 1980, the fifth anniversary of Chiang's death, the enormous 76-meter-high (250-ft) Memorial Hall dominates the landscaped grounds. Inside is an imposing 25-ton bronze statue of the late president. From morning until late evening, the adjacent park is full of life – seniors chatting under a shady tree or feeding the beautiful fat carps in the placid fish ponds, mothers with children strolling the walkways, newlyweds taking the inevitable wedding photos.

The main entrance to the Memorial Hall is a magnificent arch, in traditional Ming style, that towers 30 meters (100 ft) high and stretches 75 meters (250 ft) across. One feature of the memorial are the 18 different styles of traditional Chinese windows, at eye-level along

Chiang Kaishek Memorial Hall.

the entire length of the perimeter wall.

Part of the cultural center complex, and standing amidst beautiful grounds, are the **National Opera House**, built in Chinese Palace style, and the **Concert Hall**. The Memorial Hall itself closes at 5pm, but the park grounds remain open for evening jaunts or jogs.

The **National Museum of History**, on Nanhai Road, contains 10,000 Chinese art objects dating from 2000 BC to modern times, including a fine sampling of Chinese currency. This interesting museum is less crowded than its counterpart, the National Palace Museum. After touring its exhibits, visitors can stroll the grounds of the **botanical gardens** next door, containing hundreds of species of trees, shrubs, palms and bamboo. Adjacent to the Museum of History are the **National Science Hall** and **National Arts Hall**.

A short distance further south, on Chungching Road, the **Postal Museum** makes philatelists happy with its extensive stamp collection.

West of the Chiang Kaishek memorial and near the river is the oldest and most famous of Taipei's myriad temples, **Lungshan**, or Dragon Mountain, a reference to the large collection of toothsome creatures on its busy roof. The temple is on Kuangchou Street, close to the Tanshui River in the heart of old Taipei and southwest of the Taipei Railway Station. It was built early in the eighteenth century to honor Taiwan's patron deities, Kuanyin and Matsu.

The building was inadvertently hit by an Allied air raid in 1945. So intense were the flames from the incendiary bomb that they melted the iron railings surrounding the large camphor-wood statue of Kuanyin. The hall was totally destroyed – yet the wooden statue somehow withstood the searing flames, except for a bit of ash and debris around its feet. The main hall was rebuilt, in 1957, enveloping the statue that gazes with unceasing equanimity at worshippers from its spot on the main altar. Devotees attribute the survival of the statue to the supernatural powers of the deity herself, the goddess of mercy.

Lungshan courtyard.

In addition to the miraculous carving of Kuanyin, the temple is renowned for its fine stone sculpture, woodcarving and bronze work. Only the top performers in annual island-wide carving competitions are permitted to perform maintenance and restoration work on the temple buildings.

Especially striking are the 12 main support columns that hold up the central hall. They appear to come alive with their dragons hewn from solid stone. Open until late at night, Lungshan is usually packed with worshipers, a place to witness traditional Chinese rites.

Markets: A good way to absorb the city's traditions is to take in the public markets. Most are open from dawn until midnight, selling an amazing variety of fresh vegetables, fragrant fruits, meats, fish, poultry, spices and condiments. At night, the fresh-produce vendors retire from the scene, to be replaced by scores of food stalls on wheels. These instant cafes serve every conceivable kind of Chinese snack food, at reasonable prices. The most exotic night market of all is the two-block-long lane in the Wanhua district called **Snake Alley** by tourists, which flock to the street by the bus load. Only a few minutes' walk from the Lungshan temple, this alley's main thoroughfare is known to everyone else as Huahsi Street.

The Western sobriquet stems from the nature of business conducted by some of the street's vendors, their shops stacked with cages of hissing snakes. The vendors flip open the cage tops and deftly whip out snakes to sell. Customers watch as the chosen snake is strung live on a wire, stretched taut and literally unzipped open before their eyes with a small knife.

Blood and bile from the squirming snake are squeezed into a glass containing potent spirits and herbs. For customers who are keen on seeking an additional "kick", the vendor will even add a few drops of poison venom to the mixture. The carcasses of the gutted snakes are left to hang in the night, while the concoction is drunk by men who believe the potion strengthens the

Tattoo art and snake snack, Snake Alley.

eyes and the lower spine, eliminates fatigue and, inevitably, promotes male sexual vitality. Later, the meat is taken back to the kitchen for snake soup, a tasty and nourishing dish.

Other than the snakes, the alley offers countless fortune-tellers, vendors of herbal potions, tattoo parlors, fresh-fruit stalls and hawkers of baubles and bangles. It also has good restaurants specializing in fresh seafood.

The Jaoho Street night market, near Sungshan Railway Station in the east of the city, is easily accessible, although all the hustle there may be too much for some visitors. Farther afield is the Shinlin market, one of Taipei's largest and most complete. It sprawls across several acres north of the Grand Hotel, in the suburb of Shinlin. Despite the occasionally appalling appearances of these markets, the food is uniformly safe for consumption – culinary cleanliness is an ancient Chinese tradition.

North of the city: Nestled in the foothills, several kilometers to the northeast of the Grand Hotel and past the Martyrs'

Shrine, is the most popular and important attraction in Taipei, if not in all of Taiwan. An imposing complex of beige-brick buildings, topped with green and imperial-yellow slate roofs, houses the **National Palace Museum**. The building is impressive, and the treasures within are unimaginable. Next to the museum is a small, but perfectly styled and very attractive, *chin-shan-yuan* Chinese garden, worth a stroll.

Displayed in the Palace Museum – the exhibitions change from time to time – are some 6,000 works of art representing the zenith of 5,000 years of Chinese creativity. And these are just a fraction of the more than 700,000 paintings, porcelains, bronzes, rubbings, tapestries, books and other art objects stored in nearly 4,000 crates located in vaults that are tunneled into the mountain behind the museum.

The National Palace Museum opened in 1965. But the history of its treasures, which reads like a John le Carré thriller, can be traced back more than 1,000 years, to the beginning of the Song

National Palace Museum.

dynasty (AD 960–1279). The founder of that dynasty established the Hanlin Academy to encourage literature and the arts. The emperor's brother and successor later opened a gallery, where some of the items in the current collection were first housed. The gallery was then established as a government department for the preservation of rare books, old paintings and calligraphy. This imperial gallery was the prototype for Taipei's collection.

The Song collection was transported from Beijing to Nanjing during the Ming dynasty, then back again, foreshadowing the collection's many moves in the twentieth century. The collection expanded considerably during the Qing dynasty (1644–1911). The Qing emperors were avid art collectors. The majority of items in the present collection are the result of their effort to seek out China's most important treasures.

But the real intrigues began in November, 1924. The provisional Nationalist government in Beijing gave the last surviving Manchu emperor, Puyi, and his entourage of 2,000 eunuchs and ladies two hours to evacuate the Imperial Palace. Then the government had 30 young Chinese scholars and art experts identify and inventory the overwhelming collection of art treasures that had been hoarded within the palace for more than 500 years.

It took the scholars two years just to sort out and organize the collection. In the meantime, the government formally established the National Beijing Palace Museum and began displaying some of the treasures.

By the time the task of identifying all the priceless objects was completed in 1931, the Japanese had attacked northwest China, in Manchuria, and threatened Beijing. The art collection had, and still has, enormous symbolic value to whomever possesses it, bestowing a measure of political legitimacy upon its owners. To prevent the Japanese from seizing the collection, the government carefully packed everything in 20,000 cases and shipped it, in five trains, south to Nanjing.

Carved wooden cups.

Thus began a 16-year-long odyssey. The priceless treasures were shuttled back and forth across the war-torn face of China by rail, truck, ox cart, raft and foot, always a few steps ahead of pursuing Japanese and, later, Communist troops. Incredibly, not a single item was lost or damaged. A representative selection of the best items was shipped to London for a major art exhibition in 1936 – prompting an uproar among China's intellectuals, who feared the foreigners would never return the works. But all made it back to China.

The following year, the Japanese occupied Beijing and threatened Nanjing. Once again, the precious collection was loaded aboard trucks and transported in three shipments over hills, rivers and streams to China's rugged western mountains.

After the Japanese surrender in 1945, the Nationalist government brought the pieces back to Nanjing. But when Communist control of the mainland appeared imminent in 1948, 4,800 cases of the most valuable pieces were culled from the original 20,000 cases and sent for safekeeping to Taiwan. They were stored in a sugar warehouse in Taichung, where they remained until the Chungshan (Sun Yatsen) Museum Building, in Waishuanghsi, opened in 1965.

Among the items cached are 4,400 ancient bronzes, 24,000 pieces of porcelain, 13,000 paintings, 14,000 works of calligraphy, 4,600 pieces of jade, 153,000 rare books from the imperial library, and 390,000 documents, diaries and old palace records. Massive steel doors lead to the catacombs in the mountain, where the steel trunks are stacked one atop the other. One semicircular tunnel is 190 meters (610 ft) long, the other 150 meters (490 ft). The temperature is kept at a constant 18°C (64°F), and dehumidifiers line the corridors.

Little by little, the Palace Museum has been revealing most of the secrets of its vaults. Paintings are rotated in special exhibitions every three months; other objects, like Hindustan jades and *ting* bronzes, are rotated at two-year intervals. The museum's permanent collection includes artifacts from tombs in Hunan province, along with bronzes, oracle bones, ceramics, porcelains and paintings. Enamels, jade, small carvings, lacquers and more paintings are displayed on the third floor.

There are famous pieces such as the *feitsui* jade cabbage stock – carved during the Qing dynasty, complete with camouflaged grasshopper – and a unique set of 79 wooden cups, carved paper-thin so that all can be held in a single large cup. There's an amazing collection of miniatures carved from wood and ivory. One tiny cruising yacht, only five centimeters long and three centimeters high, has crew and guests carved into its interior cabin.

Almost directly opposite the National Palace Museum, just a few minutes' walk away, is the **Chinese Culture and Movie Center**, which provides insight into medieval Chinese architecture, costume and folk art. Feature films are also sometimes made here; the architectural compositions and other motifs conform perfectly to the Chinese idea of typically Chinese.

Left, vault of National Palace Museum. **Right**, Taipei's hotels climb higher each year.

NORTHERN TAIWAN

Taipei's sights and traffic monopolize most of a traveler's time in the northern part of Taiwan. But an excursion beyond the city will offer another side of life on the island. Taiwan's northernmost tip, especially, is a microcosm of Taiwan, with its mountains, waterfalls, volcanic past, beaches, paddy fields, villages and temples.

The fastest route of escape from Taipei lies up nearby **Yangming Shan**. About 40 minutes' drive via winding roads north of the city, Yangming is known as the local Beverly Hills. Large numbers of wealthy industrial tycoons, movie stars and entrepreneurs, as well as expatriate businesspeople, live here in luxurious villas clinging to the cliffs in the cool climes above Taipei. Originally called Grass Mountain, the name was changed to honor a philosopher, Wang Yangming (1472–1529).

Halfway up the main road, a sign points left toward White Cloud Villa, an orchid garden with a selection of both modern sculptures and magnificent orchids. Especially worth seeing is the private museum containing exhibits of naive art from all over the world. The villa's mountain-top restaurant provides panoramic views of Taipei.

The mountain-top is crowned by **Yangmingshan National Park**. This well-maintained park features walkways that wind through colorful gardens of trees, bushes, fragrant flowers and grottos. From the middle of February until the end of March, an annual spring-flower festival is held in the park, with the entire mountain awash with cherry blossoms and carpeted with bright, flowering azaleas. (For a small fee, visitors can enter the park on foot. People in automobiles pay more.)

The park gets very busy on Sundays and holidays, particularly during spring and summer.

A less lofty but an equally-entrancing retreat a few minutes from Taipei is the suburb of **Peitou** (pronounced *bay tow*). It nestles snugly in lush green hills north of the city, and can be reached via twisting back roads from Yangming Shan, or from Taipei via a much-less-scenic route that passes through the suburb of Tienmou. (Peitou will soon be a stop at the MRT's Red Line.)

Peitou literally means Northern Sojourn. It has a Japanese feel that has lingered ever since the Japanese turned the town into a resort for their officers and magistrates at the turn of the century. More recently, Peitou was notorious as a getaway for large groups of men from Japan. The attractions were Peitou's therapeutic hot springs, and women tending aching muscles.

Prostitution was once legal here, but ended (in theory) in 1979 when the Taipei city council passed an often-shelved resolution prohibiting the practice. Although this measure has not entirely succeeded in sweeping the "fallen flowers" from the streets, it has improved Peitou's overall ambience; now, families and couples enjoy the unequaled delights of this unique village.

Almost all hotels in the area feature

hot sulfur-spring water that runs directly from the tap into tiled tubs, sunken or above ground. Some also have large *furo*-styled pools for groups. After a stint in these hot tubs, a professional massage completes the revival. (As in Japan, massage is one of the traditional occupations of blind people in China and Taiwan.)

Peitou is easy to explore on foot. A street leads directly to Hell's Valley, where the steamy, open sulfur pits offer a first-hand look at the natural activity responsible for the area's hot springs. It is sometimes not open, unfortunately. But when it is, visitors can boil fresh eggs in the medicinal waters that gurgle through the sulfur-stained rocks. Such specially-prepared eggs and other snacks are also on sale at the hawker stands that flank Hell's Valley entrance.

After walking through the center of town, with its city park and Chinese pavilion, strollers will come to a traffic island. The right-hand fork proceeds past the New Angel Hotel, near to which Chiyen Road offers access to a chal-lenging diversion: a climb up tranquil **Phoenix Mountain**.

Those who venture up Chiyen Road to the mountain eventually come to a large double staircase guarded by two enormous lucky dogs. The stairs lead to the **Chen Memorial Garden**, whose chief attraction is its tranquility. The paved pathway behind the garden is the start of the exhausting mountain ascent. From the summit, there are sweeping views of Taipei, Peitou and the surrounding countryside. Trekkers find well-marked hiking paths leading in four directions from the top of Phoenix Mountain; all lead to main roads.

Beyond the Chen Memorial Garden is the **Monastery of Central Harmony**, a complex of pavilions, halls, arcades, shrines, statues and gardens. Buddhist monasteries like this one are peaceful retreats set in nature's lap.

Attractions within easy reach of Peitou include another impressive temple and mountain: **Hsingtien Temple**, which stands high on the road that runs between Peitou and the coastal town of **Hell's Valley.**

Tanshui. It has the same name as its sister temple in downtown Taipei, but the setting is considerably more scenic, with a landscaped garden covering the entire hill behind the temple. The main hall and subsidiary shrines are as lavishly decorated as any in Taiwan, but better maintained than most. The ruling deity here is the red-faced Kuan Kung.

Another place to consider is the **Hsiaoyiokeng Fumarole** nature preserve, with its dense stands of bamboo. The park's volcanic past can be seen in its valleys, plateaus, and peaks. The highest point is the **Chihsing Shan** (Seven Stars Mountain), at 1,200 meters (4,000 ft) in altitude. A steep, but not dangerous, path leads to the top, where the view is remarkable.

Famous for bird- and butterfly-watching is the area of Tatun Shan and Mientien Shan.

The route back to Taipei passes the **Chungshan Hall** complex, opened in 1966 as a conference center, as well as the buildings of the **Culture University**, built in traditional Chinese style.

The western horizon of northern Taiwan is dominated by a 475-meter-high (1,560-ft) mountain, the **Goddess of Mercy Mountain**, as its profile resembles that of Kuanyin (Guanyin) from a distance. Visitors who make the steep climb to its peak will be rewarded by breathtaking views of the island's northern coastline, and of the Taiwan Strait.

The mountain can be reached by taxi or bus from Taipei. The climbing path starts at a small town at the foot of the mountain. Plantings of tea, tangerines and bamboo mark the lower slopes. About halfway up the mountain are two Buddhist temples.

Northern routes: The drive along Taiwan's northern coastline rewards visitors with its scenic natural sights, and with charming farm towns and fishing villages. The entire route can be covered comfortably in a single day of driving from Taipei.

Two major roads skirt this coastline, meeting in Keelung northeast of Taipei to form a wide arch around Taipei. A recommended route is to proceed north-

Jamming, Yangmingshan National Park.

west from Taipei to Tanshui, then eastward through Paishawan, Chinshan, Wanli and Yehliu, then to Keelung. From this harbor town, travelers have the option of taking a quick highway back to Taipei. From Keelung, it is also possible to continue on a southeast coastal course to Pitouchiao, Fulung and its excellent beach, and Toucheng, then return north to Taipei past waterfalls and via Hsintien.

On the way to Tanshui, alongside the Tanshui River, is **Kuantu** with its eye-catching, red-colored 550-meter-long (1,700-ft) bridge. Directly on the river and close to a cliff is an extremely large temple complex, **Kuantu Matsu**, one of the most important of its kind in Taiwan. It is worth a stroll around, with a viewpoint high above the river accessed via a tunnel through the cliff.

The terminus of the North Coast Highway is a town with a rich historical heritage, **Tanshui** – together with Kuantu, a popular day-trip from Taipei. The town was the main point of contact in northern Taiwan between the Chinese and foreign traders during its heyday as the island's major port, in the nineteenth century. Even before that, the Spanish – who had occupied Keelung – extended their claim to Tanshui, where in 1629 they built a fort, **San Domingo**, on one of the hills close to the river. (Local residents had another name for the fort: Hung Mao Cheng, or Fort of the Red-Haired Barbarians.) Today, the old British headquarters, built in 1876, stands on the same lofty site.

Taiwan regained possession of the site when the British closed their consular compound, in 1972. Remnants of the fort's cannon and eight-foot-thick walls still stand, and the building itself has become an interesting museum.

In addition to the Spanish and British, Tanshui was occupied by the Dutch in the seventeenth century, bombarded by French warships in 1884, and claimed by the Japanese in 1895. Before they left, the Japanese built the island's first golf course in Tanshui, now known as the Taiwan Golf and Country Club. Opened in 1919, the club remains popu-

Butterfly kite.

lar among visitors and residents alike. Tanshui's streets are narrow, the shops old-fashioned, and the life-style a bit on the old-fashion side.

Tanshui's biggest draw is its fresh seafood. Strategically located at the confluence of the Tanshui River and the Taiwan Strait, fishermen make a prosperous living here. Many seafood stalls, and small but good seafood restaurants, are eager to serve up fresh delicacies. Point to what is desired, and they prepare it. Sunsets from the river bank are quite exquisite.

A short drive north from Tanshui is **Paishawan Beach**. Because of its proximity to Taipei, it pulls huge crowds on summer weekends. Otherwise, it is a convenient spot to swim and sunbathe. The beach has snack bars, changing rooms and a nearby hotel. Paishawan is famous with windsurfers.

The North Coast Highway rounds the northernmost nib of Taiwan. From here on, the China Sea extends to the horizon. After passing Fukwai Cape, at Taiwan's northernmost point, a natural

Northern coast.

wonder appears: **Shihmen** (Stone Gate), an impressive natural erosion form, with an eight-meter-high (25 ft) opening. Shortly afterwards, the highway turns in a gentle southeasterly direction toward **Chinshan**, site of a once-popular beach that has been reduced to nothingness by fierce storms and tidal action.

Even more evidence of the forces of nature are apparent at **Yehliu**, literally Wild Willows. The white, yellow and brownish sandstone promontories here, directly in front of the pounding ocean, have been etched into all manner of artistic shapes by weather and erosion. The terrain is other-worldly, attracting crowds of curious onlookers from the big city of Taipei.

In fits of poetic fancy, the Chinese have given appropriate names to some of the rock formations over the years. There's a queen's-head rock that could pass for the profile of the ancient Egyptian sovereign, Nefertiti. There are a dinosaur, griffin and fish, and even the famous lost shoe of Cinderella. Some of the swirls and bumps in the rock faces

look a lot like eggs, left here to hatch by some ancient sea serpents.

To cope with the crush of visitors and to attract even more, **Ocean Park** was opened near the entrance to Yehliu. Here, the usual contingent of dolphins, seals and other aquatic animals perform as at any sea park around the world.

The highway runs through **Wanli** and on to the port of Keelung. En route, there's a modern recreation park with full facilities, Green Bay Seashore Recreation Club. The club is open to the public for a nominal fee. The main attraction is its beaches, and the bay itself offers parasailing, hang-gliding and sailing. Equipment for these activities can be rented. The Green Bay Club also provides an amusement park for children and several dozen beach-side bungalows. These expensive, overnight accommodations should be booked well in advance.

Taiwan's northernmost city and second-largest port is **Keelung**, junction for the North Coast and Northeast Coast highways, and the northern terminus of the North-South Highway. Its natural harbor has 40 deep-water piers and three mooring buoys that can handle vessels up to the 30,000-ton class. The port has excellent facilities for the loading and unloading of container ships; the container depots are massive. About 80 million tons of freight are handled here annually. Only Kaohsiung, in the south, has more extensive port facilities.

Like Tanshui, Keelung has long been a crossroads for Taiwan's contacts with the rest of the world. Local brigands, Japanese pirates, Spanish conquistadors, Dutch soldiers, American traders and Japanese imperialists have all made Keelung their base during the past three centuries. Keelung's 400,000 inhabitants are basically a blue-collar lot, wedded to the port trade and its offspring industries. But its setting and history make it an interesting stop.

Keelung's main point of interest is an enormous white **statue and temple of Kuanyin**. The 22.5-meter (74-foot) statue is propped up on a 4-meter-high (14-ft) pedestal that enables the deity to **Keelung.**

168

watch over the entire city. Her stature is increased by placement high on a hill in **Chungcheng Park**. Two finely-proportioned pavilions grace a knoll next to the statue. Stairs inside the statue lead to a perch for a view.

An alternate return route to Taipei, instead of the highway, is a narrow but scenic road that winds from Chinshan through the Yangming Shan area.

The Northeast Coast Highway moves out from Keelung eastward to coastal enclaves like **Juipin** and **Pitouchiao**, located on a stone bluff overlooking the Pacific Ocean. Like Yehliu, to the west of Keelung, its rock formations make for spectacular blends of land and sea.

A few minutes' drive south of Pitouchiao lies **Yenliao**. A historical monument here was erected in honor of the Chinese soldiers and civilians who died resisting Japan's 1895 invasion, which led to Japan's colonial occupation of Taiwan.

Fulung, the next stop on the Northeast Coast Highway, belies the notion that Taiwan's best beaches lie only in the southern reaches of the island. The white sand beach here hugs the northern shore of a cape that juts into the Pacific Ocean. Because of its location, the sun rises on the right and sets on the left as one looks out to sea.

To further enhance the setting, the cove is entirely surrounded by rolling green hills. Enthusiastic strollers will find that the shoreline stretches for kilometers in both directions. About 100 meters (300 ft) inland, a river runs parallel to Fulung Beach, in effect forming a secondary beach. A bridge leads to the seashore, and sailboats and windsurfing boards can be rented.

The route south from Fulung to Toucheng passes a wonderfully-ornate Daoist temple that faces the sea, Celestial Palace Temple.

Toucheng is a tiny coastal village, with a modest beach resort, that is usually less crowded than Fulung or other northern beaches. As the road skirts the shore, travelers get a look at an offshore island called **Kueishan Tao** – Turtle Mountain – for obvious reasons.

Keelung Harbor.

One of the area's attraction, however, lies not along the sea, but in the hills behind Toucheng. About five kilometers (3 mi) behind the village is **Hsinfeng**, or New Peak Falls. The falls are 500 meters beyond the main entrance to the complex, inside a canyon. By stepping carefully down the rocky ledge, swimmers can slide into the refreshing water that cascades 50 meters (160 ft) down a stone chute.

The other principal attraction of this lovely region is the **Chiaohsi hot springs**, which once had a long-standing reputation among local libertines as "a great place to pick wild flowers." Although the "garden" has mostly gone to seed, a few hardy "perennials" still blossom. Small restaurants scattered about the town specialize in fresh seafood. Two temples cater to the faithful in Chiaohsi. Further down the main road is the Temple of Heavenly Accord.

Less than 10 minutes' drive into the hills behind the Chiaohsi is **Wufengchi** (Five Peaks Flag Scenic Region). Vendors around the parking lot sell the area's sought-after products of dried mushrooms, preserved plums and other fruits, fresh ginger and medicinal herbs.

Among the latter is a furry little doll with four "legs" formed by roots, and two "eyes" made with buttons. The vendors call it Golden Dog Fur. It's actually a fern-plant that roots in stone and grows from remote cliff sides. When rubbed into cuts, scrapes, lacerations, sores and other festering skin wounds, it stops the bleeding immediately and promotes rapid healing with a minimum of unsightly scarring.

The trail from the parking lot leads to **Wufengchi Falls**, a vine-and-fern-spangled waterfall that cascades musically in sprays and sheets down a 60-meter (200-ft) cliff. A viewing spot faces the falls from across the stream. Cement steps lead up along a side of the canyon, enabling one to get close enough to cool off in its stinging spray.

Highway 9 continues south from Chiaohsi to the bright little country town of **Ilan**, becoming the town's main street of temples, shops and such. A half-hour Kueishan Tao.

south of Ilan lies the international seaport of **Suao**.

A lovely ride back toward Taipei is in store for travelers who double back up the Northeast Coast Highway to Erhcheng. It is worth making a detour into the Chingingu Valley, where a resort complex nestles among the beautiful scenery. Highway 9 then continues to twist and turn through the spectacular central mountain range, revealing vistas of spellbinding beauty as it zigzags back to Taipei.

Near the Taipei suburb of **Hsintien**, south of the city, is the **Chihnan Temple**, one of the most important landmarks in the north. This Temple of the Immortals has been under constant construction and expansion for nearly 100 years. Perched on a lush green hillside, it exemplifies the concept of a temple as a magic mountain peak. There are supposedly 1,000 steps along the winding approach to the temple. The temple is home for about 50 Buddhist monks. Near Chihnan Temple, keep an eye on the rolling green hills – many are coated with tea bushes. And if they are in flower, stop and take a closer look at the camelia-like blossoms.

South from Hsintien, in the opposite direction from Taipei, the mountainous retreat of **Wulai** is the best place in northern Taiwan to witness Atayal traditional culture. Beyond the town, a suspension bridge hangs across a river. From here, a footpath and mini-train take visitors to the Clear Flowing Garden, where a waterfall cascades into a deep gorge. Local ethnic minorities perform traditional music and folk dances in the garden.

A cable car carries visitors across the gorge to a place in the mountains appropriately called **Dreamland**, which has additional ethnic performances, a lake for rowing and fishing, plenty of places to eat, and an amusement park for children. Nearby hot springs provide therapeutic bathing.

Traditional tribal arts and crafts, wild mountain mushrooms, Chinese herbs, spices and souvenirs are available in the parks, and in stores in Wulai, whose

Dreamland, Wulai.

many restaurants offer exotic fare such as wild boar, deer, pheasant, snake and freshwater eel.

South of Taipei: Southwest of Taipei are several other places well worth a stop. Only 20 kilometers away from Taipei is the busy old town of **Sanhsia**, with streets snaking around old brick buildings and the famous Tsushih Temple, originally built in 1770. The temple was in ruins after World War II, but it is now reconstructed, with new and perfectly-carved stone decorations, making it one of the finest examples of Chinese temple art.

A short hop away is the small town of **Yingko**, a potter's heaven. Some of the factories allow tours, giving a chance to watch how "muddy" clay will be transformed into a beautifully-painted Chinese vase, worth a dominant position in the Ming or Qing court. Many shops line the narrow, usually crowded streets, selling everything from simple earthenware to the finest porcelain, from ordinary teapots to delicate figures. Some is predictable, some is exquisite.

Several other attractions within hailing distance of Taipei – and all to the south – beckon travelers. Fifty kilometers (30 mi) away to the southwest, down Highway 3 and near the town of Tahsi, is **Tzu Hu** (Lake Mercy), temporary resting place of the late Chiang Kaishek. His body rests above ground in a heavy granite sarcophagus in his former country villa, awaiting the day when political conditions permit returning his body to his birthplace in mainland China, in Zhejiang province.

The location, thick with acacia forests and bamboo groves, reflects the bucolic beauty of Taiwan's countryside. A lot of people visit the lake each year to pay respects to the late president. The villa and grounds are open only by prior arrangement (bring passports), but visitors are free to wander around the lake and its surroundings anytime.

The **Shihmen Reservoir** nearby offers motorboat rides and a restaurant. The Shihmen Dam, completed in 1964, was built with American aid.

One of the main attractions to the south of Taipei, beyond Tahsi and near Lungtan, is **Window on China**. On a site covering 10 hectares (25 acres), the most important buildings and temples in Taiwan, as well as many notable buildings in mainland China, have been erected in miniature.

Totalling 130 in all, the buildings are on a scale of 1:25, and are populated by some 50,000 miniature – and artificial – people, some of whom perform parades or dances to music. A recently-added section features famous buildings from all parts of the world. Vegetation is provided by countless bonsai trees grown to proportionally-correct sizes.

Window on China is one of the top attractions of Taiwan, and one of the best places in the world to study Chinese architecture, as it demands little travel to compare various buildings and styles. There are a number of restaurants on the site, and visitors can also visit the adjacent **Taiwan Folk Arts Theater** to experience a cross-section of Chinese culture.

Some distance south – on Highway 3, about halfway between Taipei and

Chiang Kaishek's sarcophagus.

Taichung – is **Shihtou Shan** (Lion's Head Mountain), 20 kilometers (12 mi) east of the North-South Highway. It is a pleasant excursion for travelers bound for central Taiwan. When viewed from the proper angle, the peak does bear a resemblance to the king of beasts. But the mountain's main significance is as a center of Buddhism; most of the temples here were built directly in natural caves during the past 75 years.

From the arched entrance above the parking lot, it is possible to hike up to the lion's head, then down along its spine, visiting the temples and other sights along the way. From the old stone arch at the entrance, 1,500 steps lead up to the top, or head. From there, a path leads down to the tail of the lion. The round-trip walk takes about three hours, with the last part as an enjoyable stroll through flower-scented forests and patches of bamboo.

The first main temple on the path is the **Chunghua Tang**. Hearty, healthy vegetarian meals cooked by Buddhist nuns are available in several of the temples on the route. Two temples offer rooms and meals at fixed prices.

The main shrine hall of the first temple, just above the dining room, rises on beautifully-sculpted stone columns that depict celestial animals and ancient Buddhist legends.

The massive multi-storied structure just beyond the temple is the **Kaishan Monastery**, a different kind of study and activities center for resident monks and nuns. Feel free to inspect the ornate temples, observe monks and nuns at their daily duties, and listen to the sounds of the forest.

Another steep path winds up around the lion's "mane" to the Moon-Gazing Pavilion, serving well its purpose on both dark starry nights and moon-lit nights. From there, the paved trail cuts down past several more cave-temples, the Pagoda of Inspiration, monastic quarters, bridges and viewing terraces. The rustic cave-shrines of the Water Screen Convent are the last major sights on the trail, which deposits hikers back on the road near the parking lot.

Pagoda, Shihtou Shan.

CENTRAL TAIWAN

Less than an hour out of Taipei, travelers on the southbound highway begin to see dramatic changes in the surrounding countryside. Factories are fewer, lush farmland more prevalent. The gray tones of the capital give way to green patchworks of ripening rice, fruit plantations and vegetable plots.

Central Taiwan, roughly covering the region from Miaoli to Chiayi, west of the Central Mountain range, boasts the most varied terrain on the island. From the summit of snow-capped Yu Shan, the Jade Mountain, the landscape drops 3,952 meters to the harbor at Taichung. The alluvial plain that divides the highlands from the Taiwan Strait is filled by vast green rice fields, and plantations of bananas, pineapples, papayas, sugar cane, tea and other crops.

Taichung: The urban center of central Taiwan is Taichung, whose name means, not coincidentally, Central Taiwan. The pace and pressure of modern metropolitan Taipei are replaced here by a quieter, slower life. Taichung is what Taipei once looked like, before the big boom of the 1970s.

Taiwan's third-largest city and on the island's western side, Taichung has a population of around 100,000 people. Located on the plain about 20 kilometers (13 mi) from the coast and 100 kilometers (60 mi) south of Taipei, Taichung enjoys the island's best year-round climate, without the seasonal extremes of heat and cold that mark the north and south.

The opening, in 1975, of Taichung Harbor was a significant regional event. Central Taiwan was then linked to international markets and suppliers of natural resources. A 10-lane expressway connects downtown Taichung with the coastal harbor. Another response to the area's importance as a manufacturing and business center was the opening of the World Trade Center, in 1990.

Taichung was founded in 1721 by immigrants from the Chinese mainland. They originally named it Tatun, or Big Mound. The city's current name was adopted by the Japanese after they took possession of Taiwan in 1895. Today, 20-hectare (50-acre) **Chungshan Park** occupies the hillock upon which the original settlement was built. The two pavilions rising above the lotus-filled lake are a Taichung landmark.

Although Taichung is neither as scenic nor as diverse as Taipei, it has numerous points of interest. The **Martyrs' Shrine**, on Shuangshih Road northeast of Chungshan Park, was erected in 1970. Its design provides a superb example of the harmony and balance inherent in classical Chinese architecture. Many locals claim it is even more outstanding than the martyrs' shrines in Hualien or Taipei. Protected by two bronze guardian lions, the Martyrs' Shrine commemorates 72 Chinese beheaded in 1911 by the tottering Manchu court, on the eve of the republic's revolution.

Next to the Martyrs' Shrine is Taichung's tranquil **Kong Miao**, or Confucian Temple. While every major city in Taiwan – and China – has a shrine

Preceding pages: picking tea near Tunpoling. **Left,** Central Cross-Island Highway view. **Right,** the long road to a rice harvest.

hall dedicated to the great sage, this one is notable for the constrained design of its roof. In this shrine, the eaves – rather than flaring audaciously heavenward – curve gently downward, cleaving close to the earth. And indeed, earth, not heaven, was the sage's prime concern.

On the altar of the shrine is a simple black-stone stele with the name of Confucius engraved in gold on its smooth, otherwise unadorned surface. Although he believed in spirits and deities, Confucius insisted that people should steer as clear of them as possible.

Every year on 28 September, the birthday of Confucius, this temple hosts a colorful spectacle of ancient rituals, archaic costumes, and 2,000-year-old music played on antique instruments.

The **Paochueh Temple**, on the northern edge of the city on Chienhsing Road, contains one of the largest and fattest Buddha images in all Taiwan. This is the proverbial happy Buddha, the golden shimmering Milofo. (In other Buddhist traditions, he is known as Maitreya, the Buddha of the future.) Milofo sits laughing on a massive pedestal in one corner of the temple compound, towering 30 meters (100 ft) above the ground. Smaller statues of the same Buddha are scattered around interesting Buddhist iconography. In the main shrine hall are three Buddha images, protected at the gate by a brace of fierce guardians. Within the hollow pedestal of the giant pot-bellied Milofo is a room used for meetings. In the adjacent building are several thousand cremation urns, making it a place of remembrance.

The **Natural Science Museum**, northwest of Chungshan Park and off Taichung Road, has an interesting Space Theater. The **Museum of Art**, west of Chungshan Park on Wuchuan Road, has 24 expressive galleries and is Taichung's premier cultural institution.

Taichung's main **shopping district** is located along Chungcheng Road, west of Chungshan Park and between the railway station and Wuchuan Road. There are silk and satin shops, fresh-produce markets, and a number of interesting herb shops, redolent with the

**Martyrs'
Shrine.**

pungent aromas of potent medicinal plants. In the evening, a colorful night market is open on Chunghua Road. Taichung's night life is not as colorful as that of Taipei, but there are popular watering holes along Wenhsin Road.

A 20-minute drive northwest of downtown Taichung, on Taichung Kang Road, is **Tunghai University**. The entire wooded 139-hectare (345-acre) campus was built according to the architectural style of the Tang dynasty, the period regarded as China's golden age of culture and the arts. This subtle and restrained style differs radically from the sometimes garish style that prevailed in China after the Ming period. Almost all campus buildings are constructed in the square, squat, colonnaded Tang style, with plain tile roofs. A modern departure is the abstract Christian Chapel, designed by the famous Chinese-American architect I.M. Pei to symbolize a pair of hands touching in prayer.

Just 10 kilometers (6 mi) northeast of Taichung lies a somewhat interesting example of landscape gardening, the **Encore Garden**. The colorful flower gardens are decorated with copies of famous European statues, and in evenings, a fountain lit by multicolored lights dances to classical Western or South-American rhythms.

A short detour 40 kilometers (25 mi) north of Taichung is **Sanyi**, a small town stretched along one main road that parallels the expressway. Shops sell large selections of high-quality wood carvings, as Sanyi is home to many of Taiwan's best woodcarvers. It is impressive to watch how these craftsmen can transform a large tree root, for example, into a masterpiece, all the while following the wood's natural grain.

Across the island: North and east of Taichung, the **Central Cross-Island Highway** stretches for 200 kilometers (120 mi), from Tungshih through Taroko Gorge to the eastern coast. The Chinese claim no visit to Taiwan is complete without a trip across this road, for it displays – with striking beauty – the full gamut of the island's rainbow hues: lush tropical valleys and snow-capped

Confucian Temple, Taichung.

peaks, alpine forests and rocky ravines, steamy hot springs and roaring rivers, mountain lakes and the shimmering sea.

The highway was completed in 1960 at the cost of 450 lives. Ten thousand laborers, most of them retired servicemen who had fought on the mainland in the 1940s, struggled four years to complete the road.

In two places, the highway forks. At Lishan, it traverses the upper spine of the Central Range to reach Ilan and the Northeast Coastal Highway, 110 kilometers (70 mi) away; at Tayuling, it cuts south around Hohuan Shan, the Mountain of Harmonious Happiness, to Wushe and Lushan hot springs, a distance of 40 kilometers (25 mi). The latter route eventually leads back to Taichung or on to Sun Moon Lake.

The western half of the Central Range, between Kukuan and Lishan, sometimes resembles Switzerland more than subtropical Taiwan. Visitors should let the terrain guide their choice of clothes: a sweater or jacket is often a welcomed encumbrance at these altitudes.

The first 20 kilometers (12 mi) from **Tungshih** lead past a series of alternating rice fields and vineyards. The first notable village is **Kukuan**, or Valley Pass, a hot-springs resort lying at about 1,000 meters (3,300 ft) above sea level. Having undergone major tourist development in recent years, Kukuan features numerous hotels and inns, and restaurants and handicraft shops. A roaring river careens in an aquatic symphony over a boulder-strewn riverbed, slicing right through the village. Hot mineral water is piped directly into the private baths of hotel rooms, but there are no big communal or outdoor pools. Though this water is not as hot as the springs on the east coast, a soak in it is therapeutically effective and relaxing.

Rather than mineral water, however, Kukuan's major attraction is the two-kilometer walk though Dragon Valley. The walk begins with the crossing of a teak suspension bridge over the river. The path weaves past a cave-pen of Himalayan black bears, a house-sized cage of acrobatic monkeys, a pair of **Kukuan.**

dignified Manchurian cranes, and numerous other denizens of an outdoor zoo. It proceeds through sculpted shrubbery and brilliant bougainvillea to the Mahjong Terrace of the Eight Immortals, high atop a crag overlooking the river, and the Goddess of Mercy Grotto, a shrine set in a bend in the gorge. A serene white ceramic statue of Kuanyin rests within. Here, she is in her usual meditation posture, sitting in repose on a lip protruding from the rocky face of the gorge across the river, with her hands held in a benevolent *mudra* (gesture), the deep rumble of the river for her mantra, and the phantasmagoric face of the gorge as her mandala, or mystical meditation scroll. A shrine gate and altar are set just beneath her by the path for anybody who cares to burn an incense stick. Look for the small bridge nearby; across this bridge, two small wooden pavilions hugging the cliff-side offer a rest spot.

Around the next bend, the gorge terminates in a narrow canyon strewn with automobile-sized boulders. Here, the impressive 75-meter-high (250-ft) Dragon Valley Fall cascades into the stream. Even on sunny, windless days, it is always raining with a fine mist, created by the upward deflection of the waterfall's sheer force by the pool and boulders at its feet. Viewing terraces are staggered 30 meters (100 ft) up the side of the gorge opposite the falls. This is the most easily accessible of Taiwan's major waterfalls.

En route back to the village, the trail forks left to the riverside, where there is a pen full of proud peacocks and other large gaily-feathered birds. Nearby is a Chinese garden grotto with pools, fountains and mountains as its backdrop. Then make your way to an open pavilion set on top of a small stone bluff and see how the Dragon Valley stream courses into the main river. Dragon Valley merits at least half a day of meanderings to enjoy nature's sights and sounds.

Restaurants along the main highway through Kukuan specialize in steamed fresh rainbow trout.

Below, Buddha. Below right, Goddess of Mercy Grotto.

Beyond Kukuan, the highway climbs steeply a few kilometers into the Central Range. At the **Techi Dam**, a pleasant hostel clings to steep green hillsides overlooking a lake below. Tons of water gush into this reservoir beneath the impressive hydroelectric plant.

Lishan: Two hours' drive from Kukuan is Lishan – Pear Mountain – on the crest of the Central Range, near the Central Cross-Island Highway's halfway point. Highway 7, to Ilan in the northeast, begins here.

Swept by alpine breezes and drifting mists, lodges and restaurants dot the slopes of this mountain village. Most impressive is the Lishan Guest House, an alpine version of Taipei's Grand Hotel. Terraces, pavilions and sculpted shrubbery grace the spacious grounds. Lishan is enchanting in spring (between February and April), with the apple, pear and peach trees in full blossom.

An interesting side trip from Lishan is **Fushoushan Farm** (Fortunate Life Mountain Farm). Essentially a large fruit orchard spread across a hilltop, Fushoushan appears more European than Asian. The entrance to the farm is through an arched gate less than one kilometer east of Lishan village. From there, a pine-lined drive leads past a church and steeple in a five-kilometer ascent. Terraced acres of apple and pear orchards surround Western-style farmhouses. Trees are braced against the stiff mountain wind by elaborate bamboo scaffolding; individual fruits are protected in bags from insects and birds. In season, these fruits are on sale at the farm. At the entrance of the farm is a small museum of local artifacts and illustrations.

Along the Fushoushan drive is Hwakong Tienchin, a small cafe where Chiang Kaishek kept a private holiday bungalow. The road ends at Hwagang, a knoll guarded by giant wind-torn trees.

Lishan is the staging point for mountaineering expeditions to **Hsuen Shan**, Taiwan's second-highest peak at 3,884 meters (12,743 ft). Climbers normally stay overnight at the Wuling Farm, another popular mountain resort offering **Hohuan Shan ski resort.**

spectacular views of the surrounding peaks, before making the final summit ascent. The four-day, round-trip expedition requires a special permit and prior permission from the Alpine Association, in Taipei.

Still on Highway 8 and thirty kilometers (20 mi) beyond Lishan, the village of **Tayuling** straddles the highest point of the highway, at an elevation of 2,600 meters (8,530 ft). East of here, the highway descends rapidly past Wenshan Hot Springs and through the Taroko Gorge to the east coast.

Tayuling is the junction for Highway 14, which cuts south from **Hohuan Shan**, the Mountain of Harmonious Happiness, and continues to the Lushan Hot Springs and Wushe (Jenai). Hohuan Shan, looming 3,420 meters (11,220 ft) above sea level just nine kilometers (5 mi) south of Tayuling, is Taiwan's only winter ski resort. For about two months each year, from January to early March, heavy snowfall turns the mountain white. A 400-meter-long (1,300-ft) lift carries skiers up the slopes. The Pine Snow

Hostel provides accommodation; equipment rentals are available. Even in the heat of summer, temperatures up here rarely rise about 15°C (60°F). Hiking, mountain climbing and hot-springs bathing are the most attractive recreational activities at that time of the year.

Further on, the settlement of **Wushe** (Jenai) is embraced by the tall peaks of the Central Range. Although its name means Foggy Community, it is renowned for its crystal-clear alpine air, as well as the profusion of wild-cherry and plum blossoms that shower the village in early spring.

Far below, the green mirror of Wushe Reservoir is surrounded by abrupt mountain escarpments. The Chinese word for landscape is *shanshui* – literally, mountains and water – and this lake is a perfect example. A trail leads from the village to the lake, where only shore-fishing is permitted. In Wushe village are a few local inns and ethnic minority handicraft shops.

Wushe made its mark on Taiwan's history in 1930, when minority-group

Wushe
Reservoir.

tribes residing there staged a bloody but futile uprising against Japanese occupation forces. The Japanese, with modern weaponry, killed 1,000 of the tribesmen, but not before losing 200 of their own. A memorial plaque in the village commemorates the massacre.

Lushan Hot Spring snuggles in the valley below Wushe. Lushan village straddles a turbulent stream traversed by a suspension footbridge. Hot-spring inns lie along the banks of both sides of the river.

On the far side of the river, just beyond the last hotel, a trail leads past a pair of waterfalls to the smoldering source of the spa's hot water. The simmering puddles that have formed in crevices around the source are hot enough to boil eggs, and many visitors do just that. The water lends flavor and vital minerals to the eggs, making them highly nutritional.

Lushan village is famous for its tea, medicinal herbs, petrified-wood canes, wild-blossom honey and dried mushrooms. Potent medicinal deer-horn shav-ings, tanned deer skins and other products that are either very expensive or unavailable in Taipei are common purchases here. The best place to stay is the Lushan Garden Guest House, on the left across the river. This is the only establishment with large, old-fashioned Japanese-style tubs, ideal for lengthy soaks and big enough for a whole family.

South of Lushan and Wushe is **Puli**, a village known as the exact geographical center of Taiwan. On its outskirts, Chenghuang Temple is a monastery founded in 1924, standing in a grove of palms. Nearby, a marked turn-off leads three kilometers up a pretty valley to Carp Lake, a pleasant picnic spot devoid of people, except straw-hatted farmers. These horticulturists specialize in growing edible and medicinal fungi on wooden planks and shaded arbors.

Sun Moon Lake: Taiwan's most enduringly popular honeymoon resort is Sun Moon Lake, 750 meters (2,500 ft) above sea level and in the western foothills of the Central Range. Entirely enfolded in mountains and dense tropical foliage, **Lushan.**

the lake takes the shape of a round sun when viewed from some of the surrounding hills, or of a crescent moon when seen from other heights. Under sunny skies, the dreamy landscape of turquoise waters, jade-green hills and drifting mountain mists lends itself well to the moods and passions of honeymooners and other amorous couples flocking to the lake's shores.

The lake was formed in the early twentieth century, when the occupying Japanese built a dam for hydroelectric production. Prior to that, there had been a major tribal settlement in this area; traces remain on the lake's south shore.

Its beauty notwithstanding, Sun Moon Lake's popularity often leaves it crawling with bus-loads of package tourists from Taipei and abroad. However, there are a number of hillside trails and shoreside walks for privacy.

The best way to enjoy the scenic beauty of Sun Moon Lake is to rise at daybreak and walk, drive or take a cab along the road that winds around the lake. At dawn, the crowds are still snoozing, and early birds have the lake to themselves.

A good starting point for an exploration of the lake is the Sun Moon Lake Hotel, perched on a high embankment overlooking the lake. Heading east and south, the road leads first to the majestic **Wenwu**, a temple of martial and literary arts. This Daoist shrine, dedicated to Confucius and the two great warrior deities Kuan Kung and Yueh Fei, is built into the hillside in three ascending levels. The two largest stone lions in Asia stand sentry at the entrance, and the portico is graced by two full-relief windows of carved stone, depicting the celestial dragon and tiger. A viewing terrace at the rear of the temple allows unimpeded vistas of the lake. The sea of golden tiles on the temple roofs is indicative of the scale and ambition of Chinese temple architecture.

The shrine to Confucius occupies the upper rear hall, with decorative motifs drawn from Chinese folklore antedating by centuries the arrival of Buddhism in China. Symbolic of the ultimate subservience of the sword to the pen, the

Sun Moon Lake.

temple's martial shrine sits slightly lower than the literary shrine. Within are the red-faced Kuan Kung, sometimes incorrectly referred to as the god of war, and the white-faced Yueh Fei, a Song-dynasty patriot and military hero who attempted, without success, to recover the empire from the barbarian nomads.

The temple complex is interesting for its complicated layout, with various pavilions and side halls connected by ornate passages and stairways. Throughout the grounds stand potted bonsai trees, tropical flowers, and shrubs sculpted to resemble animals. The 4.5-meter-tall (15-ft) gods at the entrance, carved from solid wood and colorfully painted, rank among the best in Taiwan.

Further along the road, a bronze statue of Chiang Kaishek gazes across the lake to the Pagoda of Filial Virtue. Preening peafowl scream from a peacock garden. Still further on, the drab and commercial Tehuashe Aboriginal Village sits by the lake shore.

High on a hill near the southern end of the lake, the **Hsuanchuang Temple**

houses some of China's most precious Buddhist relics. This temple was built for safekeeping and preservation of the relics, known as *ssu li-tze*.

Devout Buddhists believe that small kernel-shaped pieces – found among the ashes of highly-accomplished Buddhist monks and Daoist adepts after their cremations – are formed by the forging of spirit and energy after a lifetime of intensive meditation and other spiritual disciplines. The ashes of the historical Buddha, Sakyamuni, yielded 12 cups of these tiny black-and-white pebbles, some of which are enshrined in the Hsuanchuang Temple. Flames will not consume them, it is said, nor will steel sledgehammers crack them. Of course, Western science thumbs its nose at the Buddhist explanation, insisting that they are kidney or gall stones. (One interesting exhibit is in a separate shrine hall. A monk's body refused to decay after his death and his hair continued to grow; he was encased in solid gold and placed in his own shrine hall.)

The *ssu-li-tze* nuggets have other unusual properties. The two that were carried to this site by monks during the Nationalist retreat of 1949 have not remained static over the centuries. It is claimed that they have expanded, contracted, or even generated new kernels, depending upon how much prayer and offering is performed. There are now seven little nuggets enshrined at the temple. The relics are kept within a miniature jewel-encrusted pagoda of solid gold on the altar of the main shrine hall. A tiny light illuminates the nuggets inside the pagoda. (An attendant reports that one of the kernels is beginning to shrink and disappear due to insufficient visits by the faithful.)

Also in the main shrine hall are a gilded reclining Buddha and a handsome statue of Hsuanchuang himself. This Tang-dynasty monk made a pilgrimage to India that was immortalized in the classical Chinese novel, *Journey to the West*. After 17 years of Buddhist study, lecturing and travel in India, Hsuanchuang returned to the imperial Chinese capital of Chang'an (now Xi'an) in 645. Over the next two decades, he **Pagoda of Filial Virtue.**

translated 1,335 sutras from the Sanskrit language into classical Chinese, thus playing a major part in bringing the Buddhist religion to China.

On the second floor of the Hsuanchuang Temple is a shrine to Kuanyin, the goddess of mercy. On the third floor, another small golden pagoda protects a shard of Hsuanchuang's skull-bone, looted from China by the Japanese during World War II. In 1955, a Japanese monk was dispatched to return the bone – its age and authenticity verified – at Chiang Kaishek's request. Upon handing over the relic, the monk-messenger died; his ashes are kept in a wooden pagoda nearby.

Atop a hill beyond the Hsuanchuang Temple stands the ornate, nine-tiered **Tzuen**, the **Pagoda of Filial Virtue**. It was erected by Chiang Kaishek in memory of his mother, and hence the name. An uphill walk through cool glades of bamboo, fern, maple and pine leads to the foot of the pagoda. From here, there are spectacular views of the entire lake and surrounding scenery.

Last stop on the lake-side jaunt is the Glory of Mystery Temple, a minor shore-side shrine. Below this temple is a dock from which rowboats or motor launches can be hired for short cruises to Kuanghua (Glory of China) Island. This lovely, wooded islet has an open pavilion on it.

The specialty of restaurants on Sun Moon Lake is fresh carp – braised, steamed or highly spiced. Sun Moon Lake produces a unique carp called the President Fish – bony but delicious.

Forest heights: There are three important experimental forests in the mountains of Central Taiwan. The Huisun Forest, with its towering trees and flowering shrubs, managed by Chunghsing University, is in the highlands north of Puli. The Alishan forest of cypress, cedar and pine is accessible from Chiayi. But the **Hsitou Bamboo Forest**, a side trip off Highway 3 between Taichung and Chiayi, may be the most interesting of the trio.

Forty percent of Taiwan's supply of raw bamboo and bamboo products come

Hsitou Bamboo Forest.

from this 2,485-hectare (6,150-acre) forest research station, operated by the National Taiwan University. There are many varieties of bamboo in this green forest, along with vast tracts of cypress, cedar and pine. The station cultivates and distributes more than one million tree shoots annually for Taiwan's extensive reforestation projects.

Visitors to Hsitou can stroll along paved footpaths shaded by leafy canopies. At 1,150 meters (3,770 ft) above sea level, this is a favorite spot for hikers and campers. Motor vehicles are strictly prohibited within the recreation areas.

One of the most popular walks leads to the remains of a sacred tree, 3,000 years old and 46 meters (150 ft) high. University Pond features a bamboo bridge arching gracefully over carp-filled water. A seven-kilometer (4 mi) trek leads to a remote ravine with a lovely waterfall. For the hardy, the resort of Alishan, to the south, is a full day away by foot, but this excursion requires a permit and equipment.

Souvenir shops in Hsitou village, which is a popular honeymoon retreat, sell bamboo products and other mountain goods – mushrooms, tea and herbs. There are two guest houses, operated by the government forestry bureau, and an alpine hostel, managed by the China Youth Corps, built entirely of bamboo and local wood. Bamboo shoots are, of course, the specialty of the resort's single restaurant.

Leaves of tea: Returning towards Taichung, and just before **Nantou** at the village of Mingchien, Highway 16 meets Highway 3. Not far away, about ten kilometers further, the **Sungpoling** (Pine Bluff) tea-production region spreads across a hilly plateau. Despite the name, there aren't many pines on this bluff. Instead, groves of areca palm and giant bamboo shelter large tea plantations. At most times of day, women wearing straw hats and bandannas can be seen plucking the tender leaves and buds from these green shrubs, dropping them into huge baskets carried on their backs. Between the tea plantations are fields of pineapples and banana trees, giving the entire plateau a shimmering green glow.

The main street of Sungpoling village is lined with tea shops offering a service known locally as Old Folks' Tea, as only old folks (and travelers) seem to have the time to enjoy it. Samples of many varieties of tea are brewed in tiny clay pots and poured into thimble-sized cups, with constant infusions of hot water to keep the flavor strong and fragrant. Bulk teas are available for purchase, along with traditional paraphernalia for brewing. Tea connoisseurs are assured of falling in love with the area.

Tungting, a young leaf from the highest plantations above Sungpoling, is regarded as Taiwan's best tea. It has a superb flavor, subtle fragrance and practically no bite. Those who buy bulk tea in Sungpoling get the same wholesale price as major Taipei retailers, which varies a great deal, depending upon quality. The more expensive the blend, the better the bargain.

In addition to its famous tea, Sungpoling has one other attraction: a Daoist temple known as the Palace of Celestial Mandate. Some of the most exquisite stone sculptures in central Taiwan, depicting Daoist legends and Chinese folklore, comprise the portico. Of special interest, carved in full relief from solid stone, are two huge, round windows that brace the temple – one depicting the celestial dragon and the other the tiger, a duo found in all Daoist temples. The intricate ceiling inside the hall and the finely-painted 4.5-meter (15-ft) solid wood doors are impressive.

South of Taichung: In **Tsaotun**, about 20 kilometers (12 mi) from Taichung, the Handicraft Exhibition Hall contains an extensive display of local handicrafts and modern manufactured goods. The four-story, air-conditioned building houses bamboo and rattan furniture, Chinese lanterns, lacquerware, ceramics, stonecraft, woodcraft, curios, jewelry, cloisonné and textiles. All items on display are for sale at fixed prices.

Another two kilometers from Tsaotun is **Chunghsing** village, seat of Taiwan's provincial government. Taipei, while regarded by the Taiwanese as the temporary capital of the Republic of China, is not the center of provincial affairs.

(Both the People's Republic and the Republic of China consider Taiwan a province of China; both, of course, have differing versions of exactly how the arrangement should be implemented.)

Thirty minutes by road southwest of Taichung is the typical country town of **Changhua**, notable for the impressive Buddha image atop **Pakua Shan**, Eight-Trigram Mountain. This rather sterile-sounding name derives from the combinations of broken and unbroken sticks used by the Chinese in traditional divining procedures.

The 30-meter-high (100-ft) concrete Buddha image meditates serenely atop a five-meter-tall (16-ft) lotus dais. It took five years to complete and required 300 tons of concrete. The concrete Buddha itself is hollow, with life-size dioramas of Sakyamuni Buddha's life built into the walls. The second floor features the story of his birth, the third his enlightenment under the bodhi tree, the fourth his discourses and teachings, and the fifth his death and entry into nirvana. Behind the Buddha image is a palatial three-story temple, one of the largest in Taiwan. Within it is an impressive collection of gilded icons. In the shrine hall on the top floor is a large golden statue of the Buddha, attended by two disciples. Beside this main hall are a traditional octagonal pagoda of eight tiers and an ornate three-tiered pavilion of classical design.

Close to the town of **Huatan**, south of Changhua and about 15 kilometers from the Changhua expressway exit, is an interesting place to explore the island's indigenous mysteries. Founded in 1990, the **Taiwan Folk Village** has several original structures of traditional architecture, dismantled at their original sites and rebuilt on the grounds. Moreover, there are nearly 100 reconstructions of various ethnic minority buildings. A visit here offers probably the best introduction to traditional crafts. A full day is needed to see and enjoy the activities. Buses depart regularly from Changhua bus station, next to the railway station.

Lukang: West beyond Changhua, the ancient harbor of Lukang lies sleepily

Pakua Shan.

on the shores of the Taiwan Strait. The most popular port of entry during the Qing dynasty (1644–1911) for waves of Chinese immigrants from Fujian province, Lukang was abruptly closed down by the Japanese in 1895. Thereafter, silt and sand rendered the harbor useless for commercial shipping; fishing is now the major activity. The town is a day-excursion from Taichung.

Tradition is at its best in Lukang. Narrow residential lanes have changed little since the Qing dynasty days. Artisans can still be seen fashioning furniture with ancient tools and techniques, in open-front shops.

Altar tables, shelves, ornaments, beams, eaves and other furnishings and fixtures are hewn into shape, then finished with elaborate detail at numerous workshops lining the main street. The fragrance of freshly-sawn camphor and wet lacquer drifts everywhere. Incense is also produced in Lukang, and it is interesting to view the creation of the enormous coils that hang from temple ceilings and burn for days.

The oldest temple in Lukang, and one of the oldest in Taiwan, is **Lungshan Temple**, the Dragon Mountain Temple, dating from the eighteenth century. It is located on Sanmin Road, just off the main avenue, Chungshan Road. The temple was constructed by early Chinese settlers as an expression of gratitude to Kuanyin, the goddess of mercy, for their safe passage from the mainland. Kuanyin is enshrined in the main hall. The temple structure reflects a classical mainland style of a design that differs markedly from the style that subsequently developed in Taiwan. Note the elaborately-carved wooden ceilings and stone-dragon pillars.

A 200-meter stroll through quaint lanes leads to **Fengtien**, the Phoenix Mountain Temple, a small structure built in the early nineteenth century by immigrants from Fujian province. The painted guardians on the main doors are particularly excellent.

Down Chungshan Road from the Dragon Mountain Temple is the impressive – and old – **Tienhou Temple**. On the main altar, the image of Matsu, goddess of the sea, is said to have been brought here in 1684 from the original Matsu shrine on Mei Chou Island by Admiral Shih, who captured Taiwan for the Qing emperor. If true, this story substantiates the claim of Lukang's people that this was the first center of the Matsu cult in Taiwan. There are numerous other exotic icons here. Among them is the magnificent Jade Emperor in a temple of his own, in the same compound. Many more temples and shrines are tucked away among Lukang's lanes. Signs to them are posted throughout the residential maze.

Also worth a visit is the **Folk Culture Museum**, a 30-room villa that is a collector's item. Designed as a private residence by a Japanese architect in orientalized Edwardian style, it is one of the most unusual mansions on the island. Within is an interesting collection of old furniture and household fixtures, vintage photos, paintings, personal effects, costumes, books and musical instruments, and other items reflecting the life-styles of Taiwan's people.

Left, temple images, Lukang. **Right**, field worker.

PEAKS AND PLAINS OF CENTRAL TAIWAN

Chiayi straddles Highway 3, about half-way between Taichung and Tainan. In itself, this manufacturing city on the fertile western plain is not of special interest to the traveler. It is, rather, a springboard to nearby attractions.

East of Chiayi, the resort area of **Alishan** and the peak of Yu Shan (Jade Mountain) rise from the mists of the Central Range.

Alishan's popularity is due primarily to the famous sunrise view from the summit of nearby **Chu Shan** (Celebration Mountain). Indeed, it is a spectacular event. As visitors stand shivering in their jackets 2,490 meters (8,170 ft) above sea level, gazing into the graying mist, the sun suddenly peers over the horizon. Golden shafts of light pierce the dawn, skipping across the thick carpet of clouds that cover the valleys to the east. This sea of clouds springs to life like a silver screen the moment the sun glances across it, undulating in vivid hues of gold and silver, red and orange.

On holidays and weekends, the summit is overcrowded with excited and noisy visitors – several thousand of them. Such days are not the days to witness an idyllic sunrise. On any given day, nonetheless, hundreds of people make the predawn ascent, usually by tour bus. By 7am, most of them will be back at the hotel for breakfast.

More often than not, however, fog and mist are so thick atop the peak that sunrise watchers find themselves floating within the clouds rather than in clear skies above them. And even if the weather on Alishan is terrible – if there are rain and clouds – most visitors will depart quite delighted.

There are two explanations, both founded in legend, for this appreciation of less-than-clear conditions.

In ancient times, clouds and rain symbolized the mating of heaven and earth. It is said that a king of Sichuan made an excursion to Wu Shan, or Sorcery Mountain, where he grew tired in the middle of the day and fell asleep. He dreamed that a woman approached, identified herself as the Lady of Wu Shan, and said, "Having heard that you have come here, I wish to share pillow and couch with you."

When the lovers later parted, the woman told the king: "I live on the southern slope of Wu Shan, on top of a high hill. At dawn I am the morning clouds; in the evening I am the pouring rain. Every morning and night I hover about these hills."

The legend established a standard for Chinese writers, who have used clouds and rain as a poetic metaphor for sexual intercourse. Clouds symbolize the essence of the woman, rain that of the man. Colorful thematic variations have enriched centuries of Chinese literature, with phrases like "After the rain had come, the clouds dispersed," and, "The clouds grew thick but the rain never came."

But there is one reason, even more compelling than the sensual imagery, that draws Chinese to mountain retreats

several times a year, regardless of weather conditions. Drifting mountain mists are regarded as possessing extraordinary curative powers, due to their high concentration of *qi.*

Qi (pronounced *chee*) is the life-force or vital energy, the most fundamental of all Chinese physical and spiritual concepts. Qi is considered the basic force that animates all forms of life. The most potent qi, it is believed, rises in the atmosphere and clings as mist to the mountains, like cream rising to the top of milk. The legend of Wu Shan further reinforces this concept, suggesting that mists are the vital essence emitted during the mating of heaven and earth on high mountain peaks.

From time immemorial, Chinese have cultivated the custom of *deng-gao* – ascending high places. They believe the qi found in the mist strengthens their longevity and virtue. One of the most ancient of all Chinese characters – *hsien,* for immortal – combines the symbols for man and mountain. And while the practical and urban Chinese are unlikely to become mountain-top ascetics, they are convinced of the restorative powers of high-altitude mists.

Rain and mist, however, may not hold the same delight for foreign visitors as for the Chinese. Not to worry; there are other reasons to visit the Alishan area. The region is blanketed with thick forests of red cypress, cedar and pine, some of them thousands of years old. When these ancient plants finally fall to rest, the Chinese let sleeping logs lie. The great gnarled stumps and petrified logs form some of Alishan's most exotic sights. Some of these suggest romantic images and have been named accordingly: Heavenly Couple and Forever United in Love are two examples. The walking paths and grottoes behind Alishan House incorporate several of these formations, and there are many more on the trails.

A 3,000-year-old sacred tree, once 50 meters (160 ft) tall and 23 meters (76 ft) at its girth, was hit some decades ago by lightning, but its remains are still remarkable. Another tree, called the Three-

Sunrise over Alishan.

Generation Tree, may indeed be a natural wonder: a tree growing in a tree, growing in yet another tree.

Perhaps Alishan's greatest attraction for Western travelers is the long train ride to the mountain resort from Chiayi. Antique narrow-gauge diesels, especially restored for this route, cover the zigzagging 70 kilometers (45 mi) in about three hours. The rails cross 114 bridges and pass through 49 tunnels, one of them 770 meters (2,500 ft) long. At the mountain-top depot are several coal-burning locomotives that still haul passengers and lumber through the mountains, all the while belching smoke and piercing the air with shrill whistles.

It is best to book train tickets in Taipei and reserve a room at the Alishan House hotel one week prior to arrival. The Taiwan Forestry Tourism Corporation office, across the street from the main railway station, can make all arrangements. There are other inns at Alishan, but the Alishan House, under the aegis of the forestry tourism people, is the oldest, and the most charming and picturesque. Its Shanghai-cuisine dining room has the best food in the area.

Alishan is the billeting post of mountaineering expeditions to **Yu Shan**, the Jade Mountain. At 3,952 meters (12,966 ft) in altitude, Yu Shan is the highest mountain in Asia east of the Himalaya, south of the Russia's Kamchatka Peninsula and north of Borneo's Mount Kinabalu. Yu Shan is far more visited than the others, however. Indeed, as Taiwan's favorite alpine resort, Yu Shan can lure visitors by the thousands. Even higher than Japan's majestic Mount Fuji, this peak was called New High Mountain during the 50 years of Japanese occupation. Its original name was restored by the Chinese in 1945.

Prior permission to climb this peak, now within a national park, is required from the Alpine Association, in Taipei. Treks to Yu Shan, of course, require proper alpine clothing, hiking shoes, backpacks and sufficient stamina.

From Alishan village, there is a road leading 20 kilometers (12 mi) to **Tungpu**, a remote hot spring nestled in

Sunrise watchers atop Chu Shan.

the mountains at 2,600 meters (8,500 ft) above sea level. There is a rustic hostel there for overnight stays; another hostel is high on the mountain slopes, at about 3,300 meters (10,800 ft) elevation. Four full days should be allotted for this breathtakingly-beautiful trip.

Using his head: After journeying into the mountains, other trips might seem anticlimactic. But temple-lovers, especially those proceeding south from Chiayi, or heading to or from Alishan by road, may want to stop at **Wufeng Temple** to pay respects.

Wufeng, perhaps the only historical personage revered by both Chinese and the ethnic minorities, was an eighteenth-century Chinese official. Born in 1699 to a merchant family in mainland Fujian province, he emigrated to Taiwan as a youth and studied, in great detail, the customs and dialects of indigenous people. Appointed official interpreter and liaison between Chinese settlers on the plains and recalcitrant tribes in the mountains, he worked tirelessly to end feuding between the two camps.

The tribes followed the disturbing practice of invading the plains every year, after reaping the bounty of their mountains, to harvest Chinese heads as sacrifices to their gods. Wufeng, wise at the age of 71, devised a courageous scheme to end the practice.

On a certain day and at a certain place, he told his tribal friends that they would see "a man wearing a red hood and cape, and riding a white horse. Take his head. It will appease your gods." The tribal warriors followed his instructions, lopping off the head of the mysterious rider. Only after removing the red cowl did the warriors discover that the man they had killed was none other than their old friend, Wufeng. This act of self-sacrifice so moved and terrified the local chief that he called a conclave of all 48 of the tribal headmen in the Alishan region. They agreed to ban the practice of head-hunting.

This story obtains more depth by a visit to the Wufeng Temple. Within it is a small museum of artifacts and a series of large oil paintings, with English- **Hostel near Yu Shan.**

language captions, recalling the life and times of Wufeng. Nineteenth-century minority life-styles are depicted in a collection of vintage photographs.

An enormous memorial garden, commemorating the peace established between Chinese and minority groups through Wufeng's efforts, was built in 1984. The garden contains clusters of traditional dwellings, grottoes, and an artificial lake. Wufeng's birthday is celebrated with elaborate ceremonies on 12 November each year.

About 15 kilometers (9 mi) south of Wufeng Temple, a short distance off Highway 3 to Pingtung, is the rustic hot-spring spa of **Kuantzuling**. Resting in a low mountain pass between Chiayi and Wushantou Lake, it is renowned for its therapeutic mineral waters.

Chronic skin ailments find rapid relief in the water, which is also said to relieve chronic gastrointestinal and stomach problems.

The road that runs around the mountains behind Kuantzuling village has a number of interesting sights. About five kilometers (3 mi) from the hot springs, in close proximity to one another, are the Exotic Rock and the Water-Fire Crevice. The rock is an enormous fossilized boulder the size of a house, part of a prehistoric landslide frozen in place at this spot. Bizarre fossil skeletons can be seen etched into its sides.

The crevice is more astonishing. Boiling-hot mineral water bubbles like a cauldron in concert with a constant flickering fire, the flames of which have licked the grotto black. This paradox – fire and water pouring together from the earth – looks literally like burning water and adds to its mystique.

Also in Kuantzuling area are the Blue Cloud Temple, built in 1701, the new Monastery of the Great Immortals, and the small, highly ornate Temple of the Immortal Ancestor. It is but a short drive to a medicinal herb farm, White River Reservoir and the Pillow Mountain Cable Car. Taxis cover the entire circuit from Kuantzuling.

Northwest of Chiayi, via Hsinkang and its elaborate Daoist temple, is the

Monastery of the Great Immortals, Kuantzuling.

town of **Peikang**. It is a 23-kilometer (14-mi) drive on Highway 159. Peikang's chief claim to fame is **Chaotien**, a temple dedicated to Matsu, goddess of the sea. In fact, it is probably the most extravagant of Taiwan's 385 temples dedicated to Matsu, the island's patron deity. Koxinga attributed the safe passage of his war fleet across the Taiwan Strait to the divine protection of Matsu; ever since, she has been a highly-revered deity in Taiwan.

Chaotien, the Palace Facing Heaven, is probably the wealthiest temple on the island. More than three million pilgrims visit every year, leaving large sums of cash in annual donations. During the April or May festival week commemorating Matsu's birth (the 23rd day of the third lunar month), the town is the site of a fascinating display of ancient folk religion and traditional customs.

This festival period is the most exciting time to visit the temple. Throughout the year, however, the staccato bursts of firecrackers, gongs and drums often make it sound like a battlefield. Religious rites are performed with a pomp and ceremony that has not changed significantly in 1,000 years. One particularly colorful (and frequent) ritual involves the parading of a holy icon in a gilded, silk-tasseled palanquin. When the procession returns to the temple gates, the deity is welcomed back amid thick clouds of incense, exploding firecrackers, and a cacophonous din of gongs, cymbals, drums and flutes.

Four stone lions and four Immortals mounted on dragons guard the front gate of the temple. But it is the roof that demands study. There may not be a livelier, more colorful set of eaves and gables on the island. Hundreds of glazed ceramic figures cavort among miniature mountains, palaces, pagodas and trees, depicting tale after tale from folklore. On the central roof are the Three Star Gods of Longevity, Prosperity and Posterity – the three cherished goals of the Chinese people in this life. The pagoda on the main beam of the central shrine hall symbolizes communion of heaven and earth. The roof beams on the side halls have pairs of gamboling dragons pursuing the elusive Pearl of Wisdom.

Within the temple courtyard stands a three-tiered pagoda, where paper offerings are burned. Pilgrims pay real money to temple vendors for ersatz paper money, incense and other gifts for the gods. Thus, the temple fills its coffers with legal tender, the gods benefit from the symbolic offerings, and the pilgrim is blessed by both.

There are many tall image cones (known as Buddha mountains) bearing the names of the temple's financial patrons, lit like Christmas trees and standing in pairs at the temple's altars. Most temples have only two such cones, but the Peikang temple has 12, clear evidence of its immense following and generous patronage. The offering tables are heaped high with meat, fish, poultry, fruit and candy, incense, wine, real cash, and even bottles of soft drinks – conveniently uncapped so that the essence might reach the gods.

An open-air market occupies the narrow lanes surrounding the temple, selling everything imaginable.

Left, Chaotien temple, Peikang. Right, image cones, Chaotien temple.

TAINAN

Tainan is to Taiwan what Kyoto is to Japan, and Kyongju to Korea. The city was capital of the island from 1663 to 1885, and its history, and thus its modern flavor, is inextricably linked with the exploits of Koxinga.

Known in Taiwan as Cheng Chengkung – Lord of Imperial Surname – Koxinga was a Ming loyalist at odds with the new Manchu Qing court. He fled to Taiwan, landing near Tainan in 1661 with 30,000 troops in 8,000 war junks. He besieged the Dutch fort at Anping, eventually driving the Dutch from the island. The Ming stronghold that he established lasted three generations, until his grandson finally capitulated to the Manchu court.

Koxinga brought more than troops to Taiwan. He carried a camphorwood icon of Matsu, which still sits in the shrine to this goddess at Luerhmen (Deer Ear Gate), where Koxinga first landed. Moreover, his entourage included about 1,000 writers, artists, musicians, craftsmen and master chefs, whose function it was to launch a Chinese cultural renaissance in Taiwan. (A similar group of scholars and artisans followed Chiang Kaishek to Taiwan in 1949.)

Today, Tainan remains highly conscious of its rich cultural legacy. For decades a sleepy town of temples and pleasant memories, Tainan currently is rising in a concerted effort to restore its former glory. Under a forward-thinking administration, Taiwan's fourth-largest city of just under one million people is focusing into a tourist mecca. Light industry, agriculture, fishing and tourism are all encouraged in the area, but large industrial plants and their accompanying pollution are kept at arm's length. The goal is to maintain a clean and cultured city, a showcase for visitors. The authorities are especially determined to protect the scenic beauty and delicate ecological balance of Tainan's tropical coastline.

While Tainan is Taiwan's most socially-progressive city, it is also its most traditional. A maze of narrow lanes, courtyards and garden walls are tucked into hundreds of shrines and temples. Native *pai-pai* religious festivals are observed far more frequently and extravagantly than in the north, and most residents prefer to speak the native Taiwanese dialect instead of Mandarin.

As the most "civilized" city in Taiwan, Tainan naturally excels in that most civilized of all Chinese pursuits – cuisine. After dinner, many Tainanese retire to sip coffee at the cozy, chic cafés found all over the city, or relish a cup of tea in one of Tainan's unique tea houses. Overall, Tainan is far more sedate at night than Taipei or Taichung.

Temples, of course: Most of Tainan's chief points of interest are concentrated in the old downtown section, stretching east to west between Chihkan Towers and the railway station, north to south between Chungshan Park and Koxinga's Shrine. It is a pleasant city to explore by foot, day or night.

Temples are the hallmark of Tainan. The sobriquet City of a Hundred

Temples is a modest understatement. In fact, there are 220 major temples and countless minor shrines scattered throughout the town and surrounding countryside. Most are marked by an arched gate or a wall plaque, on which the temple's formal name is inscribed.

It is perhaps appropriate to begin at **Koxinga's Shrine**. Set in a garden compound of tropical trees and breezy pavilions, the shrine was built in 1875 by imperial edict from the Manchu Qing court in Beijing. This was a landmark event: it indicated that the former Ming resistance leader had been forgiven, and now had been deified as a national hero.

A statue of Koxinga stands in the central shrine hall, flanked by those of his two most trusted generals. In the colonnades are enshrined the 114 loyal officers who followed him to Taiwan. The rear shrine hall houses an altar to Koxinga's mother, accompanied by young princes. An attached museum displays antiques, pottery, paintings, documents and costumes reflecting the life and times of Koxinga.

Left in ruins following the Japanese occupation, the shrine was restored after World War II, and again in 1962. Major memorial festivities for this father of modern Taiwan are held three times a year – on 12 February (the Dutch surrender to Koxinga), 29 April (day of retrocession) and 27 August (Koxinga's birthday). The shrine, located on Kaishan Road, is open daily.

Three blocks from Koxinga's Shrine is Tainan's **Confucian Temple**, the oldest temple for the sage in Taiwan. It was built in 1665 by Cheng Ching, Koxinga's son, as a center for the Chinese cultural renaissance in Taiwan. Restored 16 times since then, it still stands out as Taiwan's foremost shrine to Confucius, reflecting a classical architectural style otherwise seldom seen on the island.

It is set in a tranquil garden compound. Arched gates and corniced walls divide the complex into a series of courtyards, each with its own halls and special functions. Originally, these courtyards served as schools for the branches of classical Chinese studies.

Tainan Boy Scouts.

Confucius is enshrined in the central Hall of Great Success, with a simple gilded stele of stone, adorned with fresh flowers and incense. Plaques bearing honorific inscriptions to Confucius from various Qing dynasty emperors also hang here. Elsewhere are shrines to Confucius' most distinguished disciples, and memorials to a host of historical heroes and famous scholars. Ancient costumes, books and musical instruments – used in formal ceremonies marking Confucius' birthday each year – are on display in the temple. The shrine is located on Nanmen Road.

When Koxinga's grandson formally surrendered Taiwan to Manchu forces in 1684, a distant relative of the last Ming emperor was living on the island with his five concubines. Learning of Taiwan's imminent fall, he committed suicide. His concubines – as an act of love and loyalty – hanged themselves on the same day. They were posthumously granted the rank of royal princesses, and the **Shrine of the Five Imperial Concubines**, on Wufei Street, was erected to commemorate them. The small shrine hall houses five doll-like, hardwood icons wearing jewels and silken finery. (The four maidens painted on the doors represent legendary figures, not the five concubines.)

One of Taiwan's oldest Buddhist monasteries is the **Kaiyuan Monastery**, built during the seventeenth century by Koxinga's son and successor, Cheng Ching, in memory of his mother. It is on Kaiyuan Road, best reached by taxi.

Sitting within the central shrine hall is a smiling, pot-bellied Milofo, the Happy Buddha. He is guarded by four enormous celestial sentries in fierce poses. The altar table boasts a very old, intricately-carved panel with coiling dragon motifs. Numerous side shrines dedicated to attendant deities contain traditional Chinese temple furnishings of sculpted hardwood. Another shrine hall with altars and image cones sits behind the main hall. At one corner, visitors may peek into a fully-equipped Buddhist vegetarian kitchen, where all the monks' meals are prepared.

Downtown Tainan.

Indeed, this is a functioning monastery as well as a public temple. Freshly-shaven monks and nuns in robes shuffle about the grounds attending to monastic chores, as they have done for century upon century in China.

Tainan's residents believe that their behavior is reported to the emperors of heaven and hell by Cheng Huang, the city deity. His small, old, and very original temple – **Cheng Huang Miao** – is located on Chingnien Road, between Chienkuo and Poai roads.

The main shrine is a fascinating jumble of smoke-stained icons, antique hardwood fixtures and intricately-hewn beams. Within is a solemn bearded statue of the deity, with life-sized statues of a warrior and a scholar standing guard on either side. In the side-wall niches are two dozen smaller icons of smooth camphorwood, clothed in silk brocade. The facial features and poses are highly individual. Behind the main shrine is a smaller hall and shrine. The side walls are lined painted clay statues, depicting famous monks and masters of the past.

The open beam-work on the temple ceiling is noteworthy. Unlike other ceilings, this one is varnished rather than painted, its surface etched with fine filigree. Relics and ritual objects hang everywhere, among them two giant abaci. The hardwood beads of each abacus are the size of melons. One hangs to the right of the main shrine, the other from the beams over the front door. These are used by the city deity to tally the merits and demerits of each citizen for his annual report to the emperors of heaven and hell.

An indispensable stop on any Tainan temple tour is the **Temple of the Jade Emperor**, one of the oldest and most authentic Daoist temples in Taiwan. Located near the corner of Mintsu, a highly-detailed facade of stone, carved in deep relief, graces the entrance to the central hall of this gaudy complex. Inside, the Jade Emperor is represented by an austere stone slab engraved with his name. To the right, an elevated shrine is dedicated to the red-faced warrior-god, Kuan Kung. It is an exquisite shrine with

Cheng Huang Miao, Tainan

finely-painted door gods and attendant dragons, side panels of sculpted stone depicting animals and Daoist immortals, a large center pagoda for burning offerings, and a circular ceiling inhabited by hundreds of carved, gilded gods.

On the left wall is a most significant fresco: a full-color reproduction of an ancient painting, depicting the third-century Daoist physician Hwa-To performing surgery on the upper arm of the wounded military hero Guankung, who stoically ignores the pain while playing a game of chess with a friend. This is the earliest record of systematic medical surgery in China. Hwa-To is not only revered as one of the fathers of Chinese medicine, he is also renowned as an accomplished Daoist adept and a master practitioner of martial arts.

Temple of the Jade Emperor.

The Temple of the Jade Emperor is one of the most ritually-active temples on the island. Exorcisms and other rites are held frequently during the day, many times involving trance mediums. Visitors need merely follow the sound of drums, gongs, cymbals and loud incantations to the rear courtyard of the temple to find these mediums trying to contact the spirits of deceased friends and relatives on behalf of anxious supplicants, beneath the beatific gaze of the Jade Emperor and his entourage.

The **Palace of the Empress of Heaven**, Tainan's downtown Matsu shrine on Yungfu Street, was built in 1683 to enshrine Taiwan's patron saint. This temple claims to be the oldest Matsu shrine in Taiwan, a boast disputed by the temple in Lukang.

Tall, well-wrought, smoke-stained statues of Matsu and her two bodyguards – former demons converted to the side of good – grace the shrine hall. Worshipped by unmarried men and women, Old Man Under the Moon is a secondary deity in the temple; it is believed that a prayer to this god will help to find a mate.

The **Hsiaopei night market** features stalls offering clothing, and scores of tiny eateries where one can feast on *hsiaochih* or on *dan-tze mien*, a local noodle soup specialty.

Tainan has ample recreational facilities for both residents and visitors. On Chienkang Road, next to the Martyrs' Shrine, is one of Tainan's showcase projects: an enormous sports and recreation center of swimming pools, tennis and squash courts, rugby and soccer fields, running and motorcycle-racing tracks, and hotel facilities.

The **Chihkan Towers** were built in Chinese-pavilion style during the Qing dynasty, on the site of Fort Providentia, an old Dutch fort. Little remains today of the original Dutch fortification, once known to local Taiwanese as the Fort of Red-Haired Barbarians. It was built in 1653 as a Dutch stronghold, but was taken over as Koxinga's administrative headquarters in 1662.

The towers, on Mintsu Road, house visual displays of Koxinga sailing across the Taiwan Strait and ousting the Dutch. Bronze statues in the attached park symbolize the surrender. Nine stone turtles in the park, bearing memorial steles, were inscribed by imperial edict in 1786 and presented to a Chinese magistrate in Taiwan for successfully suppressing an uprising.

Another centrally located park site is **Chungshan Park**, only a block from the railway station. Among the trees and paths is a pleasant landscaped pond with a miniature replica of the "marble boat" built for China's Manchu empress dowager, Cixi. The original is at the Summer Palace, near Beijing.

Also in Tainan, on Kaishan Road, is the **Antiques House**. There are four display rooms: Nature and Humanities contains fossils of rhinoceros and elephants found on Taiwan, possible evidence that the island was at one time a geographical part of the mainland; Politics and Education houses collections and documents, coins, stamps, seals, books and other artifacts relating to Taiwan's political and social history; Literature reflects scrolls, engravings, costumes, porcelain and statuaries; and Customs and Practices of the People displays household implements. First established in 1932, at Fort Zeelandia in Anping, the collection was moved

Temple of the Holy Mother at Deer Ear Gate.

three times before finding a permanent home in this former memorial house to Koxinga, in 1965.

Koxinga landed at **Luerhmen** (Deer Ear Gate), a shallow bay north of Tainan, off of Highway 17. The spot is consecrated by the elaborate **Matsu Temple**, built upon the site of an older structure. Matsu's shrine, within the main hall, is protected by enough writhing dragons to frighten away an army of devils. Her two fierce guardians, one red and one green, stand fully armed in classical martial-arts postures. Sitting before the large central icon of Matsu are a row of smaller, black camphorwood icons bedecked with finery. The one in the center is said to be over 1,000 years old, brought to Taiwan from the Chinese mainland by Koxinga.

The splendid craftsmanship that went into this temple is indicative of its high regard. In addition to the usual wooden temple doors, there are two magnificent moon-gates with nine-meter-wide (30-ft) slabs of polished blackstone etched with coiling dragons and flying phoenixes. The six-meter-tall door gods are carved of solid camphorwood and glazed with enamel and gilt. These are said to be the largest temple doors in Taiwan.

A few kilometers beyond the Matsu temple is what Tainan bills as the largest temple structure in this part of Asia: the **Temple of the Holy Mother at Deer Ear Gate**. Visitors can see its golden roof tiles shimmering in the distance long before they actually reach it.

The entry to this temple is formed by an immense two-story facade braced by a pair of large pagodas. The sculpted dragon columns that support the portico were hewn from solid stone by Taiwan's finest temple artisans. The main wall of the double-tiered shrine inside is divided into six ornate niches, each of which enshrines the icons of major deities of Taiwan. The entire shrine area is carved, etched, painted, cast and gilded in incredible detail. The altar table is a triple-length, black-lacquered, gold-gilded fantasy of intricately-carved celestial animals, heaped high with offerings to Matsu.

Temple bell-ringers.

An equally magnificent shrine hall stands behind the first, also with six major shrines in the walls and two intricately-carved altar tables. The small black wooden icons are paraded about town on elaborate palanquins during traditional festivals.

The third hall is a story taller than the first two. In the ground-floor hall are three well-crafted Buddha images. The central figure is seated on a lotus dais; the right one rides a tiger, the left one is mounted on an elephant. On the second floor are three more large Buddhas. On the third floor is an ornate triple shrine to the Jade Emperor.

The complex has been under construction for many years and is far from finished. But already it is impressive, with its massive scale and grand ambition, blending Buddhism, Daoism and the Matsu folk beliefs. The temple can be reached by following Chengkung Road from the railway station, then bearing right onto Wenhsien Road, which becomes Highway 17. A left turn on Highway 12 leads directly to the temple.

In **Anping**, a 20-minute taxi ride from downtown Tainan, are more reminders of Tainan's military past. **Fort Zeelandia** was first built by the Dutch in 1623, then heavily reinforced between 1627 and 1634. Bricks were held in place with a mixture of sugar syrup, glutinous rice and crushed oyster shells. This ingenious mixture must have worked, for much of the original foundation is still intact.

When Koxinga took possession of Fort Providentia, the Dutch retreated to this bastion, surrendering only after a nine-month siege. Over the centuries, various additions have been made to Fort Zeelandia. During the Opium Wars of the 1840s, cannons were installed and a lighthouse erected by the Chinese. From the top of the observation tower, there once was a good view of the coast. (The coastline is now several kilometers to the west, compared to the times of the Dutch colonialists.)

Two kilometers to the south of the canal, which is crossed via a bridge, stands **Yitsai Chincheng**, an old Chinese fort once used for Tainan's coastal

defenses. As with Fort Zeelandia, silt and sand accumulations have left this edifice far from the shoreline it once guarded. It was constructed in 1875 by Shen Pao-chen, commissioner of naval affairs in Fujian province, after Japanese forces had raided Taiwan on the pretext of avenging shipwrecked Okinawan fishermen killed by local minority groups.

The layout of this fort is remarkably secure. The interior ground is set lower than the exterior, and bunkers and arsenals are placed around the walls. In its heyday, the fort could accommodate 1,500 fighting men. Today, no buildings or major artifacts remain, but there is a fine collection of nineteenth-century cannons on the ramparts.

Near Fort Zeelandia, on Anpei Road and in a house once occupied by a British businessman, is the **Tainan Wax Museum**. Opened in 1981 for the 320th anniversary of Koxinga's victory over the Dutch, this museum displays typical scenes in the lives of farmers, fishermen and ethnic minorities during Koxinga's **Festival time.**

time. Clothing, implements, and other props are authentically recreated against detailed backdrops.

Into the hills: If driving the scenic inland route between Chiayi and Tainan, travelers will pass the two largest lakes in Taiwan – **Wushantou** (Coral Lake) and the **Tsengwen Reservoir**. An underground tunnel three kilometers long feeds Wushantou from the reservoir. Despite their proximity, the road connecting the lakes winds for 30 kilometers (20 mi) through pastoral landscape.

Wushantou derives its name from the countless narrow inlets that probe like fingers into the surrounding hills, making the lake's outline resemble a chunk of coral. More than 30 mountain streams flow into this 30-meter-deep (100-ft) body of water.

Swimming is not permitted, as the lake provides drinking water to the region. Boats can be rented for fishing or just cruising; in fact, the lake's main attraction is a boat tour that visits several islands, Paotzuliao Suspension Bridge and Hsikou Tunnel. A network of trails surrounds the lake. There is a small resort village, featuring a replica of Beijing's Tiantan (Temple of Heaven), and several hostels and inns.

Tsengwen Reservoir replaced Wushantou as Taiwan's largest inland body of water when it was completed in 1971. This 44-square-kilometer (17-sq-mi) reservoir also attracts boaters and hikers. Several tropical fruit plantations in the area provide delicious fresh food to this off-the-beaten-track resort. There is accommodation available at the Tsengwen Youth Activities Center.

Tsengwen is 60 kilometers (40 mi) northeast of Tainan via highways 20 and 3. Ten kilometers (6 mi) nearer to Tainan, via the same route, is the village of **Yuching**, the western gateway to the **Southern Cross-Island Highway**. This road was completed in 1972 at a cost of four years' hard labor, and more than 100 lives. Nearly as scenic as its Central Cross-Island Highway cousin, it can be traversed in a day from Yuching to Haituan, a small town 60 kilometers (40 mi) north of Taitung.

Tsengwen Reservoir.

KAOHSIUNG
AND SURROUNDINGS

Kaohsiung is Taiwan's economic showcase and a city of superlatives. It is Taiwan's largest international seaport, its major industrial center, and the only city on the island besides Taipei with an international airport. The port is the world's third-largest container port after Hong Kong and Singapore, and it also has an extremely large dry-dock for ship repairs and maintenance.

With over one million inhabitants, the city is Taiwan's second largest, and the only one besides Taipei to enjoy the status of a special municipality – equal to a province, and administered by the central government.

Kaohsiung is the southern terminus of the North-South Highway, about a four- to six-hour drive from Taipei. Kaohsiung can be reached from Taipei by train, express bus or plane. Visitors from abroad can also fly direct to Kaohsiung from Hong Kong and many other destinations.

A city of humble origins, Kaohsiung has experienced meteoric economic growth, but the concentration of heavy industry has caused considerable pollution. Kaohsiung is trying to attract and develop high-technology industries in its central districts, moving smokestack factories out to suburban industrial zones. For now, unfortunately, the city is often shrouded with smog. Fishing remains a major enterprise, with over 1,500 vessels registered here plying waters as far as South Africa. Agriculture, however, is glaringly absent in the immediate vicinity, another indication of the city's industrial orientation.

The city center is dominated by modern tower blocks, including the **Grand 50 Tower**, whose 50 stories make it one of the tallest buildings in Taiwan. Another overview of the city is atop **Shou Shan** (Longevity Mountain Park), which overlooks Kaohsiung harbor near the fishing wharves. But on most days, the views of the city itself are disappointing; only when the smog clears can they

be described as impressive, day or night. On top of Shou Shan is the Martyrs' Shrine, and next to it a series of other temples, pavilions, historical monuments and terraces.

Temple-addicts may want to include three complexes on their rounds in Kaohsiung. The **Three Phoenix Palace**, on Hopei Road, is the largest temple in the city, devoted to the demon suppressor, Li Na-cha. Stone lions stand sentry at the foot of the steps, which lead up to an elaborately-carved stone facade. The central hall contains three major icons, exquisite altar tables, and 10 large image cones that glow warmly.

Behind and above the main hall, a set of steps leads to a smaller shrine with three altars. This is a Buddhist hall: three gilded Buddha images – seated on a lotus, an elephant and a lion – share space with statues of warrior guards and the Buddha's disciples.

The **Holy Hall of Martial and Literary Arts**, a three-story Daoist temple dedicated to the deity Kuan Kung and his literary counterpart, Confucius, is

on Fu-Yeh Street. On the ground floor is a shrine devoted to the martial deities, with a number of finely-crafted hardwood altar tables. The second floor enshrines Confucius, patron of the literary arts, his name simply engraved on dignified stone steles. The third floor, wherein reside the Jade Emperor and his celestial entourage, is magnificent with wall frescoes and detailed ceiling work. Three smaller icons dressed in brocaded, jewel-encrusted dragon robes sit on a lacquered table before the shrine.

Not far away, on Yeh-Huang Street, is the **Shrine of the Three Mountain Kings**. This 300-year-old Buddhist temple is dedicated to three brothers, private tutors to a man who saved the life of the Chinese emperor.

When the emperor rewarded the man, he gave credit to his three teachers. The emperor consequently made each brother "King of the Mountain" in three mountainous regions of Fujian province. This beautiful shrine hall houses a dozen deities in a complex panoply of brilliant ornamentation.

Ship scraps: Kaohsiung is the world's largest scrapper of old ships. Armies of laborers bearing acetylene torches, saws and wrenches break down about 200 steel-hulled, ocean-going ships each year. They harvest an enormous quantity of scrap steel, nautical devices, copper wire and other parts. Those lucky enough to be in Kaohsiung when a luxury liner is being scrapped can sometimes get bargains on lanterns, clocks and other nautical artifacts. The scrap wharf is located at **Little Harbor**, 10 kilometers (6 mi) south from downtown.

There are two beaches within the Kaohsiung city limits. **Chichin Beach** has a black-sand beach that is insulated not only from the bustle of downtown Kaohsiung, but also from the murky waters of the harbor – it is located on the seaward side of a long island that forms a breakwater for the harbor. A four-minute ferry ride, from a small dock next to the entrance of the Pin-Hai fishing wharf, takes swimmers there. Near the beach is an ornate Daoist temple, dedicated to the god of medicine.

Haze over Kaohsiung Harbor.

216

Beyond Shou Shan, near the northern entrance to the harbor, lies the beach of **Hsitzu Bay**. The water is not as clean as that of Chichin, but it is a pleasant place for seaside strolls. It is near the Sun Yatsen University with its modern buildings; sports grounds and other facilities have been developed on the reclaimed land. Pedestrians can reach the university grounds through a 230-meter-long (755-ft) tunnel, a cool but windy retreat during hot summer days.

On the steep hill overlooking the harbor entrance stands the building of the **former British consulate** at Takao. After the treaty of Tianjin, the first British vice-consul to Taiwan arrived here in 1861. Five years later, the official British consulate was built on the 30-meter-high (100 ft) hill, guarding the small entrance to the harbor. Today, it is a museum that, with its photographs and models, gives a fascinating insight into the city, past and present. The view from above, looking out over the harbor to the lighthouse, erected in 1883 on Chichin island, is worth mentioning.

Nothing remains of the fortifications that once guarded the harbor.

As Taipei's leading industrial and export city, Kaohsiung is naturally a good place for shopping. Best buys are modern manufactured goods, clothing and other contemporary items, rather than arts and crafts. Most of the older shopping areas are located within walking distance of the major hotels.

A good street for window-shopping and absorbing local color is narrow **Hsinle Street**, which runs parallel to Wufu Road, between Love River and the harbor area. The street is packed with every imaginable type of contemporary Chinese shop. Side lanes lead to more colorful local markets.

Good buys in brass ship lanterns, clocks and other nautical paraphernalia can be found at Henry's, on Wufu 4th Road. A couple of doors down is a well-stocked store with top-quality outdoor camping gear. Several bookstores in this area sell popular Western novels and reference books. Pharmaceuticals and Western medicines may be found in

Simple transport.

the tiny, well-organized Health Pharmacy on Tajen Street, on the corner facing the Temple of the Three Mountain Kings. One of Taiwan's largest department stores, the gargantuan 10-story President Department Store, is on Wufu 3rd Road, near Chungshan Road, next to Central Park.

As Taiwan's number-one fishing port, Kaohsiung naturally offers excellent fresh seafood. A fine culinary evening can be enjoyed on Chichin Island, which can either be reached by ferry from the Kushan terminal, or by car, arriving at the south end via the harbor tunnel. The island is 11 kilometers (7 mi) long, but only 200 meters wide. At the northern end, dozens of seafood restaurants stand cheek-by-jowl. Whether kept on ice or alive in tanks waiting for customers to make their choice, the sheer variety of seafood is unbelievable. Hungry guests come in droves, and you can't afford to hesitate too long when a table becomes vacant, for nowhere else can one eat fish as fresh as it is here.

Concerts, symphonies, plays, exhibits and other programs are presented regularly at Kaohsiung's new **Culture Center** for the performing arts.

After Taipei, Kaohsiung has Taiwan's most active night life. The busy but pleasant **Liuho night market**, some blocks south from the railway station, offers plenty of food stalls and many bargains. Midnight ramblers on the prowl find amusement on **Fleet Street**, a one-block section of Chienhsin 3rd Road, between Wufu 4th and Kungyuan. Fleet Street caters to Kaohsiung's transient merchant seamen, and when the fleet's in, the smoky air of these clubs can grow rowdy.

Suburban sights: A 25-minute drive north of downtown Kaohsiung is **Chengching (Purity) Lake**. Similarities have been drawn between it and Hangzhou's renowned West Lake, on the Chinese mainland. A broad tree-lined esplanade leads to the Ming-style entry arch of the lake's park. An entrance fee gives access to a seven-kilometer-long (4-mi) road sweeping the circumference of the lake.

Below left, dressed for play. Below, Dragon and Tiger Pagodas.

A leading attraction at Chengching Lake is the tall and stately **Restoration Pagoda**. There are also islands, towers, bridges, pavilions, an orchid collection and aquariums, along with boating, fishing, hiking, horseback riding, golf and swimming. Just outside the entrance gate to Chengching Lake, a driveway leads uphill to the Grand Hotel.

Thirty minutes' drive north of Kaohsiung, in suburban **Tsoying**, lies another lovely body of water called **Lotus Lake**. The architectural attractions here include Kaohsiung's **Confucian Shrine**. Divided by corniced walls and moon-gates into various courtyards and garden grottoes, the complex is enclosed within a long wall, enameled in brilliant red and fringed with gold tile.

The **Spring and Autumn Pavilion**, standing on an islet connected to the south shore of Lotus Lake by a causeway, is entered through the jaws of a life-sized dragon sculpture. A stone's throw away stand the twin, seven-tiered **Dragon and Tiger Pagodas**, which also sit over the water and are joined to shore by a nine-corner bridge. A Daoist temple dedicated to Kuan Kung is located directly opposite the entrance to the Spring and Autumn Pavilion.

Into the hills: No visitor should miss **Fokuang Shan**, at least an hour's drive northeast of Kaohsiung in lush rolling hills. Better known as Light of Buddha Mountain, this is the center of Buddhist scholarship in Taiwan.

The complex consists of several shrine halls surrounded by cool colonnades, pavilions and pagodas, bridges and footpaths, libraries and meditation halls, ponds and grottoes, and exquisite Buddhist statuary. Near the entrance, the tallest Buddha image on the island – 32 meters (105 ft) high – is surrounded by 480 life-sized images of disciples.

The major shrine hall is known as the **Precious Hall of Great Heroes**. The size of a larger theater, this hall has no artificial lighting. Sunlight enters through windows running the entire circumference of the hall, along the tops of the walls. Enshrined within are three 20-meter-tall (66-ft) Buddha images,

Spring and
Autumn
Pavilion.

seated in meditation and displaying various *mudras* (hand gestures). Every inch of wall space is neatly compartmentalized into thousands of tiny niches, each containing a small Buddha illuminated by a tiny light bulb. Other items in this cavernous hall are a huge drum and bell hanging in the corners from wooden frames, and a pair of towering 10-meter (30-ft) image cones bearing the names of the temple's donors.

The second major shrine is the **Hall of Great Pity**. It houses a white Kuanyin *bodhisattva* standing on a lotus dais. From a vial in her hand, she pours the sweet nectar of wisdom and compassion. Other sites within the complex include Kuanyin's Pond for Releasing Living Creatures; the Nine Grades Cave; the Pure Land Cave with colorful dioramas; the Precious Bridge; the Hall of Great Wisdom; and the Pilgrims' Parlor, with inexpensive lodging and vegetarian meals.

Fokuang Shan is nestled amidst a dense bamboo forest. The shortest route there from Kaohsiung is via Highway 1, through Fengshan, then north on Highway 21. Public buses run frequently between Kaohsiung and Fokuang Shan.

A further half-hour drive along Highway 21, beyond Light of Buddha Mountain and in the direction of Chishan, is a small park called **Three Peach Mountain**. Meandering footpaths lead through a maze of gardens and rock formations. Aviaries display various wild fowl of the island. There is also a deer pen and the Dragon Cloud Temple, a Buddhist shrine.

Beyond the mountain village of **Chishan**, another 15 minutes' past Three Peach Mountain, exotic **Butterfly Valley** is near the village of **Meinung**. Taiwan is one of Asia's most magnificent butterfly kingdoms, and in this valley, on sunny spring days, the creatures once fluttered as thick as snowflakes. Meinung is most noted for handcrafting oil-paper umbrellas, decorated with calligraphy or colorful paintings. The prices are reasonable and the craftsmen more than willing to explain and demonstrate their ancient art.

Chengching Lake.

Somewhat off the beaten path is the **Kangshan Hot Spring**, also known as Crest Mountain. It lies about an hour's drive north of Kaohsiung in the rolling green foothills of the Central Range. Carbonic hot springs fill the two full-sized swimming pools of the Takangshan Spring Resort.

Nearby is an exotic soft-rock formation called Moon World; it looks like something from another planet, especially under the light of a full moon. One of the most interesting, if not unusual, sites is the Mud Volcano, a small crater filled with thin mud, through which gas occasionally bursts, spilling mud bubbles out of the crater.

This bizarre landscape can be reached by exiting the North-South Highway at Kangshan, then following Highway 177 east towards **Ahlien.** The hot-spring resort lies about five kilometers (3 mi) beyond this small village.

Outlying islands: As Taiwan's major port city, Kaohsiung is also the gateway to various offshore islands under the jurisdiction of the Taiwan government.

It is easy to discover **Penghu**, the Pescadores Islands, the Isles of the Fishermen, situated between Taiwan and the mainland. The sixteenth-century Portuguese sailors who first put Taiwan on European maps – as Formosa – also gave these islands their name. This 64-island archipelago, covering only 130 square kilometers (50 sq mi) of land, has a colorful history. Nearly every army that has attacked Taiwan has used the Penghu as their springboard. During the Mongul Yuan dynasty, Chinese pirates used these islands as a base from which to sack ships plying coastal waters. Ming authorities finally suppressed the piracy and established a trading post here, and early Hakka settlers stopped here en route to Taiwan. Then, in rapid succession, the Dutch, Koxinga, the Manchu Qing, and the Japanese took control of the archipelago, en route to the main island of Taiwan.

Over the years, treacherous coral shoals surrounding Penghu have claimed countless ships. These shipwrecks – and the periods of foreign occupation – help

Mist over Penghu Islands.

to account for the nearly 150 temples and assorted monuments dotting the otherwise barren islands.

Today, Penghu forms Taiwan's only island-county. Half of the archipelago's population of 150,000 live in **Makung**, the county seat on the main island of Penghu. Fishing is the primary source of income; the only crops that grow on these flat, windswept islands are peanuts, sweet potatoes, and sorghum, used for making potent Kaoliang liquor. Makung has a number of attractions, including the old town wall and its gates, and a number of old temples. Hidden in the alleys of the old town is the Four-Eyed Well, which has four openings instead of one, so that the ropes of the buckets don't get entangled.

The Crossing Sea Bridge joins the islands of Paisha and Hsiyu. With a total length of 5.5 kilometers (3 mi), it is the longest bridge between two islands in Asia. On the ramp at the Paisha end stands a holy banyan tree, which is steeped in legend. Worth seeing on Hsiyu is the **Hsitai Fort**, dating from 1883, with its massive casemates. There are superb swimming beaches near **Lin Tou Park** and along the shoreline of **Shihli**, 14 kilometers (9 mi) south of Makung. Stone grottoes, caves and fishing coves are found along the shore.

Visitors can make an interesting side trip to the **Isle of the Seven Beauties**, a 20-minute flight from Makung. According to local lore, seven virtuous beauties of the Ming period drowned themselves in a well on this island, to protect their chastity from marauding pirates. A shrine was erected to their memory, called the Tomb of the Seven Virgins.

Excellent fresh seafood is available at restaurants throughout the Pescadores. There are daily flights to Makung from both Taipei and Kaohsiung.

East of Kaohsiung: Shortly after Fengshan, an extremely large bridge crosses the Kaoping River. In the dry season, only a little bit of running water is visible, but in typhoon season, the whole river bed is filled with raging waters. From the pleasant town of **Pingtung**, worth exploring with its

Below left, Kenting National Park. Below, Blessed Spirit Tortoise.

farmer markets and temples, Highway 22 runs directly to **Santimen**, 50 kilometers east of Kaohsiung.

The Paiwan village here still retains its ethnic color and customs. The neighboring village of **Peiyeh** is home of the Taiwan Aboriginal Cultural Park. Reconstructed buildings, garnished with traditional tribal songs and dances daily, have a magnetic effect on visitors.

South of Kaohsiung: Where the North-South Highway ends, Highway 17 proceeds southeasterly along the coast to Taiwan's southernmost tip at Oluanpi.

Tungkang is a lively fishing port, but not much visited by outsiders. The port is filled with fishing boats, whose sheer variety of design, size and color provides a feast for the eyes. The fish market at the harbor is worth a look.

From the harbor quay, board a scheduled boat to **Liuchiuyu**, a small wooded island just off the coast. The road around this island is only 12 kilometers (8 mi) long, so a day-tour is enough time to see everything. South of Tungkang town, the village of **Linpien** is renowned for the gourmet seafood banquets served in dozens of roadside restaurants.

At **Fangliao**, Highway 17 merges with scenic Highway 1. The latter skirts the coast all the way to the southern tip. Here, the Central Range looms abruptly on the skyline.

On the inland side of the road are lush plantations and paddy fields. On the seaward side, fish farmers cultivate all manner of mollusks and ocean fish, their paddle pumps splashing ceaselessly. At **Fengkang**, Highway 9 from the east coast joins Highway 1. At **Checheng**, another road turns off toward the hot springs of **Szechunghsi** (Four Heavy Streams).

The southern tip: The coastal crescent that occupies Taiwan's southern reaches is known as the **Hengchun Peninsula.** Two arms reach into the sea: Oluanpi (Goose Bell Beak), longer and to the east, and Maotoupi (Cat's Nose Cape), stubbier and more westerly. The broad bay between the two points harbors some of the island's best swimming beaches and many scenic attractions.

Kenting Beach.

The town of **Hengchun** is situated midway between Checheng and Kenting, about nine kilometers (5 mi) from each. Impressive is the Chinese clock tower and the ancient **East Gate**, along with remains of the town wall. A short distance south, a turnoff in a westerly direction toward **Kuan Shan** leads to scenic seascapes. The Palace of Blessed Virtue is a small temple set in a charming grotto of bizarre rocks and trees. A path leads to Blessed Spirit Tortoise, a turtle-shaped rock with a green carapace formed by tenacious vines growing on top.

The roadside resort valley of **Kenting** lies between Kenting Park in the hills and Kenting Beach on the shore. There is a choice of several hotels in the area. Close by is also one of the three nuclear power stations owned and operated by the Taiwan Power Company.

In the low hills above the two-pronged peninsula sprawls **Kenting National Park**, a lovely haven for exotic flora and strange formations of coral rock. Offshore, the merging of waters of the Pacific Ocean, Taiwan Strait, South China Sea and Bashi Channel create a pastel tapestry of green and blue swirls.

Kenting National Park was first established by the Japanese in 1906, who combed the earth to find exotic species of plants to transplant here all that could thrive in this climate. The Chinese have continued to expand the collection: currently there are more than 1,200 species growing in the 50-square-kilometer (20-sq-mi) park. Paved paths and marked scenic routes interlace the park, and most trees and shrubs are identified in Latin as well as in Chinese.

Scenic points include the 100-meter-long (330-ft) tunnel through contorted rock called the Fairy Cave, and the deep gorge, opened like a sandwich by an ancient earthquake, known as One Line Sky. In the Valley of Hanging Banyan Roots, visitors enter a preternatural world where thick banyan roots stretch 20 meters (60 ft) through cliffs of solid stone to reach the earth, their green canopies whistling in the wind high above. From First Gorge, confirmed trekkers can enter the dense groves of the **Tropical Tree Preservation Area**. It takes a little over an hour to make the walk through a wild jungle world of ancient trees, dark ravines, coral-rock formations and shrieking birds.

On the beach: On the ocean side of town, **Kenting Beach** features an unspoiled white-sand beach that stretches about 200 meters (650 ft). The clear azure water is warm and gentle, perfect for swimming from April to October.

Eight kilometers (5 mi) west and south from Kenting, the cape at **Maopitou** pokes into the sea in a jumble of contorted coral-rock formations. The sea shimmers a deep sapphire blue, and the cape provides superb views of the sun-swept peninsular crescent. A rocky path cuts through the craggy formations.

Among the points of interest is the South Sea Cave. A small shrine is maintained here, and elevated sea-viewing terraces make this a fruitful stop for landscape photographers. Roadside stalls offer one of southern Taiwan's most refreshing summer drinks: green coconut water. This clear and cool refreshment, according to Chinese herbalists, has an overall *yin* or cooling effect on the internal organs.

Opposite Maopitou, **Oluanpi** arm extends for several kilometers beyond Kenting and boasts Taiwan's best white-sand beaches. Recently declared a seaside park of 65 hectares (160 acres), Oluanpi features a three-kilometer-long walking path, along with fine opportunities for swimming, snorkeling, scuba diving, fishing and even surfing. Collectors of exotic shells often find a bonanza. Outside the park, Oluanpi's rocky eastern ends in dramatic cliffs. Interesting here is the sand dune at Fengchuisha.

Fifteen minutes by car from Kenting is the **Oluanpi Lighthouse**, a landmark erected at the tip of the cape in the 1880s. It has saved countless vessels from certain peril on the notorious coral shoals that reach into the sea.

A tourist complex has been developed at the foot of the lighthouse, spreading like a growth in anticipation of visitors. There are restaurants with large carparks, and countless stalls selling food and souvenirs.

Rocky shoreline, southern coast.

THE EAST COAST

On the Pacific side of the great Central Range, which bisects Taiwan from north to south, lies the island's rugged eastern coast, unsurpassed for its contours of land, sea and sky. (Parts of this eastern seaboard look much like California's Big Sur coastline.) Insulated by a wall of mountains from the industrial and commercial developments of the western plains, eastern Taiwan remains an enclave of old-fashioned island culture, a refuge where the flavor of human feelings retains its natural taste.

East is East, and West is West, wrote Rudyard Kipling, and in Taiwan seldom do the twain meet. Everything about the east coast is different from the west and north. As if to emphasize this inherent difference, the sun rises over the ocean at around 5am, awakening the east while the west side slumbers in darkness. Then the sun abruptly disappears over the central range in the late afternoon, plunging the east coast into dusk while the rest of the island still basks in sunlight.

The sun and sea have shaped the eastern coastal life-style. People here are early-to-bed and early-to-rise sorts, their skins burnished brown by constant exposure to the strong sun, and their cheeks rosy from steady ocean winds and mountain mists. Farming and fishing – the fruits of sun and sea – remain the pillars of the east coast economy.

Eastern Taiwan's rugged mountains and deep inland valleys are home to many of the island's ethnic minorities. The raw beauty and wild terrain here appeal to their senses, much as the coast's beauty does to travelers with wanderlust for remote and unspoiled places.

On the east coast, the weather is far less predictable, seas are rougher, hot springs are hotter, mountains higher, butterflies bigger, and the people more robust than in tamer regions of Taiwan. Travelers here are still welcomed with hospitality – and curiosity.

A good place to begin an exploration of the east coast is **Suao**, Taiwan's fifth international harbor. A convenient springboard between northern and eastern Taiwan, Suao is located south along the coast from Toucheng, and is linked directly with Taipei via Highway 9. It is also the major link on the railway that connects Taipei to Hualien.

Suao is an orderly Asian seaport that looks a lot like Hong Kong's fabled harbor did half a century ago. The international port facilities occupy the northern part of the harbor town, but the local ambience is concentrated two kilometers south, in the quaint coastal enclave called Southside Suao.

Here is the island's enchanting fisherman's wharf. Timeless Chinese fishing scenes are reflected in the bright pastel paints on vintage, high-prowed fishing boats, in the hoarse cries of fishmongers, and in the heady blend of marine aromas. The marina is lined with seafood restaurants and interesting souvenir shops. By 10am, the fishing activity, however, has already subsided.

Some of the best seafood in Taiwan can be found in the restaurants along the

Preceding pages: tunnels in Taroko Gorge. <u>Left</u>, east coast, south of Suao. <u>Right</u>, Suao Harbor.

wharf's main street, a lane distinguished by its digital-clock tower (erected by the local Rotary Club) in the shape of a small lighthouse. On the ground floor of many of the restaurants is a large, open aquarium, with tanks displaying live moray eels, lobsters, crabs, turtles, jumbo prawns, flounder, tuna, shark, swordfish and several species with no equivalent English names.

South to Hualien: "Breathtaking" is not a cliché when applied to the roller-coaster, 110-kilometer-long (70-mi) route between Suao and Hualien to the south. It is literally a cliff-hanger, with the crashing breakers of the Pacific Ocean eroding the rocks 300 to 450 meters (1,000 to 1,500 ft) below the highway. Chiseled into sheer stone cliffs that rise in continual ridges, the road was first built in 1920, along the route of the original footpath that was hewn out of rock in 1875. At first, there was only one lane to cope with the convoys of automobiles, taxis, buses and trucks. Now, traffic can move freely in both directions, even if the road occasionally gets rather narrow. The journey takes between two and three hours, but the traveler is rewarded with magnificent views and a rush of adrenaline.

Travelers who forego the vehicular routes to this region have three other options to consider. A railway links Hualien with Taipei, with 90 kilometers (55 mi) of track that crosses 22 bridges and passes through 16 tunnels, one of them eight kilometers (5 mi) long. The trip takes three hours and is usually heavily booked, so tickets should be purchased in advance.

The domestic airlines fly to Hualien several times a day from both Taipei and Kaohsiung. It is perfectly possible to leave either of these cities early in the morning, tour Hualien and all of Taroko Gorge by bus or car, and return to base by nightfall.

Hualien: Those who visit Hualien will find it a pleasant, cheerful town. With 90 percent of the Hualien area dominated by mountains, the city itself – the largest settlement on Taiwan's east coast – fills the narrow strip of flat land sepa- **Ami harvest festival, near Hualien.**

rating the mountains from the sea. Hualien's greatest claim to fame is marble. Uncountable tons of pure marble are contained in the craggy cliffs and crevices of nearby Taroko Gorge. The marble is mined by engineers headquartered in Hualien, and processed both in large factories and small workshops. Local bargains include marble lamps, ashtrays, bookends, vases, goblets and just about anything else.

Hualien's finer hotels are notable for their solid-marble waste bins, marble bathrooms, marble coffee tables, and entire sidewalks of marble. Travelers visiting Hualien by air for the first time are startled by the world's only marble airport terminal. Hualien even boasts marble temples. The **Temple of Eastern Purity**, located on a hill downtown, has floors, walls, columns, and shrines all constructed of local marble. Within the main hall sit three gilded Buddhas. Behind the hall stands a modest pagoda, with a small shrine at ground level.

But Hualien's most renowned temple predates the discovery of marble here, and thus is constructed of traditional materials: the Daoist **Hall of Motherly Love**. The sculpted stonework on its facade and columns, and its painted door gods, are its most impressive elements, as in other major Daoist temples.

A very ornate shrine devoted to the Regal Mother of the West occupies the main hall. Prior to a renovation in 1983, it was braced by two of the biggest image cones on the east side of Taiwan, indicating that this temple is generously bank-rolled by big wheels from the wealthier west, in addition to more frugal east-coast donors. Two old and authentic shrines are built into alcoves on either side of the central altar, each with its own set of carved dragon columns and a pair of guardian lions.

Behind stands a four-story annex called the **Palace of the Jade Emperor**. Here, there is extensive use of marble. This remarkable building can house 2,000 pilgrims in three floors of dormitories, and can feed them in a huge ground-floor dining room. A top-floor shrine to the Jade Emperor is surrounded

Hualien street vendors.

by carved and cast icons representing every major religious tradition of China.

The Hall of Motherly Love is located near the end of Chunghua Road, just before it crosses a small canal en route to Carp Lake. Major festivities occur here on the 18th day of the second lunar month, about six weeks after the lunar New Year. At this time, thousands of pilgrims from throughout Taiwan and East Asia converge on the temple to have chronic ills cured through faith, receive the blessings of the priests, and leave donations for the temple's maintenance and expansion.

Hualien is home to Taiwan's largest ethnic minority, the Ami, numbering about 150,000. During the annual Ami harvest celebration, in late August and early September, the town is particularly festive. At other times, authentic performances of traditional tribal dances are staged for visitors in a large marble factory along the road to Taroko Gorge, and in the **Ami Culture Village**, about a 15-minute drive from downtown.

But these centers offer more kitsch than class. Those seeking authentic glimpses of Ami life should visit the little coastal town of **Fengpin**, a short drive south of Hualien. The harvest festival's opening ceremonies are especially exciting at Fengpin.

The **Martyrs' Shrine**, built into a hillside on the northern outskirts of Hualien, is an impressive architectural complex that reflects classical Chinese concepts of balance and proportion.

Hualien's favorite recreational resort is **Carp Lake**, a 30-minute drive by car southwest of the city. Set amidst tropical-fruit plantations in the foothills of the towering Central Range, this fish-shaped reservoir was created by a nearby dam. In June, the lake hosts colorful dragon-boat races. Boating and fishing are popular here, but visitors must bring their own fishing gear. Rowboats, paddle boats and motorboats are all available for rent. Anglers who manage to reel in one of the lake's famous carp can have it cooked at one of the numerous roadside restaurants. One can also shoot the rapids here, along one of the roaring

Martyrs' Shrine.

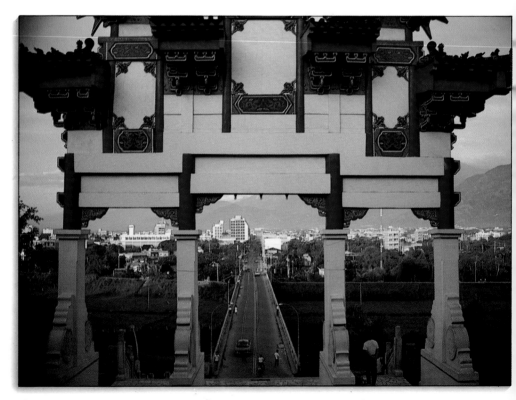

rivers cascading down to the sea from the marble gorges of the Central Range.

Taroko Gorge: Nine out of 10 people who visit Hualien usually tour Taroko Gorge, one of the most spectacular natural wonders of the world. By car, cab or bus, the route from Hualien heads north for 15 kilometers (9 mi), through vast and green plantations of papaya, banana and sugar cane. When the road reaches **Hsincheng**, it cuts westward, straight into the cavernous, marble-rich gorge of Taroko.

Taroko means beautiful in the Ami dialect, and visitors at once realize that the people who named the site were not exaggerating. A gorge of marble cliffs, through which flows the torrential Liwu River, Taroko winds sinuously for 20 kilometers (12 mi) from the coast to its upper end at Tienhsiang.

The first scenic points along the route are the **Light of Zen Monastery** and the **Shrine of Eternal Spring**. The latter is a memorial to the 450 retired servicemen who lost their lives constructing this road, known as the Rainbow of

Treasure Island. The shrine is perched on a cliff overlooking the boulder-strewn river, with a view of a waterfall pouring through a graceful moon bridge.

At **Swallow's Grotto**, the cliffs tower so tall on either side of the road that direct sunlight hits the floor of the gorge only around noon. The Fuji Cliff reels visitors' heads as they look up its sheer stone face, echoing the roar of the river below. The **Tunnel of Nine Turns** is a remarkable feat of engineering – it cuts a crooked road of tunnels and half-tunnels through solid marble cliffs.

The Bridge of Motherly Devotion is worth a stop to explore the rocky river bed, a jumble of huge marble boulders tossed carelessly down the gully by some ancient convulsion. A small marble pavilion stands on a hillock.

The final stop on the Taroko Gorge tour is **Tienhsiang**. Here, amidst natural beauty, is the Tienhsiang Lodge, where overnight lodging and meals are available. A suspension bridge near the lodge leads across the river to an exquisite pagoda perched on a peak. A few

minutes' drive beyond Tienhsiang, a series of steps at the mouth of a tunnel lead down to the dramatic setting of the **Wenshan Hot Springs**. The magnificent walk to the bottom of the gorge is an appetizer for the hot springs themselves. After a swaying suspension bridge crosses the Liwu River, steps carved into the cliff-side lead to a large hot pool lying in an open cave of solid marble, directly adjacent to the rocky, rumbling river bed.

The water is crystal-clear, despite heavy concentrations of sulfur and other minerals, which stain the rocks and waft through the air. A spring lets the hot water seep through a crack in the cave wall; a drain hole empties the pool into the river. Bathers can enjoy the sensation of hot spring and cold river water rushing simultaneously over their limbs. There are no showers or vendors to spoil the raw beauty of this spot, and large boulders provide the only cover for bathers changing their clothes. There is a guest house at the top of the gorge, at Wenshan, however. From here, the Central Cross-Island Highway continues towards Taichung.

South from Hualien: Scenery along the East Coast Highway heading south from Hualien grows more gentle and pastoral. On one side, the deep-blue waters of the Pacific either crash frothily against rocky capes or nuzzle the beaches of quiet coves. Inland, the Central Range forms a massive windscreen, sheltering brilliant green plantations and terraced paddies that cover arable land.

There are two routes connecting Hualien with Taitung. The foothill route, Highway 9, features three rustic hot springs: **Juisui, Hungyeh** and **Yuli**. It follows the railway and runs parallel to the coast, 30 kilometers (20 mi) inland. Most people, however, prefer the coastal route of Highway 11 for its greater scenic attractions.

Along the coastal route, a large, seated Buddha image, facing the sea some 15 kilometers (9 mi) south of Hualien, draws the attention of those not "templed out." Another 25 kilometers (16 mi) further is **Chichi**, the first good swimming beach south of Hualien. The small bay here has clear water for swimming, and sometimes the waves break perfectly for body-surfing. The beach is of black sand.

Just south of Chichi bay, the interested visitor can discover incredible rock formations and a tribal village. The **Hsiukuluan River** offers year-round white-water rafting in a four-hour trip, originating in the foothills next to Juisui, one of the hot springs on the inland Highway 9 route to Taitung.

About 60 kilometers (40 mi) south of Chichi and near **Changpin**, a tall and craggy cliff juts into the ocean. This cliff shelters **Pahsien**, the Caves of the Eight Immortals, while at the same time providing superb panoramic views of the east coast. Steps from the parking lot lead to where a shrine hall is built into the mouth of a large cavern facing the ocean; in an adjacent cave sit three garish pink Buddha images. The final ascent leads through bamboo thickets to the top of the bluff. Here, the trail splits. The right fork leads to the Sea Lightning Cave, a stone grotto where ascetics once lived and meditated. The left fork ascends to a topmost cave containing a crude shrine with several icons. On a clear day, sharp-eyed observers can almost see the southern tip of Taiwan.

After the exertion from the climb, the black-sand beach at the foot of the cliffs is a refreshing place for a dip. There is another beach at **Chu Hu** (Bamboo Lake), 10 kilometers (6 mi) further south.

Between Chu Hu and Chengkung, there is an outcropping of contorted coral known as **Sanhsientai**, the Terrace of the Three Immortals. A small islet is just beyond it, and an asphalt path winds through a maze of bizarre rock formations, with pavilions and picnic tables set up along the way.

According to legend, three of the Eight Immortals stopped here to rest while en route to Penglai, their island abode somewhere in the Pacific.

A few kilometers further south is the quaint old fishing town of **Chengkung**, whose name means success. Taitung is just over an hour's drive from here; tardy travelers will find comfortable if simple accommodation at local inns.

Taitung: Reached from the north by both Highway 9 and Highway 11, the sleepy seaside city of Taitung is pleasant and airy. At about the same latitude as Kaohsiung on the opposite coast, Taitung is the economic hub for the lower portion of the east coast.

Taitung is not much of a traveler's destination in itself. But it makes a convenient springboard for excursions to nearby places such as the Chihpen hot springs, Lu Tao (Green Island) and Lanyu (Orchid Island), and the East Coast Highway.

Taitung can be reached directly by air from Taipei and Kaohsiung. There are also regular train and bus services from Kaohsiung and Hualien.

Within the city limits are a few sites worth visiting, however. The most popular attraction is Carp Hill, with its **Dragon and Phoenix Temple** providing fine views of the city and sea. The temple itself is not particularly noteworthy, except for some interesting icons and a small collection of 3,000- to 5,000-year-old archaeological artifacts unearthed in the area. These stone implements include coffin slabs and hand tools, and they prove that people lived on Taiwan long before the dawn of written history. The government plans to house the artifacts in a museum.

On Chunghua Road stands a modest Matsu temple called the **Palace of the Empress of Heaven**. The Three Star Gods of longevity, prosperity and posterity smile down from the central roof beam; the ornately-enameled and gilded facade is also noteworthy.

Taitung's beach is located at the end of Taitung Road off the main avenue. The beach, however, is unsuitable for swimming, as the entire Taitung shoreline froths and churns with rough breakers, so turbulent that the water is brown with stirring sands 100 meters (330 ft) from shore. The nearest swimming beaches are either northwards along the coast, at Shanyuan, or else to the south, past Chihpen, where there are the wide-open sands of Taimali.

On the plaza in front of Taitung's railway station are several hotels with

Taitung.

adequate facilities for overnight stays. There is good seafood in the eateries along Chengchi Road.

South from Taitung: Tucked against the mountain-side at the mouth of a rugged canyon, along the rocky Chihpen River, is **Chihpen**, one of Taiwan's oldest, quaintest and most remote hot-spring resorts. Dubbed the Source of Wisdom by the Japanese, it was developed as a resort by the Japanese around the beginning of this century.

The village of Chihpen lies on the coast 12 kilometers (7 mi) south of Taitung. The hot spring is another two kilometers inland. This is almost as far away as one can get from big, bustling Taipei – in spirit and in distance – and still be in Taiwan.

The Chihpen Valley, which cuts into the steep mountains behind the spa, is reminiscent of the gorgeous wild gorges hidden deep within the remote mountain ranges of western Sichuan province, on the mainland. Here are thick forests and clear streams, steep cliffs and cascading waterfalls, bamboo groves and fruit orchards, robust mountain dwellers and exotic flora and fauna.

The inn place to stay at Chihpen is the luxury Royal Chihpen Spa Hotel, one of the most amenable hot-spring inns on the entire island. Its bronze fountain and neatly-sculpted hedges make it easily distinguishable from the other hotels lining the roadside at the resort.

The older Chihpen Hotel boasts the biggest outdoor mineral pools in all of Taiwan. Set against the tangled mountain behind the hotel, the triple pool is canopied by cliff-hanging banyans and swaying palms. It is constructed entirely of smooth cobblestones and oddly-shaped rocks. The hottest pool is unbearable for those with tender toes and other extremities. But the medium one is just right for long, soothing soaks. The hot pools are about five meters (16 ft) wide and two meters deep, and are fed directly by springs bubbling from the mountain. The adjacent cool pool, fed by a waterfall contrived to drop from an overhanging tree, is big enough to swim laps. Use of these pools is free **Chihpen hot springs.**

to hotel guests, but anyone may enter and soak there for a nominal fee.

Because it is hot and strong, the Chihpen mineral water is good for therapeutic bathing. Six soaks of 15 to 20 minutes each over a period of two days are said to alleviate the following ailments: skin irritations and festering sores, rheumatic inflammations, arthritis, lower spine and sciatic pain, weak limbs, poor circulation and sluggish digestion. Nonbelievers are urged to try the following regimen: soak in one of the hot pools for at least 15 minutes, then slide into the cool pool and swim slowly around the rim, using the breaststroke or sidestroke. Free-style swimming is too splashy here; the idea is to reach long and stretch the muscles slowly, rather than pump them full of adrenaline. Stand beneath the waterfall and feel a thousand leathery palms pound your back with a water massage, guaranteed to iron the kinks from the most tightly-knotted necks, and to loosen the stiffest shoulders. Then drift back to the hot pools and slip in for another long soak, repeating the process at least twice. It's sure to make a new person out of the weariest wayfarer.

The best times to enjoy the pools are at daybreak, when, under a rising sun, wild monkeys laugh and chatter as they gather breakfast from the trees above. Sundays and holidays are crowded days that should be avoided; this is when Chinese customarily pack their families into cars and head for the hills.

The Chihpen Valley is worth a thorough exploration by foot. A few hundred meters beyond the resort village, a sign points left towards the **White Jade Waterfall**, which lies about one kilometer up a winding paved path, which echoes loudly with the full-throated calls of birds and insects. The waters of White Jade tumble down a jumble of strewn boulders, dense growths of fern, bamboo and gnarled roots.

A few kilometers up the road from the falls stands the arched entrance to the **Chihpen Forest Recreation Area**. A swaying suspension bridge crosses the river to the park area. This wooded

Campers' tug-of-war on east coast.

world of walking trails, campgrounds, greenhouses, streams and waterfalls, and ancient "holy" trees has few visitors.

The biggest treat in the Chihpen Valley is the **Chinghueh Temple** (Clear Awakening Monastery), located up a steep hill about a kilometer from the lower hot-spring area, next door to the Royal Chihpen Spa Hotel. A brace of big elephants in white plaster stand at the foot of the steps to the elegant shrine hall. While Daoist temples display the dragon and tiger, the elephant is strictly a Buddhist motif.

Inside the hall are two of the most exquisite, tranquil and beautifully-crafted Buddha images in Taiwan. The two statues sit together, one behind the other, gazing in meditative serenity through half-closed eyes, exuding feelings of sublime harmony. The Brass Buddha, three meters (10 ft) tall and weighing one metric ton, was made in Thailand and occupies the rear of the shrine. The priceless White Jade Buddha, 2.5 meters (8 ft) tall and weighing 4.5 metric tons, is seated in a lotus flower in the foreground. This solid jade image was a gift from Buddhists in Burma (Myanmar). Along the altar and in front of the White Jade Buddha is a row of smaller but equally lovely icons.

Visitors should remove their shoes and approach across the carpet for a closer look. To the left of the altar is a small, solid-gold, jewel-encrusted pagoda encased in glass. This houses two of the mysterious relics of the Buddha known as *ssu-li-tzu*, tiny nuggets extracted from the Buddha's ashes after his cremation over 2,500 years ago. A series of graphic color prints from India are arranged along the upper walls. Captioned in Sanskrit, these illustrate milestone events in the life of the Buddha.

On the ground floor is a study hall and lecture room, where the monastic community meets to study the sutras. Next to the shrine hall is a dormitory, with communal and private rooms for visitors who wish to stay a night or two, and a dining room that serves good vegetarian cuisine. Banyans and lush green mountains surround the monastery, and silence reigns supreme.

Perhaps no stretch of major road in Taiwan is as untrammeled as Highway 24, which cuts inland and westward from Chihpen to cross the mountains towards Kaohsiung. Travelers will see a lot from the window of a coach, but it is far more convenient and pleasurable to cover this portion by private car or taxi. There is the train as well, but this spends a lot of its time in tunnels.

Continuing south along the east coast, twelve kilometers (7 mi) south of Chihpen lies the town of **Taimali**. A 100-meter-wide beach of gray sand and smooth pebbles runs for about 15 kilometers (9 mi) along the shoreline. The sparkling blue water is completely free of pollution, the surf is gentle, and privacy is as abundant as the beach itself.

Taimali is principally a fishing town, and its fishermen use unique motorized rafts. They are built by lashing together a half-dozen six-meter-long (20-ft) plastic water pipes, bracing them with bamboo and binding them with bailing wire. Noisy outboard motors provide the needed power.

Motorized rafts, Taimali.

A few kilometers beyond the village of **Tawu**, some 40 kilometers (25 mi) past Taimali, Highway 9 cuts inland to cross the lower spine of the Central Range. Having duly arrived at **Fengkang** on Taiwan's west coast, travelers can take the highway either north to Kaohsiung or south to Kenting and Oluanpi. Otherwise, beyond Highway 9's cross-island turnoff, the coast highway continues south to Oluanpi, looping northwards along the western coast towards Kaohsiung.

Island outposts: For the traveler with a taste for offbeat destinations, two islands easily reached from Taitung offer worlds far from the mainstream of Chinese civilization.

Within sight of Taitung, about 30 kilometers (20 mi) due east, is **Lu Tao**, or Green Island. Originally known in English as Fire Island – beacons burned there to prevent fishing vessels from wrecking on its coral shoals – it inherited its new name in 1949. The 16-square-kilometer (6-sq-mi) island has only recently been developed for tour-ism; it wasn't so long ago that a holiday on Lu Tao meant sitting out a long prison sentence.

The island's human history began in 1805, when a fisherman from Liuchiuyu, an island off the southwest coast of Taiwan, was blown off course. Having liked what he found, he returned to his home island and persuaded his family and friends to move to the then uninhabited island. Today, there are about 3,800 permanent residents.

The waters and reefs around Lu Tao are excellent for swimming, scuba diving, fishing and shell collecting. Glass-bottom boats offer views of coral reefs and colorful fish. Trails lead into the hills for day hikers, and a paved 17-kilometer-long (11-mi) road circles the rim of the island. The entire coastline is a tourist attraction with its ever-changing profile.

At the northeast corner of Lu Tao is the Kuanyin Cave. According to legend, an old fisherman lost his way at sea in a terrible storm, about a century ago. Suddenly, a fireball appeared in the sky

anyu coast.

that guided him safely back to shore, where he found safe haven in this cave. Within it he saw a stone that resembled Kuanyin, the goddess of mercy. Taking this as a divine sign, he prostrated himself before the stone and gave thanks for his safe return. Ever since, the cave has been sacred to island inhabitants.

Lu Tao is accessible by air or sea, with regular flights from Taitung. In addition, three ferries service the island, on infrequent schedules, from Taitung. Visitors who choose to stay over on Lu Tao will find a comfortable hostel on the southern tip of the island.

Lanyu, or Orchid Island, is the most unlikely jewel in the waters surrounding Taiwan. An island of 45 square kilometers (17 sq. mi), it is 60 kilometers (40 mi) east of Taiwan's southern tip and 80 kilometers (50 mi) southeast of Taitung.

Lanyu is home to 4,250 Yami, Taiwan's smallest minority tribe. With colorful costumes and a strongly-matriarchal society, the Yami are often regarded as the northernmost extent of

Polynesian ancestry. These people live simply from the fruits of the sea, supplementing their daily catch with taro and a few fruits. Their boats, built with hand tools and natural materials, are renowned for their decoration and crafting.

The government has constructed typhoon-proof concrete housing blocks on Lanyu, but many Yami still prefer living in their traditional homes, adapted by centuries of use to their indigenous environment. Built securely underground against hillsides or embankments – as protection from the fierce typhoons that rip across the island every year – these homes provide rooms for weaving, ceramics-making, storage and other practical functions, as well as eating and sleeping. Open pavilions are constructed on stilts for sultry summer days.

The relatively pristine condition of Yami culture is a result of Japanese non-interference in the first half of this century. During their occupation of Taiwan, the Japanese isolated the island as a living anthropological museum. Modern appliances were not permitted, and the ancient culture was preserved as much as possible in its original form. Since that time, however, there has been an increasing amount of outside influence. Indeed, the combination of Chinese business acumen and Christian missionary zeal has had a profound impact in most aspects.

The entire island can be driven around in a little over two hours. The coastal rock formations, eroded by weather and water, are particularly impressive. Formations include the Lion Rocks, the strange Beauty Stone, and the Battleship Fleet. One thing conspicuously missing, given the island's English name, are wild orchids – they have all been dug up and sold.

The best time of year to visit Lanyu is spring, a festive season when new boats are launched with much fanfare, and the Yamis' favorite delicacy – flying fish – literally leaps into their boats.

There are adequate accommodations and meals at the Orchid Island Inn, and regular flights from Taitung; the frequency of flights from Taipei or Kaohsiung depends upon demand.

Left, Yami woman. **Right**, Wenshan Hot Springs.

INSIGHT GUIDES
Travel Tips

FLY SMOOTH AS SILK TO EXOTIC THAILAND ON A ROYAL ORCHID HOLIDAY.

Watching exquisite cotton and silk umbrellas being hand-painted in Chiang Mai. Lazing in the shade in sun-drenched Phuket. This

Insight Guides portray destinations in depth, providing the complete picture and the top photography

INSIGHT GUIDE
AUSTRALIA

INSIGHT POCKET GUIDES
PLUS PULL-OUT MAP

BALI

Insight Pocket Guides focus on the best choices for places to see and things to do and include large fold-out maps

INSIGHT COMPACT GUIDE
Lon

Insight Compact Guides' portability makes them the perfect books to carry with you for on-the-spot reference

Three types of guide for all types of travel

INSIGHT GUIDES Different people need different kinds of information. Some want *background information* to help them prepare for the trip. Others seek *personal recommendations* from someone who knows the destination well. And others look for *compactly presented data* for on-the-spot reference. With three carefully designed series, Insight Guides offer readers the perfect choice. Insight Guides will turn your visit into an experience.

The world's largest collection of visual travel guides

is what holidaying in Thailand is all about. Book the holiday of your choice now, flying Thai. Smooth as silk.   **Thai**

ROYAL ORCHID *Holidays*

Getting Acquainted

The Place

Taiwan comprises the main island of Taiwan, the Penghu Archipelago (known in the west as the Pescadores), which is made up of 64 islands, and 21 other islands scattered around the main island. Together, these fill up about 36,000 square kilometers of the Pacific Ocean, with the main island alone occupying 98 percent of that area. Situated just off the southeastern coast of mainland China, Taiwan is bisected by the Tropic of Cancer.

A central mountain range runs parallel to the length of the main island of Taiwan, dividing it into east and west halves. With the Pacific Ocean on the east, which is sculpted by a dramatic coastline, the highland levels off gradually on the western side. The terraced tablelands and alluvial coastal plains, thus formed on the west coast, are home to about 80 percent of Taiwan's 22 million population.

A magnificent 3,952 meters (12,966 ft) in height is Taiwan's highest mountain, Yu Shan.

Time Zones

Taiwan Standard Time is eight hours ahead of Greenwich Mean Time, **GMT +8**. There is no daylight savings time.

Climate

Overlying both tropic and subtropic zones, Taiwan has a tropical climate in the southern and western flatlands, and a subtropical climate in the north and mountainous regions. Its location also subjects it to annual typhoons, which pass through between July and October. Most of these cause little more than strong winds and heavy rains over the island.

Taiwan's climate does not have four distinct seasons, but rather two: a hot season lasting from May till October,

and a cold season from December to March. The island remains excessively humid throughout the year and receives abundant rainfall, with the east (uplands) receiving more than the west (lowlands). Except in the northern region, where rainfall is more even, mean annual rainfall in other parts of the island range from 2,500 to 5,000 mm (100 to 200 inches).

Temperature falls with an increase in altitude: snow falls on the summits of the Central Range in the cold season, while lowland Taiwan remains frost-free.

The most pleasant times of the year for travel in Taiwan are March through May and September through November, especially in Taipei.

The People

Etiquette

The Chinese, like the Koreans and Japanese, used to bow and clasp their hands together when being introduced to someone new, but today the Western handshake has displaced the ancient custom. Nevertheless, the Chinese still shy away from boisterous greetings in public, such as hugs, kisses, and resounding slaps on the back. A firm handshake, friendly smile, and slight nod of the head are appropriate gestures of greeting.

In Chinese, a person's family surname precedes both given name and formal title. For example, in the name Li Wu-ping, Li is the surname and Wu-ping is the given name. In the expresson Li jing-li, Li is the surname and jing-li (manager) is the title. Most Chinese names consists of three characters – one surname and two given names – but many use only two. The majority of Chinese family names come from the Old Hundred Names (Lao Bai Hsing), first formulated over 3,000 years ago in feudal China. Among the most common are Li, Wang, Chen, Hwang, Chang, Yang, Liang and Sun.

During formal introductions, the Chinese today usually exchange name cards, which has become the tradition throughout Asia. In fact, many people don't even listen to oral introductions, but wait instead to read the person's card. It is a good idea to have some personal name cards printed up before traveling anywhere in the Far East. As

the Chinese say, "When entering a new land, follow the local customs".

Some of the most common titles used in Chinese during introductions are:

Hsien-sheng/Mister (as in Li *hsien-sheng*)
Tai-tai/Mrs (Li *tai-tai*)
Hsiao-jye/Miss (Li *hsiao-jye*)
Fu-ren/Madame (Li *fu-ren*)
Lao-ban/Boss (Li *lao-ban*)
Jing-Li/Manager (Li *jing-li*)

The Chinese term *ching-keh* literally means "inviting guests" and refers to the grand Chinese tradition of entertaining friends and associates with lavish generosity, usually at banquets. The Chinese are perplexed when they see Westerners call for their bill at restaurants, then pull out pocket calculators and proceed to figure out precisely how much each person at the table must contribute. The Chinese, on the contrary, almost get into fistfights while arguing for the privilege of paying the bill for the whole table. To the Chinese, inviting guests out for dinner and drinks is a delightful way to repay favors or to cultivate new business relationships, and they do so often. For one thing, this is the type of gift which the giver may always share with the recipients. For another, the very moment you've paid a hefty dinner bill, everyone at the table is immediately obliged to invite you out as their guest sometime in the near future. This way, although the bill is high when it's your turn to *ching-keh*, you only end up paying for one out of 12 banquets. In the final analysis, it all balances out, and everyone takes turns earning the "big face" that comes with being a generous host.

When toasted at dinner parties, it is well-mannered to raise your wine cup with both hands: one holding it and the other touching the base. The host would take his seat opposite (not beside) the guest-of-honor, and it is fitting to have the host's back to the door and the guest-of honor's facing it.

Tea served at the end of a meal is your host's polite insinuation that the party is over and that it is time for you to leave. So don't overstay your welcome even though your host may insist. What is mere courtesy to the Chinese is often regarded as hypocrisy to

Westerners. For example, even though it is late and the host would love to call it a day, he will gently persuade his guest to stay longer. In this case, it is up to the guest to detect from the host's tone what's the best thing to do. But this requires skill and cultural sense. An experienced traveler once ventured, "The rule of thumb is to do the exact opposite that your Chinese friend suggests". Try it if you must, but with discretion.

The Chinese Zodiac

Despite family planning programs, modern birth control, industrialization, the ascendancy of scientific thought, and other pragmatic Western social influences in Taiwan, the Chinese continue to hold great faith in their age-old cosmology. Prior to births, weddings, funerals, major business contracts, grand openings of new buildings, and other important events, most Chinese in Taiwan still consult ancient almanacs, fortune-tellers and geomancers for advice regarding auspicious days.

The Chinese calendar was first devised during the reign of the Yellow Emperor, around 2,700 BC. Thus, the Chinese are currently living in the 48th century, not the 20th, according to this ancient calendar.

In the Chinese lunar calendar, which follows the cycles of the moon rather than the sun, each year is designated by its association with one of the twelve celestial animals, along with one of the Five Cosmic Elements. The animals, in order of sequence, are the Rat, Ox, Tiger, Rabbit, Dragon, Snake, Horse, Ram, Monkey, Chicken, Dog, and Pig. The Five Elements are metal, wood, earth, water, and fire. Since each of the animals is associated in turn with each of the Five Elements, a full cosmic cycle takes 60 years to complete. Then, the sequence repeats itself once again.

Like the Western solar calendar, the Chinese lunar calendar has 12 months, each consisting of 29 or 30 days. To adjust their calendar, the Chinese add an extra month every 30 months. Each month commences with the new moon, and the full moon always falls on the 15th day. Chinese Lunar New Year occurs sometime between January 21 and February 28, and remains the single biggest holiday of the year among Chinese all over the world.

The pervasive influence of the ancient Chinese zodiac and lunar calendar on contemporary Chinese life in Taiwan today is remarkable. Most major Chinese and all local Taiwanese festivals are still determined according to the lunar calendar, which means that every year they fall on a different day on the Western calendar. If you ask a Chinese in Taiwan when his birthday is, he'll ask you whether you mean the Western sun calendar or the Chinese lunar calendar.

The dates for weddings and funerals in Taiwan are always set according to ancient Chinese cosmology. Many Chinese even refuse to travel or embark on new business ventures without considering auspicious dates. Not to do so would invite disaster.

When a modern new skyscraper goes up in Taiwan, the owners routinely consult a Chinese geomancer to determine the optimum position for the main entrance. Called *fengshui* (wind and water), geomancy is the branch of classical cosmology which helps humanity build dwellings in optimum harmony with the elements of the natural environment. Even if the building's owners don't really believe in *fengshui*, they will still follow the geomancer's advice, as they know perfectly well that many prospective buyers and renters will consult their own geomancers about the building prior to moving in.

Even the massive Chiang Kaishek Memorial Hall in downtown Taipei, with its extensive gardens and numerous gates, was laid out according to the laws of Chinese geomancy, in order to provide maximum harmony with the elements and spirits of the cosmos.

The Chinese zodiac is a complex and subtle system, which only fortune-tellers and scholars manage to master completely. But its basic tenets are applied daily in the lives of Chinese people everywhere.

The most popular aspect of the zodiac today is the description of one's basic personality traits according to which animal dominates the year of birth. Professional match-makers still refuse to introduce prospective marriage partners whose signs conflict, and businessmen often attribute unfulfilled contracts, financial failure and other problems to ill cosmology.

Rat: Charming and attractive to the opposite sex. They are hard-working, thrifty and highly resourceful, with remarkable ability to see projects through to the end. Rats hoard their money and are loathe to lend it, but they like to spend lavishly on themselves. Only in love do they grow generous. Though timid and retiring, Rats are easily roused to anger. Frank and honest, Rats also love to gossip.

Ox: Calm and quiet, the Ox inspires confidence and trust in others. Ill-tempered and volatile, the Ox tends to lose control when angry. The Ox is eloquent in speech, alert in mind, and dexterous of hand. The Ox is also stubborn and is not given to passion, which often causes problems with mates. The Ox tends to remain aloof from family.

Tiger: Tigers are courageous and powerful, with strong will-power. They command respect from others and resent authority. Yet they are sensitive and thoughtful, with deep feelings and sympathy for their friends and loved ones. They are said to repel the three evils of thieves, fire and ghosts.

Rabbit: Talented and virtuous, rabbits have conservative tendencies and display good taste. They are both clever and reliable in business, and are usually blessed with good luck. They are tender to those they love, yet often keep a distance from their families. Moody and sometimes arrogant, Rabbits tend to lead tranquil, fortunate lives.

Dragon: Energetic, healthy, and quick to react, Dragons are also stubborn and short-tempered. They are known for honesty and courage, and they inspire trust and confidence in others. Though admired by all, Dragons often worry needlessly about affection. Dragons usually get what they want and are generally the most eccentric people in the zodiac.

Snake: Intense and introverted, Snakes are often distrusted by others and have trouble communicating effectively. They are wise and deep-thinking, but also tend to be vain and selfish. Still, they offer help to those less fortunate than themselves. Money never seems to be a problem for Snakes, nor do they worry about it. They prefer their own judgement to the advice of others. Generally passionate and attractive, Snakes do not make the most faithful marriage partners.

Horse: Optimistic, perceptive and self-confident, Horses are popular with others and rather talkative. Though good-looking and intelligent, they often find themselves at the mercy of the opposite sex. They manage money well and are skillful in their work. Horses love freedom and tend to leave home early.

Ram: Blessed with excellent dispositions, Sheep make fine marriage partners. They are upright, honest and extremely generous, and show great sympathy for those struck by misfortune. They have excellent taste in fashion and are endowed with artistic talents. Gentle, compassionate, and rather shy, Sheep are sometimes puzzled by the vagaries of life.

Monkey: Clever, inventive and original, Monkeys can solve complex problems with ease. However, they are also cunning, inconsistent, and rather mischievous. They love to be the center of attention, but they have little respect for others. They succeed in almost everything they undertake, and are ingenious in handling money. Others respect them for their competence and ability to learn quickly, but their own enthusiasm for projects tends to fizzle out quickly.

Chicken: Outgoing, brave, and highly capable. Chickens embark on many projects, many of which they never complete. They are somewhat eccentric and self-righteous, with strong personal opinions. They tend to be moody, and are highly devoted to their work.

Dog: Dogs are honest, loyal, and easily trusted by others. They keep secrets very well and have a strong sense of justice. Though they don't possess great wealth, they rarely suffer for lack of funds. They tend to be somewhat cold, sarcastic, and erratic, but they are hard-working and devoted to their friends.

Pig: Honest, polite, and devoted to their tasks, Pigs also place great value on friendship and are loyal. Though quick-tempered, they hate to argue and are affectionate to their mates. They have a tendency towards laziness and love to spend money.

The Government

The Republic of China on Taiwan, as the government officially refers to Taiwan, still marches to the battle cry of Dr. Sun Yatsen, who established a governing system "of the people, by the people and for the people" early in the 20th century.

The government adopted a constitution based on those principles. It incorporates five branches of government called *Yuan* under a president. The executive Yuan resembles the cabinet of Western governments and includes ministries and other offices and departments. Law-making is the function of the Legislative Yuan. The Control Yuan has powers of consent, impeachment, censure and audit. Under the Judicial Yuan are the courts, Council of Grand Justices and other offices that uphold and interpret the law. Finally, the Examination Yuan supervises examinations and personnel.

In addition to the ROC government, the Taiwan Provincial Government and numerous county, city and ethnic minority groups have freely-elected representatives that participate in daily decision-making. The current president of the republic is Lee Teng-hui.

Planning the Trip

What to Wear

During the hot season, appropriate clothing for Taiwan should include light and loose cotton clothing, casual sportswear, and comfortable walking shoes. Men usually need not wear jackets and ties, for even during office hours, most Chinese businessmen prefer to wear leisure suits with open collars to beat the heat. You may want to bring along a lightweight jacket or dress for formal banquets and receptions, but otherwise such clothing is not necessary. If you come for business, it is better to be overdressed, so take your jacket and tie. Most modern offices are air-conditioned.

During the cold season, be sure to bring along some comfortable woolens to help protect you from the bone-chilling, moisture-laden airs of winter in Taiwan. Sweaters, woolen jackets and dresses, warm pants and socks will all come in handy during Taiwan winters, especially in Taipei. People in Taiwan tend to dress a bit more formally on winter evenings than in summer.

During both seasons, it is advisable to bring along some sort of rain-gear. It can burst out in thunderstorms at any moment without forewarning.

Entry Regulations

Visas

Visa-free entry: Citizens of Australia, Austria, Belgium, Canada, France, Germany, Japan, Luxembourg, New Zealand, Netherlands, Portugal, Spain, Sweden, United Kingdom and the United States – with passports valid at least for six month and confirmed onward or return tickets – are allowed visa-free entry to Taiwan at any of its major international ports and harbors, for a period of 14 days. It is **not** possible to extend the validity of such visas.

Visas: Foreigners applying for visitor visas must hold passports or other travel documents which are valid for application, incoming and outgoing travel tickets (or a letter from your travel agent), three photos, and documents stating the purpose of the visit (except for sightseeing or transit) and the completed application form.

Such visitor visas are good for 60 days (unless restricted to two weeks) and may be extended twice for 60 days, for a total of six months' stay. Foreigners entering Taiwan on a visitor visa may not work without official authorization.

Visitors from countries without ROC embassies or consulates may approach the designated ROC representatives in their respective countries for letters of recommendation. These letters of recommendation may then be exchanged for visitor visas at any ROC embassy or consular office en route to Taiwan, or on arrival at Chiang Kaishek International Airport or Kaohsiung International Airport, the only points of entry to Taiwan at which such letters may be exchanged for a visa.

More detailed information regarding ROC visitor visas can be obtained from the **Department of Consular Affairs**, Ministry of Foreign Affairs, 23F, 333 Keelung Road, Sec. 1, Taipei, Taiwan, Tel: (02) 729-7117.

EXTENSIONS

Be sure to apply for extensions at least one or two days before your regular visa expires. To extend a regular tourist visa in Taipei, visit the **Foreign Affairs Department**, National Police Administration, 96 Yenping S. Road, Taipei, tel: (02) 381-8341.

Customs

Inbound Declaration: All inbound passengers must fill a customs declaration form upon arrival in Taiwan.

DUTY-FREE

All personal belongings such as clothing, jewelry, cosmetics, food and similar items may be brought into Taiwan free of duty. Items such as stereo equipments, TV sets and recorders, though also duty-free, must be declared on arrival. Each passenger is also permitted to bring in duty-free one bottle (1 liter) of alcoholic beverage and one carton of tobacco (200 cigarettes, 25 cigars, or 1 pound of pipe tobacco).

GOLD & CURRENCY

On gold in excess of 62.5 grams in weight, duty will be charged.

Although unlimited amounts of foreign currency may be brought into Taiwan, passengers who wish to take excess foreign currency out again must declare the full amount upon arrival. The unused balance may then be declared on the Outbound Passenger Declaration form upon departure from Taiwan.

Otherwise, outbound passengers are limited to taking US$5,000 or the equivalent in other currencies out of Taiwan. No more than NT$40,000 per passenger in local currency may be brought into or out of Taiwan. Visitors who want to bring in more than NT$40,000 in cash must apply for a permit from the Ministry of Finance before entering Taiwan.

PROHIBITED ITEMS

The following items are strictly prohibited from entry into Taiwan:

- counterfeit currency or forging equipment
- gambling apparatus or foreign lottery tickets
- pornographic materials
- publications promoting communism or originating in the few nations or areas still under communist control
- firearms or weapons of any kind and ammunition
- opium, cannabis, cocaine, and other illegal drugs
- toy guns
- all drugs or narcotics of a non-prescription and non-medical nature
- articles which infringe on the patents, trademarks and copyrights of the rightful owners
- animals and pets

OUTBOUND DECLARATION

The outbound passenger declaration form must be completed when carrying any of the following items:

- foreign currency, local currency, gold and silver ornaments in excess of allowed amounts
- any unused foreign currency declared upon arrival
- commercial samples and personal effects such as cameras, calculators, recorders, etc., which you wish to bring back to Taiwan duty-free in the future
- computer media, diskettes, tapes, etc.

Passengers who have not declared gold, silver and foreign currencies upon arrival and are then discovered to be carrying these items in excess of the legally-designated quantities will have the excess amount confiscated by customs authorities, and may be subject to punishment by law. The designated legal limits are as follows:

- foreign currency – US$5,000 or equivalent, in cash (excluding unused portion of currency declared upon arrival)
- Taiwan currency – NT$40,000 in banknotes and 20 coins (of the types in circulation)
- gold ornaments or coins – 625 grams
- silver ornaments or coins – 625 grams
- articles that may not be taken out of the country include unauthorized reprints or copies of books, records, videotapes, and so on; genuine Chinese antiques, ancient coins and paintings; and items prohibited from entry as firearms, drugs, counterfeit currency, and contraband.

A booklet giving complete customs regulations and hints is available. For further information on Taiwan customs regulations, contact the following government office:

Inspectorate General of Customs, 85 Hsin-Sheng S. Rd, Sec. 1, Taipei. Tel: (02) 741-3181.

Outbound passengers must sometimes open their luggage for security inspection after checking in for flights. This is done at the end of the check-in counters, and if you forget to pay attention to this, your bags may not be loaded onto the aircraft.

AIRPORT TAX

All outbound passengers must pay an exit airport tax of NT$300. You must present the receipt when checking in.

Health

Effective cholera and yellow fever inoculation certificates are required for passengers coming from certain countries or have stayed more than five days in infected areas. Otherwise, health certificates are not normally required. It is very much recommended to have inoculations against Hepatitis A and in some cases. Hepatitis B well in advance if traveling to remote areas.

Currency

Coins come in denominations of NT$1, 5, 10, 50 and 100. Bills come in units of NT$100, 500 and 1,000.

Major foreign currencies can be easily exchanged for the local currency at certain banks, hotels, some shops and all authorized money dealers. In smaller towns or in the countryside, it is nearly impossible to change foreign currency into NT$. If traveling overland, change money before the trip. In smaller towns usually only the **Bank of Taiwan** changes foreign currency; the procedure is complicated, exhausting and time-consuming.

Important: Be sure to obtain receipts of all such transactions: you'll find they save you a lot of hassle with the bank, when you try to reconvert unused New Taiwan dollars on departure. Usually you will get US$ for your surplus NT$. The best for doing this job are the banks at CKS International

Airport in Taipei. There is also a bank at Kaohsiung International Airport, but with irregular opening times.

Traveler's checks are also widely accepted at most hotels and other tourist-oriented establishments. This also applies to major credit cards such as American Express, Visa, MasterCard and Diners Club.

Getting There

By Air

Taiwan lies along one of the busiest air routes in Asia, and stopovers there may be included on any round-the-world or regional air tickets at no extra cost. Many international airlines currently provide regular air service to Taiwan. Chinese travel a lot and it is a good idea to make flight reservations as early as possible.

Taipei: A lot of the international air traffic to and from Taiwan goes through the **Chiang Kaishek International Airport** in Taoyuan, about 45 minutes' drive from downtown Taipei. This is one of the safest, most well-designed airports in Asia, fully-equipped with the latest technology. While you are here, it makes sense to visit the adjoining three-story Chung-Cheng Aviation Museum. More than just a museum exhibiting models of aircraft (about 700), it offers facilities for visitors to test their flying skills or experience the sensation of flying. Also housed within its premises are dioramas and close-circuit TV displays, which trace aviation history from the time of Icarus' flight to modern-day space exploration.

Kaohsiung: In the south of Taiwan is Kaohsiung, with Taiwan's second international airport. Regular air services connect this city to several other Asian destinations.

Special Facilities

Trade Missions

The China External Trade Development Council (CETRA) is designed to assist those who wish to do business with Taiwan, and it displays the full range of products manufactured here. It is an independent, non-profit organization supported by grants from both the government and the local business associations. Its primary purpose is to promote Taiwan's growing trade with other nations. It provides facilities to local and foreign businesses, as well as to visitors with an interest in Taiwan's industries.

CETRA operates an enormous **Display Center and Export Mart** at the Sungshan Airport (domestic), in Taipei, exhibiting the full range of manufactured products available for export from Taiwan. Next to the center is an Export Mart, where Taiwan's major exporters maintain permanent representatives to discuss business and trade with interested foreigners. At the Export Mart, you may also purchase samples of various products at rock-bottom factory prices. The range and quality of the products on display there are impressive: watches and calculators; digital pen/watches and computer games; electronic components and audio-visual equipment; tools and machines; toys and sporting goods; jewelry and handicrafts; and much more. Even if you're not interested in business, it's well worth visiting CETRA's Display Center and Export Mart.

At CETRA's initiative, the **Taipei World Trade Center** (TWTC) was opened in 1989. The massive TWTC houses four complexes: the Taipei International Convention Center, which can seat 3,300 people and is also equipped with smaller meeting rooms; the Hyatt Regency Hotel, which provide 872 rooms for the luxury and convenience of business people; the exhibition hall, which can accommodate up to 1,313 display booths; and the International Trade Building, which will be able to provide professional assistance to exhibitors, sellers and buyers. The TWTC is the ultimate meeting place with all the modern amenities and essential services.

For information on specific trade shows and dates, contact: CETRA, 5 Hsinyi Rd, Sec. 5, Taipei. Tel: (02) 725-111; fax: (02) 725-1314.

Foreign Representive Offices

American Institute in Taiwan, Taipei 7, Lane 134, Hsinyi Rd, Sec. 3, Taipei. Tel: (02) 709-2000; fax: (02) 702-7675.

American Institute in Taiwan/Kaohsiung, 5F, 2 Chungcheng 3rd Rd, Kaohsiung. Tel: (07) 224-0514; fax: (07) 223-8237.

Anglo-Taiwan Trade Committee, 9F, 199 Jenai Rd, Sec. 2, Taipei. Tel: (02) 322-4242; fax: (02) 394-8673.

Australian Commerce & Industry, Rm 2605, 333 Keelung Rd, Sec. 1, Taipei. Tel: (02) 720-2833; fax: (02) 757-6707.

Australian Trade Delegation, Rm 608, 205 Tunhua N. Rd, Taipei. Tel: (02) 715-5220, fax: (02) 717-3242.

Belgian Trade Association, Rm 901, 131 Minsheng E. Rd, Sec. 3, Taipei. Tel: (02) 715-1215; fax: (02) 712-6258.

Brazil Business Center, Rm 702, 129 Minsheng E. Rd, Sec. 3, Taipei. Tel: (02) 514-9099.

Canadian Trade Office, 13F, 365 Fuhsing N. Rd, Taipei. Tel: (02) 713-7268; fax: (02) 712-7244.

Danish Trade Organization, 4F, 12, Lane 21, Anho Rd, Taipei. Tel: (02) 721-3389, 721-3397; fax: (02) 731-5120.

France Asia Trade Promotion Association, Rm 601, 205 Tunhua N. Rd, Taipei. Tel: (02) 713-8216, 713-3552; fax: (02) 717-1353.

French Institute, Rm 1003, 10F, 205 Tunhua N. Rd Tel: (02) 545-6061; fax: (02) 545-0994.

German Cultural Office, 11F, 24 Hsinhai Rd, Sec. 1, Taipei. Tel: (02) 365-7294; fax: (02) 368-7542.

German Trade Office, 4F, 4 Minsheng E. Rd, Sec. 3, Taipei. Tel: (02) 506-9028; fax: (02) 509-3979.

Indonesian Chamber of Commerce, 3F, 46-1 Chungcheng Rd, Sec. 2, Taipei. Tel: (02) 831-0451; fax: (02) 836-1844.

Institute for Trade & Investment of Ireland, Rm 7B-09, 5 Hsinyi Rd, Sec. 5, Taipei. Tel: (02) 725-1691; fax: (02) 725-1653.

Italian Trade Promotion Office, Rm 2C-14, 5 Hsinyi Rd, Sec 5, Taipei. Tel: (02) 725-1542; fax: (02) 725-1422.

Malaysian Friendship & Trade Center, 8F, 102 Tunhua N. Rd, Taipei. Tel: (02) 713-2626; fax: (02) 718-1877.

Manila Economic & Cultural Office, Rm 803, 47 Chungshan N. Rd, Sec. 3, Taipei. Tel: (02) 585-1125; fax: (02) 594-6080.

Netherlands Trade & Investment Office, Rm B, 5F, 133 Minsheng E. Rd, Sec. 3, Taipei. Tel: (02) 713-5670; fax: (02) 713-0194.

New Zealand Commerce & Industry Office, Rm 812, 333 Keelung Rd, Sec. 1, Taipei. Tel: (02) 757-7060; fax: (02) 757-6972.

Norway Trade Office, 11F, 148 Sungchiang Rd, Taipei. Tel: (02) 543-5484; fax: (02) 561-9044.

Saudi Arabian Trade Office, 65, Lane 2, Yangteh Ave, Sec. 2, Taipei. Tel: (02) 833-2942.

SIngapore Trade Office, 9F, 85 Jenai Rd, Sec. 4, Taipei. Tel: (02) 772-1940; fax: (02) 772-1943.

Spanish Chamber of Commerce, 7F-1, 602 Tunhua S. Rd, Taipei. Tel: (02) 325-6234; fax: (02) 754-2572.

Swedish Industries Trade Representative, 96 Chungshan N. Rd, Sec. 2, Taipei. Tel: (02) 562-7601; fax: (02) 531-9504.

Swiss Industries Trade Office, Rm 1614, 333 Keelung Rd, Sec. 1, Taipei. Tel: (02) 720-1001; fax: (02) 757-6984.

Useful Addresses
Tour Operators

Taipei travel agencies operate daily bus-tours for travelers. All buses are air-conditioned, and all tours include bilingual guides. Tickets for these tours may be obtained through any hotel travel desk, or by contacting these agencies directly:

Edison Travel Service, 4F, 190 Sungchiang Rd, Taipei. Tel: (02) 563-5313; fax: (02) 563-4803.

Golden Foundation Tours Corp., 8F, 134 Chunghsiao E. Rd, Sec. 4, Taipei. Tel: (02) 773-3266; fax: (02) 773-4994.

South East Travel Service Co., 60 Chungshan N. Rd, Sec. 2, Taipei. Tel: (02) 567-8111; fax: (02) 564-2256.

Practical Tips
Emergencies
Medical Services

Although medical treatment and dental work cost far less in Taipei than in any Western country or Japan, the quality of medical facilities and services is excellent and up-to-date.

HELP

The following telephone numbers are useful for visitors to Taiwan:
Fire, tel: 119
Police, tel: 110
Traveler info, tel: (02) 717-3737 (from 8am to 8pm)
Foreign Affairs, National Police, tel: (02) 396-9781.
Foreign Affairs, National Police offices:
Taichung, tel: (04) 220-3032.
Kaohsiung, tel: (07) 221-5796.
Tainan, tel: (07) 222-9704.
Keelung, tel: (032) 252-787.

Weights & Measures

In both public markets and small shops throughout Taiwan, vendors still weigh and measure things with traditional Chinese units. If on your own without an interpreter, the following conversion table will help figure out the unit price of items.

Length: The Chinese "foot" is called a *chir*.
1 *chir* = 11.9 inches or 0.99 feet = 0.30 meters
1 *jang* = 10 *chir*
Weight: The Chinese "pound" is called a *catty* or *jin*.
1 *jin* = 1.32 pounds or 0.6 kilograms = 21.2 ounces or 600 grams
The Chinese "ounce" is called a *liang*.
1 *liang* = 1.32 ounces or 37.5 grams
Area: The Chinese measure area in units of *ping* and *jia*.
1 *ping* = 36 square feet (6' x 6')
1 *jia* = 2.40 acres

Electricity in Taiwan is 110v (60 cycles).

Business & Banking Hours

Official **government** business hours in Taiwan are 8.30am–12.30pm and 1.30–5.30pm, Monday through Friday, and 8.30am–12.30pm on Saturday, with Sunday closed.

Hours for **banks** are 9am–3.30pm Monday through Friday, and 9am–noon on Saturday, with Sunday closed.

Commercial **business** hours are 9am–5pm Monday through Friday, and 9am–noon on Saturday, with Sunday a day off.

Department **stores** and large shops stay open from 10 or 11am until 9 or

10pm Monday through Saturday, and usually close on Sunday. Many smaller shops and stalls keep longer hours and remain open all week.

Museums are usually closed on Mondays.

Tipping

Generally speaking, heavy tipping is not expected in Taiwan, although token gratuities are always appreciated. Hotels and restaurants automatically add 10 percent service charge to bills, but this money rarely gets distributed among the staff, so a small cash tip of 5 to 10 percent is always welcome in restaurants.

Taiwan taxi drivers do not get upset if you do not tip them, but it is customary to let them "keep the change" in small coins when paying the fare. Taxis still cost far less in Taipei than most places, but the cost of gas and maintenance here is quite high, so drivers appreciate even the smallest tips.

The only places in Taiwan where heavy tips are routinely expected are in wine-houses and dance-halls, where big tipping wins you "big face" and big favors from the ladies.

Media

Despite Taiwan's exotic ambience and traditional culture, it is a modern, highly developed place with complete international services. You need never lose contact with the outside world while traveling in Taiwan, although many visitors prefer to do just that.

Newspapers and Magazines

Two English-language newspapers are published daily in Taiwan: *China Post* (morning) and *China News* (afternoon). In addition to international and regional news culled from major wire services, as well as local features written by their own staff, these newspapers carry financial news, entertainment sections, sports reports and guides to English programs on TV and radio. Most hotel newsstands carry both.

The Government Information Office publishes an illustrated monthly magazine in English, *Free China Review*, which features articles on Chinese culture, travel in Taiwan, and other aspects of life in the Republic of China. Beyond this, the only English

249

periodicals published locally are devoted exclusively to industrial and financial news.

Foreign periodicals available in Taiwan include *Time*, *Newsweek*, *Life*, and several fashion magazines, all of which are sold at English bookstores and hotel newsstands. All foreign publications brought into Taiwan are subject to official government censorship, so don't be surprised if you discover a page or two missing from your magazine.

Radio

There is only one radio station in Taiwan which broadcasts programs entirely in English. International Community Radio Taipei (ICRT) broadcasts popular Western music and other programs in English 24 hours, with international news reports provided on the hour. Phone (02) 861-2280 for details of the broadcasts, on an island-wide frequency of FM 95.3. Chinese radio stations broadcast a wide variety of music, both Western and Chinese.

Television

There are four television stations which broadcast scheduled programs throughout Taiwan, where there is currently an average of one television set per household. These stations are China Television Co. (CTV), Chinese Television System (CTS), Taiwan Television Entreprise (ITV), and People Broadcasting Corporation (PBC). All stations broadcast exclusively in Chinese, but they frequently schedule English-language films and programs from the West. Check the local English-language newspapers for details regarding English-language films and programs on Chinese television.

Postal Services

Taiwan boasts one of the fastest, most efficient postal services in the world. Mail is collected and delivered every day all year, and all incoming mail is sorted and distributed within 48 hours of arrival. Many first-time residents have been astounded on seeing the local postmen trudging through driving rain and howling winds during a major typhoon to deliver a single letter to a remote hillside house. Letters mailed to the United States from Taiwan usually arrive at their destinations within

five to seven days of posting. Local mail is delivered within 24 to 48 hours.

Taipei's **Central Post Office** is located at the North Gate intersection, close to the Taipei Railway Station. This is the best place to collect and post mail in Taipei. This office also provides inexpensive cartons and packing services for parcel posting. Post offices in town are open from 8am until 6pm on Monday through Friday, 8am until 1pm on Saturdays. They are closed on Sundays.

Stamps may be purchased at the mail counter of any hotel in Taiwan, and letters may be dropped in any hotel or public mail box, of which there are many in Taiwan. Local mail goes in the green boxes, and international airmail goes into the red boxes. Current rates for letters addressed to destinations in Europe/America are NT$15–17 for letters under 10 grams (plus NT$13–14 for each additional 10 grams), NT$11–12 for postcards, and NT$12–14 for aerograms. Postal rates change from time to time, so be sure to inquire before posting your cards and letters.

Taiwan's decorative and commemorative postage stamps are highly prized in the world of philately. Charming Chinese themes, such as landscape painting, porcelain and calligraphy, are often incorporated into the design of stamps.

Telecoms

Telephone, Fax and Telex
Country Code: 886

Long-distance calls within Taiwan can be made from private or public pay phones by using the following local area codes:

Taipei area, inc. Keelung	02
Kaohsiung	07
Changhua County	04
Chiayi	05
Hsinchu	035
Hualien County	038
Ilan County	039
Miaoli County	037
Nantou County	049
Penghu County	06
Pingtung County	08
Taichung	04
Tainan	06
Taitung County	089
Yunlin County	05

Local city calls may be dialed from any public pay telephone, of which there are many in Taiwan. Local calls cost NT$1 for three minutes, after which the line is automatically cut off. For further conversation, drop in another coin for local calls and dial again. But the best is to use a telephonecard, which will cost you NT$100. Most phones are card phones, and you can phone until the card's cash amount is exhausted.

International calls: On private phones, the overseas operator may be reached by **dialing 100**. Direct-dialing is available from some phones, especially in hotels. International direct dialing rates are calculated every six seconds. Overseas phone calls may also be made at ITA **(International Telecommunications Adminstration)** offices. The main office in Taipei is open 24 hours, seven days a week, and is located at 28 Hangchou S. Rd, Sec. 1, Taipei, tel: (02) 244-3780.

Facsimile: Fax-services are available 24-hours for Taiwan or overseas at the ITA main office. Hotels also provide fax services to guests, often charging an additional fee.

Telegrams: Both international and domestic telegrams may be sent from the main ITA or branch offices, or from the mail counter of major international tourist hotels. ITA offers both Urgent (12 hours) and Ordinary (24 hours) telegram services.

Visitors who wish to register local cable addresses in Taiwan should do so at ITA's main office.

Telex: Services are available at the main office of ITA, and at major international tourist hotels.

Tourist Offices

Tourist Information

Service and information centers for visitors are located at both the Chiang Kaishek International Airport, in Taoyuan outside of Taipei, and the Kaohsiung International Airport in Kaohsiung. Receptionists at these information counters speak English, and they can help with transportation, accommodations, and other travel requirements.

There are two organizations in Taiwan which oversee and promote the tourism industry. The **Tourism Bureau**, a branch of the Ministry of Communications, is the official government organ responsible for tourism in Taiwan. The **Taiwan Visitors Association** is a private organization that promotes Taiwan tourism abroad and provides travel assistance to visitors in Taiwan. Since neither of these organizations is blessed with a generous budget, the facilities they offer to travelers are limited. Nevertheless, they do their best to assist the inquiring traveler.

At the Sungshan Airport (domestic) in town, you'll find the **Travel Information Service Center**. This facility is designed primarily to provide information on foreign countries to the ever-growing volume of outbound Chinese travelers from Taiwan. However, in addition to audio-visual and printed information on 55 countries, the center also offers a 25-minute audio-visual presentation on the most outstanding tourist attractions in Taiwan. You could also visit the center to familiarize yourself with the culture and conditions of your next Asian destination. The center is open from 8am until 8pm daily, including Sundays and holidays.

Tourist Information Offices

To obtain information regarding tourism in Taiwan, write to the Tourism Bureau's head office in Taipei, or to one of its overseas representatives.

Hong Kong: Rm 904, 9F, Wingshan Tower, 173 Des Vouex Rd, Central, Hong Kong. Tel: (852) 258-10933; fax: (852) 258-10262.

Japan: Tawian Visitors Association, A-9, 5F, Imperial Tower, Imperial Hotel, Uchisaiwai-cho 1-1-1, Chiyoda-ku, Tokyo 100. Tel: (03) 3501-3591/2; fax: (03) 3501-3586.

Korea: Taiwan Visitors Association, Rm 904, 9th Fl., Kyungki Bldg, 115, Samgak-Dong, Chung-Ku, Seoul. Tel: (02) 732-2357/8; fax: (02) 732-2359.

Singapore: Taiwan Visitors Association, 5 Shenton Way, #14-07, UIC Bldg, Singapore 068808.

USA: Tourism Representative, Travel Section, Taipei Economic & Cultural Office,

166 Geary St. (Suite 1605), San Francisco, CA 94108 USA. Tel: (415) 989-8677, 989-8694; fax: (415) 989-7242.

1 World Trade Center (Suite 7953), New York, NY 10048 USA. Tel:

(212) 466-0691/0692; fax: (212) 432-6436.

333 North Michigan Ave (Suite 2329), Chicago IL 60601 USA. Tel: (312) 346-1038; fax: (312) 346-1037.

Airlines Serving Taiwan

Australian Asia, 3F, 101 Nanking E. Rd, Sec. 2, Taipei. Tel: (02) 522-1001; fax: (886-2) 531-1649.

British Asia, 5F, 98 Nanking E. Rd, Sec. 2, Taipei. Tel: (02) 541-8080; fax: (886-2) 563-7425.

Royal Brunei, 3 F, 101 Nanking E. Rd, Sec. 2, Taipei. Tel: (02) 522-1001; fax: (886-2) 531-1649.

Canadian International, 4F, 90 Chienkuo N. Rd, Sec. 2, Taipei. Tel: (02) 503-4111, (06) 236-8243, (04) 329-4322, (07) 251-1391; fax: (886-2) 502-5403.

Cathay Pacific, 12F, 129 Minsheng E. Rd, Sec. 3, Taipei. Tel: (02) 715-2333, (03) 398-2502, (04) 321-2999, (07) 201-3166; fax: (886-2) 719-7736.

China Airlines, 131 Nanking E. Rd, Sec. 3, Taipei. Tel: (02) 715-1212, (03) 398-2451, (07) 282-6141; fax: (886-2) 398-2451.

Continental, 3F, 167 Fuhsing N. Rd, Taipei. Tel: (02) 715-2766; fax: (886-2) 557-0764.

Delta, 3F, 50 Nanking E. Rd, Sec. 2, Taipei. Tel: (02) 551-3656; fax: (886-2) 531-7364.

EVE Air, 1&2 F, 166 Minsheng E. Rd, Sec. 2, Taipei. Tel: (02) 501-1999, (03) 398-3005; fax: (886-2) 501-3999.

Air France, 13F, 167 Fuhsing N. Rd, Taipei. Tel: (02) 718-1631; fax: (886-2) 719-3578.

Garuda Indonesia, 1F, 66 Sungchiang Rd, Taipei. Tel: (02) 561-2311, (03) 398-2977; fax: (886-2) 523-8920.

KLM, 1 Nanking E. Rd, Sec. 4, Taipei. Tel: (02) 717-1000, (03) 383-3034, (07) 226-4210; fax: (886-2) 383-4229.

Lufthansa, 3F, 90 Chienkuo N. Rd, Sec. 2, Taipei. Tel: (02) 503-4114; fax: (886-2) 509-5827.

Malaysia, 1&2 F, 102 Tunhua N. Rd, Taipei. Tel: (02) 716-8348; fax: (886-2) 712-9312.

Mandarin, 13F, 134 Minsheng E. Rd, Taipei. Tel: (02) 717-1230, (03) 398-2620, (07) 231-5186; fax: (886-2) 717-0716.

Air New Zealand, 5F, 98 Nanking E. Rd, Sec. 2, Taipei. Tel: (02) 531-3980;

fax: (886-2) 560-4637.

Northwest, 7F, 168 Tunhua N. Rd, Taipei. Tel: (02) 716-1555, (03) 398-2471, (07) 272-5505; fax: (886-2) 719-0237.

Philippine, 2F, 90 Chienkuo N. Rd, Sec. 2, Taipei. Tel: (02) 505-1255, (03) 398-2419, (07) 251-1381; fax: (886-2) 509-6183.

Qantas, 3F, 101 Nanking E. Rd, Sec. 2, Taipei. Tel: (02) 522-1001; fax: (886-2) 531-1649.

Russian, Suite 3, 5F, 181 Fuhsing N. Rd, Taipei. Tel: (02) 718-9311; fax: (886-2) 719-9204.

Sempati, 174 Chunghsiao E. Rd, Sec. 3, Taipei. Tel: (02) 396-6910; fax: (886-2) 391-3934.

Singapore, 148 Sungchiang Rd, Taipei. Tel: (02) 551-6655; fax: (886-2) 523-5955.

South African, Rm 1203, 12F, 205 Tunhua N. Rd, Taipei. Tel: (02) 713-6363, (03) 383-4716; fax: (886-2) 713-9478.

Thai, 2F, 152 Fuhsing N. Rd, Tapei. Tel: (02) 717-5200, (03) 383-4131, (07) 215-5871; fax: (886-2) 713-1910.

United, 12F, 2 Jenai Rd, Sec. 4, Taipei. Tel: (02) 703-7600; fax: (886-2) 709-7564.

Viet Air, 47 Jenai Rd, Sec. 2, Taipei. Tel: (02) 393-0677; fax: (886-2) 395-0543.

Embassies and Consulates

Taiwan Foreign Missions

South Africa 1147 Schoeman St, Hatfield, Pretoria 0083, Republic of South Africa. Tel: (002-27-12) 43-6071.

Taiwan Overseas Representative Offices

Australia: Taipei Economic and Cultural Office,

B407-408 World Trade Center, Cnr. Spencer & Flinders Streets, Melbourne, Vic. 3005, Australia. Tel: (002-61-3) 621-2981.

Suite 1902, Level 19, M.L.C. Center, King St, Sydney, N.S.W. 2000, Australia. Tel: (002-61-2) 223-3207.

Unit 8, Tourism House, 40 Blackall St, Barton, ACT 2600, Australia. Tel: (002-61-6) 273-3344.

Austria: Taipei Economic and Cultural Offica, Institute of Chinese Culture, Vienna, Austria, Praterstr. 31/150G, A-

1020 Wien, Austria. Tel: (002-43-1) 212-4720-4.

Belgium: Taipei Economic and Cultural Office, Avenue Des Arts 41, 1040 Bruxelles, Belgium. Tel: (002-32-2) 551-0687.

Brunei: Far East Trade and Cultural Center, No. 5, Simpang 1006, Jalan Tutong, B.S. Begawan, Brunei Darussalam. Tel: (002-673-2) 653-410.

Canada: Taipei Economic and Cultural Office,
Suite 1202, 151 Yonge Street, Toronto, Ontario, M5C2W7, Canada. Tel: (002-1-416) 369-9030.
#2008 Cathedral Place, 925 W. Georgia Street, Vancouver B.C. V6C 3L2, Canada. Tel: (002-1-604) 689-4111.
45 O'Connor Street, Suite 1960, Ottawa, Ontario, K1P 1A4 Canada. Tel: (002-1-613) 231-5080.

Denmark: Taiwan Economic and Cultural Office, Falkoner Alle 53, 5 Sal, 2000 Copenhagen F Denmark. Tel: (002-45-31) 197-511.

Finland: Taiwan Economic and Cultural Office, Bulevardi 1A 22, Helsinki 00100, Finland. Tel: (002-358-0) 680-1216.

France: Association pour la Promotion des Echanges Commerciaux et Touristiques avec Taiwan, A.S.P.E.C.T., 78 Rue de l'Universite, 75007 Paris, France. Tel: (002-33-1) 443-98820.

Germany: Taipei Wirtschafts-und Kulturburo,
Berliner Str. 55, D-10713, Berlin, Federal Republic of Germany. Tel: (002-49-30) 861-2754, 861-2576.
Villichgasse 17, IV. OG, 53177 Bonn, Federal Republic of Germany. Tel: (002-49-228) 364-014/8.
Mittelweg 144, 20148 Hamburg, Federal Republic of Germany. Tel: (002-49-40) 447-788.
Tengstrasse 38/2 stock, 80796 Munchen, Federal Republic of Germany. Tel: (002-0-89) 271-6061.

Great Britian: Taipei Representative Office in the UK, 50 Grosvenor Gardens, London, SWIW OEB, England, UK. Tel: (002-44-71) 396-9152.

Hong Kong: Chung Hwa Travel Service, 4th Fl., Lippo Tower, Lippo Center No. 89, Queensway, Hong Kong. Tel: (002-852) 525-8315.

Ireland: Taipei Economic and Cultural Office, 1st Fl., 10-11 South Leinster St, Dublin 2, Ireland. Tel: (002-353-1) 678-5413.

Israel: Taipei Economic and Trade Office in Tel-Aviv, 270 Hayarkon St, Tel-Aviv 63504 Israel. Tel: (002-972-3) 544-0250.

Italy: Instituto Cultutrale Ed Economic Di Taipei, Via Sardegna 50, II P. Int. 12, 00187 Roma, Italia. Tel: (002-396) 474-1613.

Malaysia: Taipei Economic and Cultural Office in Malaysia, 9.01 Level 9, Amoda Bldg, 22 Jalan Imbi 55100, Kuala Lumpur, Malaysia. Tel: (002-60-3) 242-5549, 241-0015.

Netherlands: Taipei Economic and Cultural Office, Javastraat 46-48, 2585 AR, The Hague, The Netherlands. Tel: (002-31-70) 346-9438.

New Zealand: Taipei Economic and Cultural Office,
11F, Norwich Union Bldg, Corner Queen & Durham Streets, Auckland, New Zealand. Tel: (002-64-9) 303-3903.
P.O. Box 10250, The Terrace, Wellington, New Zealand. Tel: (002-64-4) 473-6474.

Norway: Taipei Economic and Cultural Office, Riddervolds gate 3, 0203 Oslo 2. Tel: (002-47) 225-55471.

Philippines: Taipei Economic and Cultural Office in the Philippines, 28th Fl., Pacific Star Bldg, Sen. Gil J. Puyat Ave, Cnr. Makati Ave, Makati, Metro Manila Philippines. Tel: (002-63-2) 892-1381.

Russia: Representative Office in Moscow for the Taipei-Moscow Economic and Cultural Coordination Commission, 5th Fl. 24/2 Korpus 1, Tverskaya St, Gate 4, Moscow, Russian Federation. Tel: (002-750-3) 9563786.

Singapore: Taipei Representative Office in Singapore, 460 Alexandra Rd, #23-00 PSA Bldg, Singapore 119963. Tel: (002-65) 278-6511.

Spain: Oficina Economica y Cultural de Taipei, Madrid Espana, c/o Rosario Pino 14-16, 18 Dcha., 28036 Madrid, Espana (Spain). Tel: (002-34-1) 571-4729.

Sweden: Taipei Mission in Sweden, Wenner-Gren Center, 4tr., Sveavagen 166, S-113 46 Stockholm, Sweden. Tel: (002-46-8) 728-8513.

Switzerland: Delegation Culturelle et Economique de Taipei, Monbijou-strasse 30 3011 Berne Switzerland. Tel: (002-41-31) 382-1523.

Thailand: The Far East Trade Office, 10th Fl., Kian Gwan Bldg (1), 140 Witthayu Rd, Bangkok, Thailand. Tel: (002-66-2) 251-9393.

United States: Taipei Economic and Cultural Representative Office in the United States (TECRO),
4201 Wisconsin Ave, N.W., Washington D.C. 20016-2137. Tel: (002-1-202) 895-1800; fax: (002-1-202) 363-0999.
99 Summer St, Suite 801, Boston, MA 02110. Tel: (002-1-617) 737-2050; fax: (002-1-617) 737-1684.
2746 Pali Highwaay, Honolulu, Hawaii 96817. Tel: (002-1-808) 595-6347; fax: (002-1-808) 595-6542.
3731 Wilshire Blvd., Suite 700, Los Angeles, CA 90010. Tel: 002-1-1213) 389-1215; fax: (002-1-213) 383-3245.
9th Fl., 801 Second Ave, New York, N.Y. 10017. Tel: (002-1-212) 697-1250; fax: (002-1-212) 490-3802.
555 Montgomery St, Suite 501, San Francisco, CA 94111. Tel: (002-1-415) 362-7680, 362-7683; fax: (002-1-415) 362-5382.

Vietnam: Taipei Economic and Cultural Office,
2D VAN Phuc Hanoi, Vietnam. Tel: (002-844) 234-403.
No. 68 Tran Quoc Thao St, District 3, Ho Chi Minh City, Vietnam. Tel: (002-848) 299-343.

Getting Around

From the Airport

Taipei: The CKS International Airport is about 45 km (28 mi) southwest of Taipei. An airporter bus connects the CKS international Airport with the Taipei Sungshan Airport (domestic), located north from downtown. The journey time is 45 to 60 minutes, the costs per person NT$111. The buses are running frequently every 10 to 20 minutes between 6.20am and 10.30pm. From the Sungshan Airport bus terminal you are only 10 to 20 minutes (depending on traffic) by cab from most major downtown hotels.

A taxi from the CKS International Airport to downtown Taipei will cost at least NT$1200. For the trip from Taipei to the CKS International Airport the drivers are allowed by law to add a 50% surcharge over the fare shown on the meter.

Kaohsiung: The easiest and best transport is a taxi to the downtown hotels. The airport, located to the south of Kaohsiung, is very close to the city center.

Domestic Travel

By air

Regular scheduled domestic air service in Taiwan is provided by the international flag-carrier China Airlines (CAL), by Far Eastern Air Transport (FAT) and many more domestic airlines. In total, 8 domestic airlines are serving Taiwan and its islands.

Strict security measures are enforced on all domestic flights within Taiwan, and all foreign passengers need to show their passports prior to domestic boarding.

For bookings and other information before arriving in Taiwan, call a travel agent directly. For flight reservations and ticketing in Taiwan, it is the best way to go directly to an airline office; second-best is a travel-agent.

Buses

A special fleet of deluxe express buses serves Taiwan's major towns and cities. Between Taipei and Kaohsiung are frequent scheduled buses. By departure time, almost all buses are fully booked. Come early and wait in a long line for a ticket, or bad news.

The best way to purchase reserved-seat bus tickets in advance is to go directly to the appropriate bus company and buy them one or two days prior to departure. Most hotel travel desks and local travel agencies can make arrangements.

Railway

The Taiwan Railway Administration maintains an extensive railroad network which runs around the island and connects all major cities and towns. Usually the trains are full, and if you do not like to stand the whole trip, a seat reservation is necessary. But without a travel agent, to get one is quite complicated and time-consuming.

The Railway Administration offers three types of services:

Fu Hsing (FH) – air-conditioned, limited express; **Chu Kuang (CK)** – first-class, air-conditioned, express; and **Tsu Chiang (TC)** – electrical multiple units and air-conditioned.

Reservations for first-class express trains in Taiwan must be made at least one, but no more than two, days prior to departure. However, although you may purchase round-trip tickets in advance, reservations for the return trips must be made upon arrival at your destination, also one to two days in advance. Even for local trains, it is highly advisable to purchase tickets at least several hours in advance, and preferably a full day prior to departure. In all cities and towns, advance train tickets may be purchased directly at the main railway station by lining up before the appropriate window. Most hotels and travel agencies will arrange advance train reservations.

Do not expect to see too much on a train ride. Most locals close the windows with the curtain to get some sleep. And they probably will complain heavily if "your" window remains open and sun is shining on "their" head.

Taxis

Sometimes it seems as if there are as many taxis in some towns in Taiwan as people. Stand on the curb and wave your arm in the street: within moments a taxi will glide to a halt by your feet, and the door will automatically swing open as the driver pulls a lever inside.

All taxi fares are calculated according to the meter. Drivers are allowed to charge for waiting time in traffic. If you wish to retain a taxi for a full day, or for a long, round-trip excursion to a specific destination, ask a hotel clerk to negotiate either a set fee for the whole day or discount on the meter fare.

Taiwan taxi meters calculate both time and distance to determine the fare. The meters have three windows. The top left window shows the time taken in minutes and seconds. Top right indicator is the distance in kilometers. The large right window meter shows the fare in NT dollars. From 11pm to 6am, there is an additional 20 percent charge.

Small towns and villages have fixed rates for the use of a taxi within a certain area. It is best to ask locals for the correct rate; even Taiwanese travelers have to do it this way, if they don't want to be overcharged.

Note: Although Taiwan's taxi drivers are almost uniformly friendly and polite, they tend to drive like maniacs. And some are rude also. Many tourists have their wits scared out as their taxi drivers weave carelessly between speeding buses and trucks, narrowly missing pedestrians, run through red lights, careen through swarms of buzzing motorcycles, and screech blindly around corners.

Unfortunately, this sort of driving is the rule rather than the exception in Taiwan. Should you get a particularly reckless driver; tell him to pull over immediately, pay him the fare on the meter (with no tip), and hail another cab. There is never a shortage of cabs in Taipei, day or night, rain or shine.

Very few taxi drivers in Taiwan speak or read English sufficiently well to follow directions given in English. Have your destination written out in Chinese before venturing out by cab. Hotel name cards, local advertisements, even restaurant match-boxes will also suffice to get you around town by taxi.

Car Rentals

It's best to rely on public transportation such as buses, taxis and tour-coaches to get around Taiwanese cities and towns. Trying to drive yourself around the city is a needless risk and could spoil your day. But if you plan an extended tour down-island or along the northern coastline, then renting a car is a fine way to go, for you'll see many more sights and enjoy the freedom to stop whenever and wherever you wish. The North-South Expressway runs like a spinal column down the center of the island from tip to tip, giving access by car to cities and scenic sites along the way. Local roads lead out to the mountains, mineral spas, temples, and other destinations along Taiwan's tourist trail.

Before renting a self-drive car, it is usually the best to ask the hotel for some rental-car company suggestions. You also can phone an Avis, Budget or Hertz reservation center before your trip to Taiwan.

If you like to splurge a bit and see the island in true comfort and convenience, the best way is by air-conditioned (or heated) limousines, driven by chauffeurs who also act as personal guides and interpreters. Any hotel travel desk or local travel agency can arrange a chauffeured limousine. The cost varies accordingly to the type of car.

Motoring Advisories

No matter how well you drive, Taiwan traffic bears the utmost attention. The Chinese have a strong faith in fate, and a big appetite for face. The former factor makes them take incredible chances on the road, while the latter drives them to take up even the slightest challenge from other drivers. The roads themselves are well maintained, however, and give convenient access to all of Taiwan's scenic treasures. With a little bit of luck, you should have no problems on the road if you bear in mind the following points:

• There are millions of motor scooters on the roads, and they constitute the single greatest hazard to automobile drivers. The most spine-chilling sight on the road is a husband and wife on a 90cc motor scooters with five or six infants hanging from the handlebars, gas-tank, fenders and mother's shoulder, speeding through rainy streets among trucks and buses. Steer clear of these.

• Also steer clear of all military vehicles. Military drivers are notorious for their careless driving on public roads. Regardless of the circumstances, military vehicles always have the right of way, and they know it.

• Though roads down south are well marked, the instructions are often in Chinese. So look for route numbers instead of place names, and match them with those on your maps. Route numbers are also inscribed on the stone mileage indicators set along the roadsides.

• Stop and ask directions when in doubt. The further south you drive, the friendlier the people become, and someone is always there to help. Don't attempt to pronounce place names in the countryside, because often people there don't understand Mandarin, at least not when it is spoken by foreigners. Show them the Chinese characters, and their eyes will light up with instant recognition, for these are universal symbols to Chinese the world over.

• Keep your gas-tank at least a third full at all times. In the more remote mountainous and coastal regions, gas stations are few and far between, and often closed at night.

Rapid Transit System

Construction of Taipei's Mass Rapid System began in 1988, when the French contractor started work. First finished was the Mucha–Sungshan Airport Line. It is one of six lines scheduled for Taipei, totaling 88 km (55 mi). The MRT system is scheduled for completion in 1999, but it has encountered many problems. Nevertheless, it is fun to take the Mucha Line and see downtown Taipei from above the traffic. Tickets on the Mucha-Line cost you NT$20 to 35, depending upon distance.

Travel in Taipei

Buses

One of the first things you'll notice in Taipei is the incredible number of public buses on the streets. For budget-minded travelers, buses provide frequent and inexpensive means of transportation to any point within or outside the city limits.

However, unless endowed with an extra measure of Asian patience, it is advisable to avoid the buses during heavy rush hours, which fall between 7.30–9.30am and 5–7pm.

There are two types of city buses: regular and air-conditioned. The regular bus costs about NT$10 per ride and the air-conditioned bus slightly more. Tickets and tokens should be purchased in advance at the little kiosk which you will find at or close to all bus-stops.

City bus service runs continously from about 6am until 11.30pm. To signal the driver to stop at an upcoming station, pull the bell cord. There are so many buses and bus routes within metropolitan Taipei that it is best to ask a hotel clerk or local aquaintance for directions before venturing out. Some bus stops in Taipei have a computer-information machine, indicating in English which buses to take to reach your final destination.

All buses are designated by code numbers, which indicate their routes and final destinations. Once you know the numbers, it is quite easy to get around on buses.

Where to Stay

Hotels

Chinese hotels are renowned for attentive, gracious service rendered with a spirit of pride and genuine desire to please. Visitors are treated as personal guests rather than anonymous patrons, and hospitality is approached more as an art than as an industry. However, Western travelers occasionally encounter frustrations. One reason is the ever-present language barrier: though uniformly trained in English, most Chinese hotel staff understand very little. Yet they'll avoid losing face by pretending to understand, then promptly forget about it. Another reason is cultural: Chinese priorities often differ from a Westerner's, and what seems of vital importance to you, such as punctuality, may seem trivial to the Chinese.

Tourist hotels in Taiwan are ranked in two categories: International Tourist and Regular Tourist. The former offers greater luxury and more varied facilities, while the latter offers lower rates and simpler services.

The hotels in Taipei are extremely expensive. Singles or twins will cost, in international tourist hotels, between NT$4,000–9,000. In Kaohsiung, the cost per room is between NT$2,500–5,000. At other places, expect to pay between NT$1,000–4,000 per night.

Taipei

LUXURY

The Ambassador, 63 Chungshan N. Rd, Sec. 2. Tel: (02) 551-1111; fax: (02) 561-7883. 428 rooms; indoor swimming pool, golfing, banquet and convention facilities, roof-top bar lounge with superb views, convenient access to shops, cocktail lounge.
Asiaworld Plaza Hotel, 100 Tunhwa N. Rd. Tel: (02) 715-0077; fax: (02) 713-4148. 1057 rooms; huge hotel with 27 bars and restaurants, cinemas, theater restaurant, fitness center, underground parking, convention facili-

ties, department stores, shopping mall with 500 boutiques.

Brother Hotel, 255 Nanking E. Rd, Sec. 3. Tel: (02) 712-3456; fax: (02) 717-3344. 268 rooms; excellent Cantonese *dim-sum* restaurant, roof-top lounge, well-maintained rooms.

Far Eastern Plaza Hotel Taipei, 201 Tunhua S. Rd, Sec. 2. Tel: (02) 378-8888; fax: (02) 377-7777. 422 rooms; two health clubs and swimming pools, shopping mall with 130 shops adjacent to the hotel

Grand Formosa Regent Taipei, 41 Chungshan N. Rd, Sec. 2. Tel: (02) 523-8000, fax: (02) 523-2828. 552 rooms; 10 different restaurants, health spa and fitness center, roof-top swimming pool.

Hilton International Taipei, 38 Chunghsiao W. Rd, Sec. 1. Tel: (02) 311-5151; fax: (02) 331-9944. 393 rooms; polished, professional service in all departments, award-winning food & beverage facilities; lively disco; sauna, roof garden, jacuzzi pools.

Grand Hyatt Taipei, 2 Sunghsou Road. Tel: (02) 720-1234; fax: (02) 720-111. 872 rooms; next to the convention center, good parking, fitness center with outdoor pool.

Howard Plaza Hotel, 160 Jenai Rd, Sec. 3. Tel: (02) 700-2323; fax: (02) 700-0729. 606 rooms; elegant decor, continental ambience, outdoor swimming pool, health center, sauna, shopping mall.

Lai-Lai Sheraton, 12 Chunghsiao E. Rd, Sec. 1. Tel: (02) 321-5511; fax: (02) 394-4240. 705 rooms; large hotel with many facilities including disco-club, health-club, and several restaurants.

President Hotel, 9 Tenhwei St. Tel: (02) 595-1251; fax: (02) 591-3677. 421 rooms; popular among businessmen; access to nightlife area and highway.

The Ritz Taipei, 155 Minchuan E. Rd. Tel: (02) 597-1234; fax: (02) 596-9222. 200 rooms; small hotel with personalized service, good European food and beverage facilities.

Hotel Royal Taipei, 37-1 Chungshan N. Rd, Sec. 2. Tel: (02) 542-3266; fax: (02) 543-4897. 202 rooms; sauna, health club, swimming pool, shopping arcade, in the heart of the old business center.

The Sherwood Taipei, 111 Minsheng E. Rd, Sec. 3. Tel: (02) 718-1188; fax:

(02) 713-0707. 350 rooms; best hotel in Taiwan, health center with indoor pool and jacuzzi, fitness center and sauna, late check-out until 3pm, four restaurants and a bar, next to the modern business and banking center.

Fortuna Hotel, 122 Chungshan N. Rd, Sec. 2. Tel: (02) 563-1111; fax: (02) 561-9777. 304 rooms.

Fortune Dragon Hotel, 172 Chunghsiao E. Rd, Sec. 4. Tel: (02) 772-2121; fax: (02) 721-0302. 312 rooms.

Gloria, 369 Linshen N. Rd. Tel: (02) 581-8111; fax: (02) 581-5811. 220 rooms.

Golden China Hotel, 306 Sungchiang Rd. Tel: (02) 521-5151; fax: (02) 531-2914. 216 rooms.

The Grand Hotel, 1 Chungshan N. Rd, Sec. 4. Tel: (02) 596-5565; fax: (02) 594-8243. 530 rooms.

Imperial Hotel, 600 Linshen N. Rd. Tel: (02) 596-5111; fax: (02) 592-7506. 327 rooms.

Taipei Miramar, 420 Minchuan E. Rd. Tel: (02) 505-3456; fax: (02) 502-9173. 584 rooms.

Mandarin Hotel, 166 Tunhwa N. Rd. Tel: (02) 581-1201; fax: (02) 712-2122. 351 rooms.

Hotel Rebar Holiday Inn Crown Plaza, 32 Nanking E. Rd, Sec. 5. Tel: (02) 763-5656; fax: (02) 767-9347. 300 rooms.

Riverview, 32 Nanking E. Rd, Sec. 5. Tel: (02) 311-3131; fax: (02) 361-3737. 201 rooms.

Santos Hotel, 439 Chengteh Rd. Tel: (02) 596-3111; fax: (02) 596-3120. 287 rooms.

United Hotel, 200 Kuangfu S. Rd. Tel: (02) 773-1515; fax: (02) 741-2789. 248 rooms.

Astar Hotel, 98 Linshen N. Rd. Tel: (02) 551-3131; fax: (02) 537-1814. 40 rooms.

China Hotel, 14 Kuanchien Rd. Tel: (02) 331-9521; fax: (02) 281-2349. 122 rooms.

Cosmos Hotel, 43 Chunghsiao W. Rd, Sec. 1. Tel: (02) 361-7856; fax: (02) 311-8921. 245 rooms.

Empress Hotel, 12 Tehhwei St. Tel: (02) 591-3261; fax: (02) 592-2922. 68 rooms.

First Hotel, 63 Nanking E. St, Sec. 2.

Tel: (02) 541-8234; fax: (02) 551-2277. 163 rooms.

Flowers Hotel, 19 Hankow St, Sec. 1. Tel: (02) 312-3811; fax: (02) 312-3800. 200 rooms.

Gala Hotel, 186 Sungchiang Rd. Tel: (02) 541-5511; fax: (02) 531-3831. 150 rooms.

Kilin Hotel (Best Western), 103 Kangting Rd. Tel: (02) 314-9222; fax: (02) 331-8133. 300 rooms.

Leofoo Hotel, 168 Changchun Rd. Tel: (02) 507-3211; fax: (02) 508-2070. 238 rooms.

New Asia Hotel, 139 Chungshan N. Rd, Sec. 2. Tel: (02) 511-7181; fax: (02) 522-4204. 102 rooms.

Paradise Hotel, 24 Hsining S. Rd. Tel: (02) 314-2122; fax: 314-7873. 144 rooms.

Kaohsiung

Ambassador Hotel, 202 Minsheng 2nd Rd. Tel: (07) 211-5211; fax: (07) 281-1115, (07) 281-1113. 457 rooms.

Grand Hi-Lai Hotel, 266 Chengkung 1st Rd. Tel: (07) 216-1766; fax: (07) 216-1966. 450 rooms.

Grand Hotel, 2 Yuanshan Rd, Cheng-Ching Lake. Tel: (07) 383-5911; fax: (07) 381-4889. 108 rooms.

Kingdom Hotel, 32 Wufu 2nd Rd. Tel: (07) 551-8211; fax: (07) 521-0403. 312 rooms.

Linden Hotel Kaohsiung, 33 Szuwei 3rd Rd. Tel: (07) 332-2000; fax: (02) 336-1600. 400 rooms.

Major Hotel, 7 Tajen Rd. Tel: (07) 521-2266; fax: (02) 531-2211. 200 rooms.

Summit Hotel, 426 Chiuru 1st Rd. Tel: (07) 384-5526; fax: (07) 384-4739. 210 rooms.

Buckingham Hotel, 394 Chihsien 2nd Rd. Tel: (07) 282-2151; fax: (07) 281-4540. 144 rooms.

Duke Hotel, 233 Linsen 1st Rd. Tel: (07) 231-2111; fax: (07) 211-8224. 100 rooms.

Alishan

Alishan House, 2 West Alishan, Shanglin Village, Wufeng Hsiang, Chiayi. Tel: (05) 267-9811; fax: (05) 267-9596. 60 rooms.

Changhua

REGULAR TOURIST

Changhua Hotel, 48 Chungcheng Rd, Sec. 2. Tel: (04) 722-4681; fax: (04) 724-6474. 50 rooms.

Chiayi

INTERNATIONAL TOURIST

Gallant, 257 Wenhwa Rd. Tel: (05) 223-5366; fax: (05) 223-9522. 106 rooms.

Chihpen

INTERNATIONAL TOURIST

Hotel Royal Chihpen Spa, Long Chuien Rd, Ween Chuien Village, Peinan Hsiang, Taitung Hsien. Tel: (089) 51-0666; fax: (089) 51-0678. 182 rooms.

Hsinchu

BUDGET

Chinatrust Hsinchu Hotel, 106 Chung-yang Rd. Tel: (035) 26-3181; fax: (035) 26-9244. 182 rooms.

Hsitou

INTERNATIONAL TOURIST

Le Midi Hotel, 1 Midi St, Neihu Village, Luku Township. Tel: (049) 612-088; fax: (049) 612-031. 245 rooms.

Hualien

INTERNATIONAL TOURIST

Astar Hotel, 6-1 Meichuan Rd. Tel: (038) 326-111; fax: (038) 324-604. 167 rooms.
Chinatrust Hualien Hotel, 2 Yungsing Rd. Tel: (038) 221-171; fax: (038) 221-185. 237 rooms.
Marshal Hotel, 36 Kungyuan Rd. Tel: (038) 326-123; fax: (038) 326-140. 303 rooms.
Parkview Hotel, 1-1 Lingyuan Rd. Tel: (038) 222-111; fax: (038) 226-999. 360 rooms.

Ilan

REGULAR TOURIST

Hill Garden Hotel, 6 Tehyang Rd, Chiao Hsi, Ilan. Tel: (039) 88-2011; fax: (039) 88-2454. 67 rooms.
Lion Hotel, 156 Chungshan Rd, Lotung, Ilan. Tel: (039) 55-1111; fax: (039) 57-6954. 54 rooms.

Keelung

REGULAR TOURIST

Hua Shuai Hotel, 108 Hsiao 2nd Rd. Tel: (02) 422-3131; fax: (02) 422-3140. 69 rooms.

Kenting

INTERNATIONAL TOURIST

Caesar Park Hotel, 6 Kenting Rd, Hengchun Town, Pingtung Hsien. Tel: (08) 886-1888; Fax: (08) 886-1818. 237 rooms.

REGULAR TOURIST

Kenting Hotel, 101 Park Rd, Kenting, Hengchun Town, Pingtung Hsien. Tel: (08) 886-1370; fax: (08) 886-1377. 250 rooms.

Kukuan

REGULAR TOURIST

Dragon Valley Hotel, 138 Sec. 1 Tong-kuan Rd, Hoping 424, Kukuan. Tel: (04) 595-1325; fax: (04) 595-1226. 250 rooms.

Lishan

BUDGET

Lishan Guest House, 91 Chungcheng Rd, Lishan. Tel: (04) 598-9501; fax: (04) 598-9505. 107 rooms.

Orchid Island

BUDGET

Lan Yu Hotel, 9 Jenai St, Hongtou Village, Lan Yu, Taitung Hsien. Tel: (089) 732-111; fax: (089) 732-189. 45 rooms.

Penghu–Pescadores

REGULAR TOURIST

Poa-Hwa Hotel, 2 Chungcheng Rd, Makung. Tel: (06) 927-4881; fax: (06) 927-4889. 78 rooms.

Pingtung

BUDGET

Ping Tung First Hotel, 3/F, 15 Chung-hua Rd, Pingtung. Tel: (08) 733-9933; fax: (08) 733-9936. 59 rooms.

Sun Moon Lake

INTERNATIONAL TOURIST

Chinatrust Sun Moon Lake Hotel, 23 Chungcheng Rd, Sun Moon Lake, Nantou. Tel: (049) 855-911; fax: (049) 855-268. 116 rooms.

REGULAR TOURIST

El Dorado Hotel, 5 Mingsheng St, Sun Moon Lake, Nantou. Tel: (049) 85-5855; fax: (049) 85-6656. 54 rooms.

Taichung

INTERNATIONAL TOURIST

Evergreen Laurel Hotel, 6 Taichung Kang Rd, Sec. 2. Tel: (04) 328-9988; fax: (04) 328-8642. 354 rooms.
National Hotel, 257 Taichung Kang Rd, Sec. 1. Tel: (04) 321-3111; fax: (04) 321-3124. 404 rooms.
Park Hotel Taichung, 17 Kungyuan Rd. Tel: (04) 220-5181; fax: (04) 222-5757. 125 rooms.
Plaza International Hotel, 431 Taya Rd. Tel: (04) 295-6789; fax: (04) 293-0099. 305 rooms.

Tainan

INTERNATIONAL TOURIST

Tainan Hotel, 1 Chengkung Rd. Tel: (06) 228-9101; fax: (06) 226-8502. 152 rooms.

BUDGET

Redhill Hotel, 46 Chengkung Rd. Tel: (06) 225-8121; fax: (06) 221-6711. 120 rooms.

Taitung

BUDGET

Lion Hotel, 572 Chunghua Rd, Sec. 1. Taitung. Tel: (089) 328-878; fax: (089) 322-378. 43 rooms.

Taoyuan

INTERNATIONAL TOURIST

CKS Airport Hotel, P.O. Box No. 66, CKS Airport. Tel: (03) 383-3666; fax: (03) 383-3546. 510 rooms.

Wuling

BUDGET

Wuling Farm Guest House, 3-1 Wuling Rd, Hoping Hsien. Tel: (04) 590-1183;

fax: (04) 590-1085. 65 rooms.

Taitung

REGULAR TOURIST

Jyh Been Hotel, 5 Lungchuan Wen-Chuan Village, Pinan. Tel: (089) 512220; Taipei: (02) 331-5982; fax: (089) 513067. 20 rooms.

Youth Hostels

If you're willing to sleep in dormitories, eat in cafeterias, and travel exclusively by bus, then you can actually tour Taiwan for as little as US$100 per day by utilizing facilities operated by the **China Youth Corps** (CYC). CYC operates a series af Youth Activity Centers and Youth Hostels around the island, and the budget-minded travelers may avail themselves of these facilities. Information and reservations for the hostels and activity centers may be arranged by writing or calling CYC headquarters at 219 Sungkiang Rd, Taipei, tel: (02) 502-5858; fax: (02) 501-1312. For an updated address list, contact the **ROC Tourism Bureau** offices overseas or the **Domestic Tourism Bureau** in Taiwan.

Due to the popularity of these facilities, groups and individuals from overseas who wish to use them should make reservations well in advance. They usually remain fully-booked from July through September, and from January through February. If you have not made prior arrangements, then at least be sure to call ahead to your next intended stop to make sure that hostel accommodations are available.

Rates for room and board vary at different centers, but on the average three meals a day can be had for about NT$250, the price range is between NT$300 to 6,000, with an average of about NT$1,000 to 1,500 per night. Most of these establishments also offer private rooms at higher rates, and some even have spacious bungalows for small groups.

Guest Houses

There are a number of guest houses in the Taipei area which function as small hotels or inns and provide inexpensive accommodations. Weekly and monthly rates may be arranged as well. Ask the **Domestic Tourism Bureau** service centers for addresses and details.

Eating Out

What to Eat

Dining out remains the single greatest pleasure Taiwan holds in store for the traveler. Whether you opt for Chinese or Western cuisine, Japanese sushi or Korean barbecue, the restaurants of Taiwan have something tasty for every palate. The happy marriage of China's highly sophisticated culinary products has given birth to a restaurant industry which never fails to delight even the most experienced epicure. Naturally, when in Taiwan, it's best to do as the Chinese and go for gourmet Chinese cuisine. But if you prefer Western food, the restaurants listed below will serve you a good meal with proper service. Though almost any Chinese eatery in Taiwan serves good food, many of the so-called Western restaurants serve fare that looks and tastes like a careless melange of East and West.

All the restaurants listed are located in Taipei, where travelers generally spend most of their time and do most of their gourmet dining. Once you've mastered dining out in Taipei, you'll be able to make it on your own down-island, where the choice of restaurants and cuisines is less confusing.

When traveling down south, it's generally best to stick with Chinese food, as demand for Western cuisine in the south is not yet sufficiently strong to support genuine gourmet Western restaurants.

Types of Cuisine

Northern Style (Beijing, Mongolia). Recommended dishes: Beijing Duck, Lamb and Leek, Hot and Sour Soup, Celery in Mustard Sauce, Cold Shredded Chicken with Sauce, Sweet and Sour Yellow Fish, Steamed Vegetable Dumplings.

Southern Style (Cantonese). Recommended dishes: Roast Duck, Poached Chicken with Onions and Oil, Greens with Oyster Sauce, Steamed Whole Fish, Assorted *dim-sum*, Roast Pigeon, Cabbage with Cream.

Eastern/Coastal Style (Shanghai). Recommended dishes: West Lake Vinegar Fish, River Eel Sauteed with Leek, Braised Pork Haunch, Sauteed Sweet-Pea Shoots, Drunken Chicken, "Lionhead" meatballs, Braised Beef Loin.

Western/Central Style (Hunan, Szechuan). Recommended dishes: (Szechuan) Steamed Pomfret, Chicken "Duke of Bao", "Grandma's" Beancurd, Fragrant Egg-Sauce, Duck Smoked in Camphor and Tea, Twice-cooked Pork. (Hunan) Frog Legs in Chilli Sauce, Honey Ham, Beggar's Chicken, Minced Pigeon in Bamboo Cup, Steamed Whole Fish.

Taiwanese Food. Recommended dishes: Steamed Crab, Poached Squid, Fresh Poached Shrimp, Shrimp Rolls, Grilled Eel, Sashimi or raw fish, Grilled Clams, Turtle Soup.

Chinese Vegetarian Cuisine. Recommended Dishes: Try the various types of "beef", "pork" and "chicken" made entirely from various forms of soybean curd and/or different types of mushrooms, as well as fresh and crispy vegetables.

Chopsticks

There's nothing more Chinese than chopsticks. The Chinese have been using two sticks to pick up a single grain of rice and one stick to carry two buckets of water ever since time began. Nothing ever appears on the Chinese banquet table that cannot be manipulated single-handedly with a simple pair of chopsticks. Today, as the popularity of Chinese cuisine spreads throughout the world, it is considered *de rigueur* to use chopsticks when eating Chinese food. And in Taiwan you'll find abundant opportunities to practice.

The Chinese only use forks and knives in the kitchen – and when eating Western food. For their own cuisine, they prefer to have everything cut, sliced, diced, or otherwise prepared in the kitchen, so that the food is in bite-sized pieces when served. Those who wield their chopsticks too slowly often miss the choicest morsels whenever a new dish appears on the table.

Chopsticks can also be used to select choice morsels from the best dishes for the guest-of-honor or just for a friend at the table. The polite way to do this is to turn the sticks around so that you use the clean blunt ends to serve food to others.

Last but not least, using the chopsticks makes you a little more Chinese and a little less foreign in Chinese eyes, and this always improves the pleasure of traveling in Taiwan.

But due to hygienical reasons, several restaurants serve now so called set menus with portions of everything on individual plates.

Where to Eat

Restaurants in Taipei

If interested in some typical Chinese food, there are three suggestions for restaurants. The best place to try the perfect Chinese cuisine are the hotel restaurants in Taipei and Kaohsiung. The hotel restaurants are used to serving foreigners, offer nearly-perfect service, and serve probably the best Chinese food available on Taiwan. The Taipei Chinese Food Festival, held in August every year, demonstrates the skills of the hotels master chefs.

Second best suggestion for lunch and sometimes for dinner is to visit one of the many eateries on the underground floors of the main department stores. Everything is freshly-cooked and the prices are quite low. If you see one eatery with no customers waiting, it is maybe better to go to another, where you have to wait in a line. Several hundred or thousands of Chinese eating at such places can not be wrong.

The third suggestion is to go to an ordinary restaurant. But most taxi drivers will not understand unless you show them the address of the restaurant written in Chinese. Through years of experience they know that Western people like to complain even about an excellent dish, perfectly prepared, because it does not taste the same as at the Chinese restaurant back home. Moreover, Chinese restaurants cater to groups, never individuals. Four people at a table should be the minimum. Do not expect the food to be cheap. Consider also the language barrier – there are so many items on a Chinese menu that most foreigners hesitate to order something "strange", and end up with a dish like rice-and-chicken. That is also one of the reasons why some gourmet Chinese restaurants don't take Western tourists seriously.

Hotel Restaurants

CANTONESE

Ambassador Hotel (Cantonese Restaurant)
Asiaworld Plaza (Cantonese Garden)
Brother Hotel (Plum Blossom)
Grand Hyatt Taipei (Canton Garden)
Howard Plaza Hotel (Pearl River)
Lai Lai Sheraton Hotel (Shangrila Garden)
Hotel Rebar Crown (Lotus Garden)
The Regent of Taipei (Tsai Fung Shuen)
Hotel Royal Taipei (Ming Court)
Far Eastern Plaza Hotel (Hsiang Kung)

HUNAN

Hilton International (Hunan Restaurant)
Lai Lai Sheraton Hotel (Hunan Garden)
Hotel Riverview Taipei (Hunan Garden)

SHANGHAI

Asiaworld Plaza Hotel (Shanghai Castle)
Grand Hyatt Taipei (Shanghai Court)
Howard Plaza Hotel (Yangtze River)
Lai Lai Sheraton Hotel (Jade Garden)
Ritz Taipei (Tien Hsinag Lo)

SICHUAN

Ambassador Hotel (Szechuan Restaurant)
Grand Hotel (Chinese Dining Room)

TAIWANESE

Brother Hotel (Orchid Room)
Hilton International (Tiffany's)
Howard Plaza Hotel (Formosa)
Lai Lai Sheraton Hotel (Happy Garden)
Regent of Taipei (Minchiangchun Court)

Restaurants in Town

CANTONESE

An Lo Yuan, 232 Tunhua N. Rd. Tel: 715-4929.
Golden Royal Taiwan Restaurant, 404 Fuhsing N. Rd. Tel: 504-7699. 3F, 46 Tunhua S. Rd, Sec. 2. Tel: 708-0558.
74 Jenai Rd, Sec. 3. Tel: 703-7290.
Nobel House, B1, 286 Kuangfu S. Rd. Tel: 773-0095.
Sung Tung Lok, 592 Tunhua S. Rd. Tel: 700-1818.

HUNAN

Charming Garden, 3/F, 16 Nanking E. Rd, Sec. 3. Tel: 511-0916.
Special Shans Kitchen, 136 Nanking E. Rd, Sec. 3. Tel: 781-5858.
The Grand, 3/F, 206 Nanking E. Rd, Sec. 2. Tel: 506-8676.
Treasure House, 3/F, 152 Sungchiang Rd. Tel: 581-9151.

MONGOLIAN

Kublai Khan, 263 Hsinyi Rd, Sec. 2. Tel: 356-0097.
Genghis Khan, 176 Nanking E. Rd, Sec. 3. Tel: 711-4412.
Tang Kung, 2/F, 283 Sungchiang Rd. Tel: 502-6762.
Yuan Dynasty, 131 Sungkiang Rd. Tel: 507-5708.

BEIJING

Celestial, 2-4/F, 1 Nanking W. Rd. Tel: 563-2380.
Huei Bin Lou, 6/F, 90 Chunghua Rd, Sec. 1. Tel: 331-2555.
King Join Restaurant, 18 Szuwei Rd. Tel: 701-3225.
Peking Tu I Chu, 506 Jenai Rd, Sec. 4. Tel: 729-7853.
Yueh Bin Lou, 45 Chunghsiao E. Rd, Sec. 1. Tel: 321-2801.

SHANGHAI

Hsiang Garden, 6, Lane 27, Jenai Rd, Sec. 4. Tel: 771-2277.
Shanghai, 57 Tunhua S. Rd, Sec. 2. Tel: 704-4878.
Tau Tau, 57-1 Chungshan N. Rd, Sec. 2. Tel: 564-1277.
Yi Hsiang Garden, 31, Lane 221, Sungchiang Rd. Tel: 505-9565.

SICHUAN

Rong Hsing, 223 Sungchiang Rd. Tel: 506-6899.
Ting Hsing Lou, 216 Nanchang Rd, Sec. 2. Tel: 394-1101.
Yu Ho Yuan, 3/F, 289 Chunghsiao E. Rd, Sec. 4. Tel: 752-8936.

TAIWANESE

Green Leaf,
5/F, 87 Chunghsiao E. Rd, Sec. 4. Tel: 752-4652.
1, Lane 137, Chungshan N. Rd, Sec. 2. Tel: 562-0260
1, Lane 105, Chungshan N. Rd, Sec. 1. Tel: 571-3859.
Hsing Yeh, 34-1 Shuangcheng St. Tel: 596-3255.
Kang Hsi Garden, B1, 207 Tunhua N.

Rd. Tel: 717-5668.

Tainan Tan Tsu Mien, 31 Huahsi St. Tel: 308-1123.

VEGETARIAN

Chuan Shing, 111 Linsen N. Rd. Tel: 541-9075.
Fa Hua, 132 Minchuan E. Rd, Sec. 3. Tel: 717-5305.
Kuan Shih Yin, 29 Minchuan E. Rd, Sec. 2. Tel: 595-5557.
Lotus Natural Vegetarian Restaurant, 57, Lane 233, Tunhua S. Rd, Sec. 1. Tel: 741-5642.
Sui Yuan Chiu, 51 Nanking E. Rd, Sec. 2. Tel: 781-8055.

International Food

CONTINENTAL

Chalet Swiss, 1/F, 47 Nanking E. Rd, Sec. 4. Tel: 715-2702.
Olympia International, 122 Jenai Rd, Sec. 3. Tel: 754-1917.
Opus, 58, Lane 122, Jenai Rd, Sec. 4. Tel: 705-9974.
Ploughman's Cottage, 2/F, 305 Nanking E. Rd. Tel: 712-4965.
Zum Fass, B1, 55, Lane 119, Linsen N. Rd. Tel: 531-3815.

FRENCH

Elysee French, 20, Alley 33, Lane 351, Tunhua S. Rd. Tel: 781-4270.
La Seine, 14, Lane 106, Minchuan E. Rd, Sec. 3. Tel: 717-6450.

ITALIAN

Casa Mia, 628 Linsen N. Rd. Tel: 596-4636.
La Cucina, 8-2, Lane 198, Hsin I Rd, Sec. 2. Tel: 397-4176.
Ruffino Ristorante, 15, Lane 25, Shuangcheng St. Tel: 592-3355.

JAPANESE

Fukul, 60 Fuhsing N. Rd. Tel: 772-7738.
Natori, 3, Lane 199, Hsinyi Rd, Sec. 4. Tel: 705-2288.
Tsu Ten Kaku, 8, Lane 53, Chungshan N. Rd, Sec. 1. Tel: 511-7372.
Jur Aku, B1, 152 Chungshan N. Rd, Sec. 1. Tel: 561-3883.

KOREAN

Tehli, 13, Lane 160, Tunhua S. Rd, Sec. 1. Tel: 771-2728.
Long Life, 16, Lane 270, Tunhua S. Rd. Tel: 781-6639.
Seoul, 4, Lane 33, Chungshan N. Rd, Sec. 1. Tel: 511-2326.

WESTERN

Friday's,
150 Tunhua N. Rd. Tel: 713-3579.
151 Chunghsiao E. Rd, Sec. 4. Tel: 711-3579.
Jake's Country Kitchen, 705 Chungshan N. Rd, Sec. 6. Tel: 871-5289.
Jimmy's Kitchen, B1, 73 Jenai Rd, Sec. 4. Tel: 711-3793.
Ruth's, 2F,135 Minsheng E. Rd, Sec. 3. Tel: 545-8888.
Kevin, 119 Minsheng E. Rd, Sec. 3. Tel: 712-1733.
Y.Y.'s Kitchen & (kosher) Steak House, 49 Chungshan N. Rd, Sec. 3. Tel: 592-2869.

Attractions

Tours

The most popular city and island tours offered by travel agencies are briefly introduced below.

Taipei City: This half-day tour covers the National Palace Museum, Martyrs' Shrine, other city sights and offers glimpses of contemporary Chinese urban life along the way. (NT$500).
Taipei by Night: An enduring favorite, this nocturnal tour commences with a traditional Mongolian barbecue dinner, then proceeds to the famous Lungshan Temple and Snake Alley bazaar. (NT$950).
Wulai Aborigine Village: This is a half-day excursion to the colorful ethnic minority village at Wulai, about an hour's drive out of Taipei. You'll see performances, hike through lush mountain terrain, and enjoy spectacular scenery. (NT$950).
Northern Coast: A half-day tour of Taiwan's scenic northern coastline, this excursion takes you to the port city of Keelung and the fantastic rock formations at Yehliu, then proceeds down the northwest coast back to Taipei. (NT$700).
Taroko Gorge: Taroko Gorge is considered to be one of the wonders of Asia, and it remains the single most popular tourist attraction outside of Taipei.

Twelve miles of craggy canyon, enclosed by towering cliffs of marble, which soar up to 3,000 ft high. Taroko Gorge is bisected by the Central Cross-Island Highway, with 38 tunnels cut into solid rock and marble bridges. This tour goes by air to Hualien from Taipei in the morning, then heads up the gorge for a bus tour of breathtaking beauty. Lunch is served in the alpine airs of the Tienhsiang Lodge, then the bus returns to Hualien in time for performances by the Ami tribe, and a tour of Taiwan's biggest marble factory and showroom. The tour returns to Taipei by air around 5pm. (NT$4,000).
Sun Moon Lake: This two-day tour takes you to bucolic Sun Moon Lake, Taiwan's favorite honeymoon resort, located 2,500 ft above sea level in Taiwan's only land-locked county. This year-round resort is famous for its landscape, hiking, temples and pagodas. The tour departs Taipei by air-conditioned bus and arrives in Taichung for lunch. The bus then proceeds to Sun Moon Lake, about an hour's drive from Taichung, passing through green fields of sugar cane, tea, and vegetables, rice paddies, banana and pineapple plantations, and other lush scenery. After checking into a hotel, you'll go for a leisurely two-hour boat cruise on Sun Moon Lake. The second morning is free time. After lunch, the tour will drive back to Taichung and then on to Taipei, arriving back in town by nightfall. (NT$4,500 for double occupancy and NT$5,000 for single occupancy).
Central Cross Island Highway/Sun Moon Lake: The 120-mile-long Central Cross Island Highway, a remarkable feat of engineering by any standards, is known in Taiwan as the Rainbow of Treasure Island. This three-day tour commences with a morning flight to Hualien from Taipei, followed by a drive through spectacular Taroko Gorge and lunch at the Tienhsiang Lodge. It then proceeds to scenic Lishan for an overnight stay. You'll spend the next morning sightseeing, then depart for Taichung, arriving in time for lunch and some city sightseeing. Next stop is Sun Moon Lake and a second night, touring the lake on the morning of the third day. The tour returns to Taichung by bus after lunch, then onto a train for the return trip to Taipei. (NT$7,500 for double occupancy and NT$9,000 for single occupancy).

Sun Moon Lake/Alishan: This three-day tour features a visit to Alishan, a magnificent resort area of 18 peaks flanking the Central Range in central Taiwan. A 45-mile-long, narrow-gauge railway with diesel trains traverses 80 bridges and passes through 50 tunnels from the town of Chiayi up to Alishan, which at 7,500 ft in altitude is the highest railway station in Asia. From a vantage point atop Chu Shan, you can catch one of the most spellbinding views in all Taiwan: a sea of clouds swirling like water and filling the entire valley between Chu Shan and 3,952-m (12,966 ft) Yu Shan 25 miles away. The latter is the highest peak in northeast Asia and a favorite destination for mountain climbers.

This tour commences with an air-conditioned bus-ride from Taipei to Taichung, then up to Sun Moon Lake for the first night. After a morning tour of the lake, the tour proceeds by bus to Chiayi, where you'll board the mountain railway for the 3-hour ride up to Alishan for the second night. A tour of the mountain the next morning, then a return trip by rail to Chiayi.

From there, you'll board an express bus back to Taipei. (NT$7,500 for double occupancy, NT$9,000 for single occupancy).

Round-the-Island Tour: This four-day tour is an extension of the Central Cross-Island Highway tour, with the addition of a visit to the southern seaport of Kaohsiung, Taiwan's second-largest city. The first day is spent touring Sun Moon Lake. The second day returns to Taichung, then on down to Kaohsiung, including lovely Cheng-ching Lake, then flies to Hualien in the afternoon. After an overnight stay in Hualien, you'll spend the fourth day driving up Taroko Gorge, then returning to Hualien for Ami performances and a tour of the marble factory. The tour flies back to Taipei around 5pm. (NT$11,000 for double occupancy, NT$13,000 for single occupancy).

Culture

Art Galleries

These galleries exhibit works of art by both established old masters and promising young artists. They display an impressive range of styles, from traditional Chinese landscape painting and calligraphy to contemporary Western abstracts and still-lifes, and the artists employ both Eastern and Western materials and methods. For further information on art and art exhibits in Taipei, contact the **Taipei Art Guild** at 8/F, 218-2, Chunghsiao E. Rd, Sec. 4. Tel: (02) 773-6673.

A spacious **Taipei Fine Arts Museum** has been opened at 1818 Chungshan North Rd, Sec. 3. Tel: (02) 595-7656. This ultra-modern facility frequently sponsors exhibitions of arts and crafts by renowned international and local talents.

Some of the more interesting art galleries an Taipei are listed below:

Apollo Art Gallery, Apollo Bldg, 218-6 Chunghsiao E. Rd, Sec. 4, 2nd Fl. Tel: (02) 781-9332.
Asia Art Center, 117 Chienkuo S. Rd, Sec. 2. Tel: (02) 754-1366.
Cave Gallery, B1, 138 Chunghsiao E. Rd, Sec. 1. Tel: (02) 396-1864.
Crown Center, 50 Lane 120, Tunhwa N. Rd. Tel: (02) 717-1398.
East West Art Gallery, 5/F, Rm 501, 63 Chungking S. Rd, Sec. 1. Tel: (02) 314-8603.
Hsiung Shih Gallery, 5/F, 16, Alley 33, Lane 216, Chunghsiao E. Rd, Sec. 4. Tel: (02) 772-1158.
Kander Arts and Antiquities Gallery, 25-27 Chung S. Rd, Sec. 1. Tel: 314-3210.
Lung-Men Art Gallery, 3/F, 218-1 Chunghsiao E. Rd, Sec. 4, 3rd Fl. Tel: (02) 751-3170.
Ming Sheng Art Gallery, 145B Chungshan N. Rd, Sec. 1. Tel: (02) 581-0858.

Chinese Opera

Taiwan is one of the best places in the world to attend the opera, Chinese style. From the bizarre melodies mouthed by magnificently-costumed performers to the exotic orchestral accompaniment, to the astounding acrobatics and martial arts displays of the performers, a night at a Beijing opera will surely prove entertaining and educational.

There is one place in Taipei where Beijing opera is performed regularly: **National Fu Hsing Dramatic Arts Academy**, 177 Neihu Rd, Sec. 2, Taipei. Tel: (02) 796-2666.

For a taste of Beijing or Taiwan opera, try the television set – live performances are broadcast almost every day. In the back alleys of Taipei and outside the big city, keep your eyes open for the traveling opera companies that set up and perform for several days.

Dance

There is a limited amount of traditional folk dancing in Taiwan, most performed by minority groups. Snippets of ethnic dances can be viewed at the various tourism centers around the island. On the other hand, modern dance has gained popularity in Taiwan in the past decade.

The **Cloud Gate Dance Ensemble**, led by Lin Hwaimin, has spearheaded the movement. It combines both Chinese and Western techniques and ideas, choreographed to the music of contemporary Chinese performers. The group, internationally-acclaimed during tours of the world, holds regular performances in Taipei. Consult your hotel for the schedules of the Cloud Gate ensemble.

Music

Taiwan has produced numerous musicians of world-class standard. Western music is regularly performed at various venues in Taipei by the **Taiwan Provincial Symphony Orchestra** and the **Taipei Municipal Symphony Orchestra**. Consult your hotel or information desk, or such organizations as the National Music Council and the Chinese Classical Music Association for information on scheduled performances. Traditional Chinese music has its roots in both special temple rituals and folk music. Consider listening to temple music at the elaborate rituals held annually, on September 28, to celebrate the birthday of Confucius.

Handicrafts

If people were classified according to how good they are with their hands, you will definitely find the Taiwanese ranked among the top.

The Taiwanese take great pride in the things they can make with their hands: from lanterns and toys, handbags and baskets, bamboo and rattan crafts, rug and carpets, to knitwear and embroideries.

Their government shoved that pride one rung higher when it erected a four-story, air-conditioned building, housed within it a range of items that have undergone inspection for design and quality, named the building the **Handicraft Exhibition Hall** and opened it officially for public viewing in 1977. Exhibits number more than 1,500 and are from all parts of Taiwan, some produced by cottage industry, and others by regular factories. The Hall, in Tsaotun, is situated on the highway running from Taichung to the Sun Moon Lake and the Hsitou Bamboo Forest. Open daily except Mondays, national and public holidays from 9am to noon and from 2 to 5pm, the hall is well worth the visit.

While in Tsaotun, also call at the **Taiwan Provincial Handicraft Institute**, also operated by the Taiwan Provincial Government. Inside are a factory, kiln and research laboratory.

In Taipei, an excellent selection of local handicrafts are on display for sale at the **Chinese Handicraft Mart**, at #1 Hsu Chou St.. Tel: 321-7233. This is a good place to do souvenir and gift shopping.

Cinemas

It will surprise you that Taiwan residents view more films per year, per capita, than any other people in the world, including Americans. The average citizen of Taiwan sees about three full-length movies per week, and these include both local and foreign films. Taiwan is one of Hollywood's most lucrative markets, and all major Hollywood studios have permanent representatives here.

Most of the foreign films which come to Taiwan are from the United States, and they are always shown in English, with Chinese subtitles. This means that traveling movie fans need not fear a shortage of Western film entertainment when in Taiwan. On the other hand, since almost all Chinese films are shown with English subtitles, you may also enjoy local gongfu fighting movies, especially if you have never seen one before.

The daily *China Post* and *China News* carry information regarding English films currently playing in Taipei. There are usually three to five performances per day, with the last show beginning around 9pm.

The visitor will find no lack of nightlife in Taipei. The capital city offers sophisticated discotheques, cosy pubs with darts, and a host of piano bars and music lounges for night owls, insomniacs and more...

Food and drink go together in Chinese society. A night on the town usually begins with a meal, not after it. The beer, wine and spirits are ordered along with dinner. And the liquid refreshment rarely stops flowing. "When drinking among intimate friends, even a thousand rounds are not enough", proclaims an ancient Chinese proverb. Again, many of the people of Taiwan take that advice to heart. Inebriation is a form of convivial communication here, an opportunity to drop the formal masks of business and reveal the "inner person".

Since the Chinese are food fanatics who appreciate good cuisine of all kinds, Taipei boasts also a range of Western restaurants, many operated by accomplished European chefs.

MTV and KTV

Besides discos and floor shows, there are other evening diversions. Mushrooming additions to the Taipei night scene are MTV and KTV. Although the name MTV was borrowed from the American cable entertainment show, its similarity ends there. MTV centers offer a wide selection of both Western and Asian movies on laserdisc and videotape. Customers first select a movie and are then assigned to a private room equipped with state-of-the-art monitors abd stereo systems.

KTVs are based on karaoke, long a favorite form of entertainment in Japan. Now more popular than MTV, KTV venues are elegantly decorated and follow a variety of stylistic themes, from Versailles palaces to high-tech chrome-and-neon space stations. After selecting the appropriate room, customers can order fruit trays, mixed drinks, and snacks while paging through a catalog of traditional, pop, Western and Asian songs. Notepads and pens provided to jot down the desired selections, which are then keyed in via a small terminal in the room. Songs can be selected anytime and are queued in line.

Wall outlets allow for plenty of microphones. An accompanying video-tape with the text is shown on a large monitor and the system cuts out the original voice part of the song allowing customers to use their own voices instead, not always a good idea.

Pubs, bars and wine houses

Taipei abounds with pubs and bars. One of the easiest places to go bar-hopping is the Sugar Daddy Row area around Shuang Cheng Street, near the President Hotel and with lots of establishments within easy walking distance of one another.

One of the quintessential forms of post-dinner activity for groups of Chinese men is the wine house or *jiou-jia*, occasionally referred to by foreigners as "girlie restaurants". Most serve food and expect guests to order several dishes, but the main meal is usually taken elsewhere and guests begin flocking to the wine house about 9pm. The wine house specialties usually include a variety of "potency foods" like Snake Soup, Turtle Stew, Sauteed Eel or Black-fleshed Chicken. All are ballyhooed as aphrodisiacs.

At least four persons should participate in a wine house party and at least one should be a Chinese man who is familiar with the routine. Without enough guests, the party cannot reach that vital stage of excitement which the Chinese call *reh-nau*, literally "hot and noisy". A Chinese-speaking guest helps translate the nuances of the conversation and activity.

A popular method of downing liquor other than toasting is a kind of "rock, paper, scissors" finger game, in which the loser must drain his glass dry. Chinese men engage in this spirited contest in restaurants and pubs throughout Taiwan.

A guest who walks out of such a place sober is considered a cheat or a man with the "capacity of an ocean".

Bottle Clubs

A more contemporary form of Chinese nightlife is the so-called bottle club. Customers buy liquor by the bottle; it is later stored in special racks for future use. These clubs are generally posh with expensive furnishings, tasteful decor, low lights and "atmosphere". Some provide live entertainment and permit dancing Wealthy Chinese patrons popularly keep bottles of good

French cognac. Chinese businessmen often choose bottle clubs for entertaining friends and associates on corporate expense accounts.

Festivals

In addition to ancient festivals such as the Lunar New Year and the Mid-Autumn Moon Festival, and national holidays such as Double-Ten and Dr Sun Yatsen's birthday, there are scores of other local Taiwanese festivals known as *paipai* (pronounced *bye-bye*), which are colorful celebrations held in honor of local city gods and deities. There are over 100 popular city gods in Taiwan, and not only are their birthdays commemorated, each of their "death days" and "deification days" are also occasions for celebration. The sensible government therefore only recognizes the major ones and declares these official public holidays, during which most businesses and public offices are closed.

"Celebration" of *paipai* days begins with the faithful offering the best food and wine to the respective deities, and ends with the devotees themselves gorging the offerings, but not before they are sure that the deities have had their fill. This is usually the time taken for a joss-stick to burn out. Few Taiwanese remain entirely sober on these occasions, and everyone spends a lot of money to *ching-keh*, or "invite friends out". In recent years, the government has tried to dissuade the Taiwanese from indulging in such frequent and extravagant celebrations, branding the custom as wasteful, but the colorful *paipai* tradition is too deeply ingrained in the island's culture to be abandoned. Besides, the relatively well-off people of Taiwan can afford it.

National holidays, which are of more recent origin, follow the solar calendar used in the West, but most festive dates still follow the lunar calendar. Thus, they vary from year to year. Check exact dates at the time of planning for your trip.

January

Foundation Day: On January 1, 1912, Dr Sun Yatsen was inaugurated as the first President of the newly-founded Republic of China. Also on that day, China officially switched from the lunar to the Gregorian calender. This occasion is celebrated annually in Taipei with parades, dragon and lion dances, traditional music, patriotic speeches, and of course, lots of firecrackers.

Lunar New Year: Traditionally called the Spring Festival, the Lunar New Year remains the biggest celebration of the year in Taiwan, as it has for millennia in all Chinese and many Asian communities. The festival is observed in various stages for a full month, from the 16th day of the 12th month, although offices and shops generally close for only a week around the New Year's Day.

Many ancient customs are associated with the Lunar New Year. For example, all outstanding debts must be paid off before New Year's Eve; failure to do so is a grave affront and an omen of bad luck for the coming year. Many wealthy Chinese businessmen in Taiwan keep running accounts in their favorite restaurants and clubs, paying their bills only once a year, just before New Year's Eve. Another custom is exchanging gifts, especially little red envelopes (*hung-bao*) stuffed with "lucky money", the amount depending on the closeness of the relationship between the giver and taker. Everyone dresses up in new clothes at New Year – from hats down to shoes – and this symbolizes renewal and a fresh start in life for the coming year. People visit family and friends and spend a lot of money on entertainment. Indeed, local banks are often plagued with cash shortages at this time of the year. The dominant color is red, which is universally regarded as auspicious among the Chinese; red flowers, red clothing, red streamers, red cakes and candies, and the ubiquitous red envelopes appear everywhere.

At the stroke of midnight on New Year's Eve, the entire island suddenly reverberates to the staccato explosions of millions of firecrackers and skyrockets, as every temple and household in Taiwan lights the fuses which will frighten evil spirits from their thresholds, insuring an auspicious start to the New Year. The Chinese invented gunpowder for this very purpose over 1,000 years ago – long before the West ever knew of it – and the fusillades which mark the Chinese New Year make America's Fourth of July celebrations seem tame by comparison.

The stock phrase to offer all your friends and aquaintances whenever and wherever you encounter them during this period is *kung-hsi-fa-tsai* (pronounced *goong-shee-fah-tsai*), which means "I wish you happiness and prosperity". The witty rhyming retort to this greeting is *hung-bao-na-lai*, or "Hand over a red envelope!"

February

The Lantern Festival: This festival, which falls on the first full moon of the Lunar New Year, marks the end of the Spring Festival. Celebrants appear at night in the streets, parks and temples of Taiwan carrying colorful lanterns with auspicious phrases inscribed on them in elegant calligraphy. This tradition is supposed to insure against evil and illness in the coming year. The festival food associated with this event is a sweet dumpling of glutinous rice-paste stuffed with bean or date paste and called *yuan-hsiao*. Major temples are excellent places to observe the Lantern Festival in full color and pageantry. Prizes are awarded for the most beautiful and original lantern designs.

March

Birthday of Kuanyin, Goddess of Mercy: Kuanyin is one of the most popular Buddhist deities in Taiwan, Korea and Japan. Known for her compassion and love for people, she is one of Taiwan's patron protective deities. Her birthday is celebrated with colorful *paipai* ceremonies in major temples throughout Taiwan.

April

Youth Day: Originally called Revolutionary Martyrs' Day, Youth Day commemorates the deaths of 72 young revolutionaries in China in 1911.

Tomb-Sweeping Day: Traditionally calculated as the 105th day after the Winter Solstice and called the Chingming (Clear and Bright) Festival, Tomb-Sweeping Day in Taiwan is now celebrated annually on April 5, which coincides with the date of President Chiang Kaishek's death, in 1975. Therefore, April 5 is both a traditional Chinese festival and a contemporary national holiday in Taiwan.

During this festival, entire families go out to their ancestral burial grounds to sweep accumulated dirt and debris from the tombs, place fresh flowers around the graves, and perhaps plant some new trees, flowers and bushes in the area.

Buddha's Bathing Festival: This day commemorates the birth of Sakyamuni (the historical Buddha) 2,500 years ago. The festival is marked in temples throughout the island with cleansing-of-Buddha ceremonies, during which all statues of Buddha are ritually washed while monks recite appropriate sutras. Many of the icons are then paraded through the streets to the beat of gongs and drums.

Birthday of Matsu, Goddess of the Sea: One of the biggest *paipai* of the year in Taiwan, this festival is dedicated to Matsu, Goddess of the Sea, patron saint of Taiwan, and guardian deity of the island's fishermen. It is celebrated with great fanfare in over 300 temples where Matsu is enshrined. The biggest festival takes place in central Taiwan, at the Peikang temple near Chiayi. But you can also get an eye and ear full at the famous Lungshan (Dragon Mountain) Temple in downtown Taipei. Sacrificial offerings of roast pig and boiled chickens, billows of smoke from incense and burning paper money, undulating lion and dragon dances, colorful parades, and lavish feasting comprise some of the festivities dedicated to Matsu on her birthday.

May

Dragon Boat Festival: One of China's most ancient festivals, this event commemorates the death of Chu-Yuan, an accomplished poet and upright minister who plunged to his death in a river about 2,500 years ago to protest the corruption and misrule of his king, who had banished him from the court. According to the legend, upon hearing of his tragic death, the local people rowed their boats out on the river and dropped stuffed rice dumplings tightly wrapped in bamboo leaves into the water to supplicate and nourish his spirit, or to distract animals from eating him. These dumplings, called *dzung-dze*, remain this festival's major food item.

The Dragon Boat Festival is celebrated with colorful dragon-boat races, which in recent years have become a major sporting event in Taipei. Teams from all over the island, including several "foreigner teams" from the expatriate community, as well as teams from Singapore, compete for top honors in various divisions. The bows of the boats are carved into elaborate dragon-heads, and the crews row vigorously to the resounding beat of big drums placed at the back of each boat.

June

Birthday of Chenghuang, the City God: This *paipai* festival is celebrated with great pomp and ceremony at Taipei's city-god temple at 61 Tihua St, Sec. 1. The worship of city gods is a practice that has been recorded in China as far back as the early Xia dynasty (2200 BC), and remains one of Taiwan's liveliest celebrations. City gods are said to have the power to protect a city's inhabitants from both natural disasters and enemy intruders, and they also advice the Lord of Heaven and the King of Hell regarding appropriate rewards and punishments for the city's residents after death. No wonder the Chinese pay them such lavish homage!

Among this *paipai*'s colorful and highly photogenic festivities are parades with icons of the City God held high upon pedestals, offerings of whole pigs and cows stretched on bamboo racks, processions of celebrants wearing stilts and colorful costumes, lion and dragon dances, lavish feasts, and much more.

July

Chinese Valentine's Day: Chinese Valentine's Day is derived from the legend of the herd boy and the spinning girl. The herd boy (a star formation in the constellation Aquila, west of the Milky Way) and the spinning girl (the star Vega in the constellation Lyra, east of the Milky Way) appear closest together in the sky on this night, and all the magpies on earth are said to ascend to the sky to form a bridge across the Milky Way so that the lovers may cross over their brief once-a-year tryst. This is a festival for young unmarried girls and for young lovers, who observe the romantic occasion by exchanging gifts, strolling in moonlit parks, and praying in temples for future matrimonial bliss.

August

Ghost Festival: The Chinese believe that on the first day of the 7th lunar month, the gates of hell swing open, permitting the ghosts of deceased relatives to return to their earthly homes for a visit. In order to placate the spirits and discourage their mischief, trays of succulent foods are set out before each home as offering to them, and Buddhist priests are invited to every neighborhood and alley to bless these offerings and supplicate the spirits with prayer. Incense is burned and bundles of paper "clothing" and "money" are set alight for use by the spirits in the other world. These offerings are also meant to prevent the ghosts of criminals and spirits with no living relatives from entering one's home and causing trouble. It is not an auspicious time for marriage or commencing important new ventures. Rites are held daily in all Buddhist temples during the Ghost Festival, which formally ends on the last day of the 7th month, when the spirits return to their underworld abode and the gates slam shut for another year.

September

Confucius' Birthday: This is an official national holiday, celebrated as Teacher's Day, which commemorates the birth of the sage Confucius in 551 BC. Known as China's greatest teacher, Confucius continues to exert profound influence on culture and society in Taiwan. Elaborate traditional ceremonies are held every year on this day, at 6am at Taipei's Confucius Temple, complete with ancient musical instruments, formal court attire, ritual dances, and other Confucian rites as old as the sage himself.

Tickets to attend this ceremony must be arranged in advance through local tourism authorities.

October

Mid-Autumn Moon Festival: The Chinese believe that the harvest moon is the fullest, brightest moon of the year, and they celebrate its annual appearance by proceeding en masse to parks, hillsides, riverbanks and seashores to gaze at "The Lady in the Moon", nibble on tasty snacks, and drink wine. According to the Chinese legend, Chang-Er, beautiful wife of the Tang emperor Ming-Huang, one day discovered a vial of the Elixir of Immortality specially prepared for her husband and decided to take a sip. But he caught her in the act, and in order to conceal the evidence, she quickly swallowed the entire potion. It took effect instantly and with such intensity that she immediately flew up from earth and landed on the moon. She's been there ever since, and on this night her beauty radiates at her very best.

The festival is celebrated by exchanging gifts of moon cakes, which are large, round pastries stuffed with sweet-bean paste, mashed dates, chopped nuts, minced dried fruits, and other fillings. Exchanging moon cakes also has patriotic overtones, because during the successful overthrow of the Mongol Yuan dynasty by the Chinese Ming, secret plans for the insurrection were concealed in moon cakes and distributed to patriots throughout the empire prior to the uprising.

Double-Ten National Day: "Double-Ten" refers to the 10th day of the 10th month, and commemorates the overthrow of the Manchu Qing dynasty, China's last, by revolutionaries on October 10, 1911. It is by far the most important national holiday of the year in Taiwan, and it is celebrated with massive parades of military hardware and honor guards from all branches of the armed forces, aerial acrobatics by the air force's daring Thunder Tigers, commando-landing demonstrations, patriotic speeches by top government leaders, and displays of folk dancing, sword-fighting, martial arts, and other cultural activites. Most of the action takes place in the huge plaza in front of the Presidential Building, in Taipei.

Hotels and restaurants in Taipei remain packed full throughout the week prior to Double-Ten day, as tens and thousands of overseas Chinese from all over the world pour into town for the festivities. Tourists who visit Taiwan at this time should make early reservations for hotel and airline space.

Restoration Day: This national holiday celebrates the return of Taiwan to Chinese rule after the defeat of Japan in 1945, thereby ending 55 years of Japanese colonial occupation. It is marked with several major athletic events, including regional competition in soccer and basketball for the Presidential Cup awards. Other festivities include lion and dragon dances and bountiful feasting at Taipei's many restaurants and hotels.

Birthday of Chiang Kaishek: This is a national holiday celebrated in Taiwan to commemorate the birth of the late President Chiang Kaishek, in 1887.

November

Birthday of Dr Sun Yatsen: Sun Yatsen, founder and first president of the Republic of China, is regarded as the George Washington of China by Chinese throughout the world, including the Communist mainland. This holiday celebrates his birth in 1866 and is marked with solemn patriotic ceremonies and speeches.

DECEMBER

Constitution Day: This is an official national holiday which marks the day in 1947 on which the constitution of the Republic of China became effective.

Sports & Leisure

Participant Sports

In recent years, sports activities have enjoyed increasing popularity in Taiwan, which host frequent international sports events and regularly sends teams to compete abroad. The sports most easily accessible to the tourist in Taiwan are golf, tennis, and swimming.

Golf

Golf is the oldest organized sport in Taiwan, and all of Taiwan's golf clubs, some of which are close to Taipei, are open to foreign visitors for guest memberships. The clubs are open all year-round.

Arrangements for guest privileges in Taiwan's golf clubs may be made through hotel travel desks and local travel agencies, who will also arrange for regular club members to accompany or sponsor temporary guests, in those clubs whose rules require it. Clubs, shoes, caddies, and food and beverage facilities are available at all of the clubs. Further inquiries regarding golf in Taiwan may be directed to the **Chinese Taipei Golf Association**, ROC Golf Association, 12F-1, 125 Nanking E. Rd, Sec. 2, Taipei. Tel: (02) 516-5611; fax: (02) 516-3208.

Tennis

Tennis has been the fastest growing sport in Taiwan in recent years, and hundreds of new courts have been laid out around the island to meet the demand for tennis facilities. In Taipei, you'll find excellent facilities for tennis at public courts, private clubs, and several hotels. Ask your hotel for the nearest available tennis courts, if you want to try tennis in Taiwan. Or just book a hotel with its own courts. Informations also at the **Chinese Taipei Tennis Association,** ROC Tennis Association, 11F, 20 Chulun St, Taipei. Tel: (02) 772-0298; fax: (02) 771-1696.

Swimming

In addition to public beaches, there are numerous swimming pools at various hotels, clubs, and resorts around the island. For a nominal fee, you may enjoy a swim surrounded by green mountains at the **China Hotel** on Yangming Shan. For a nominal fee, you may also use the outdoor pool at the **Ambassador Hotel.** The **American Club** and the **Yangming Mountain Country Club** both have large pools, but you must be accompanied by a member to use them. There are also several public pools in the Taipei area, but they're usually crowded and noisy.

Martial Arts

Traditionally, the Chinese have kept in shape by practising various ancient forms of martial arts exercises, and in recent years these traditional forms have made a comeback in Taipei. Every morning at dawn, thousands of people pour into the parks and streets of Taipei to practice taiji, martial arts, yoga, sword dances, or simple aerobics. Visitors may also get a good work-out each morning by simply joining whatever group interests them and mimicking their gentle movements. The four most popular places in Taipei for early morning exercise sessions are **New Taipei Park** (near the Taipei Railway Station), the landscaped grounds of the **Chiang Kaishek Memorial Hall**, the compound of the **Sun Yatsen Memorial Hall**, and the hills around the **Grand Hotel**. The reason that these exercise sessions always take place at the crack of dawn is that the Chinese believe the air is most densely impregnated with *qi* (vital energy) at that time. Even if you don't participate, you should try to catch this scene at least once while in Taipei.

Mountain Climbing

Two-thirds of Taiwan is covered with lush evergreen mountains, and these rank among Taiwan's greatest attractions for mountain-climbers and trekkers. The two favorite climbs are to the 3,952 m (12,966 ft) peak of **Yu Shan** (Jade Mountain), which is the highest in Taiwan and in all northeast Asia, and to the 3,884 m (12,743 ft) summit of **Snow Mountain**, which is Taiwan's second-highest peak. Both require prior arrangements by the **Alpine Association** at 10Fl., 185 Chungshan N. Rd, Sec. 2, Taipei. Tel: (02) 594-2108; fax: (02) 593-5662.

Climbers bound for Yu Shan usually take the express train down to Chiayi, then switch to the alpine diesel train for the ride up to Alishan. From there, they proceed up to the Tungpu basecamp, where there is a hostel. The next morning they make the ascent up Yu Shan, where there is a second hostel located just 697 m (2,287 ft) below the summit. Allow yourself four days for the trip from the Alishan area to the summit of Yu Shan and back.

Snow Mountain is located north of Lishan, midway along the Central Cross-Island Highway. You can get to Lishan by driving in either from Taichung or Hualien. From there, a bus takes you to Huan Shan, in the foothills of Snow Mountain, and a car carries you up to the Wuling Farms at 1761 m (5,777 ft) altitude, where simple lodgings are available overnight.

Climbers commence their ascent of Snow Mountain the following morning and should allow four days for the trip from Lishan up to the summit of Snow Mountain and back.

For less formidable climbs, there are many scenic mountains located between Taipei and the northern coastline, which require no prior arrangements nor police permits. **Seven Stars Mountain**, at 3,675 ft, is the tallest of these gentle northern peaks.

Skiing

For two months each year (January and February), enough snow falls on the slopes of **Hohuan** (Harmonious Happiness Mountains) to permit skiing. Rising to an altitude of 11,208 ft in central Taiwan, Hohuan is easily reached by taking the Tayuling-Wushe branch of the Central Cross-Island Highway. Its amenities include the cosy Pine Snow Hostel, which accommodates 150 persons, a 400-meter ski-lift, ski instructors, and a fabulous alpine scenery which is well worth viewing, even if you don't ski. Since temperatures there never rise above 14°C (60°F), Hohuan also makes an excellent summer resort, especially for hiking and mineral baths. For further information contact: **Chinese Taipei Ski Association**, ROC Ski Association, Rm 606, 20 Chunlun St, Taipei. Tel: (02) 771-2374; fax: (02) 775-3311.

Scuba Diving and Snorkeling

An entirely new kingdom of colorful sealife unfolds for divers who plunge into the blue waters off Taiwan's coral coasts. Indeed, enormous colonies of live coral form one of the island's greatest underwater attractions, with colors in every conceivable shade of pink to purple. An astonishing variety of tropical and semi-tropical fish and molluscs; exquisitely shaped and colored conch, cone, cowrie; brightly-plumed sea lilies; and other exotic underwater life inhabit these coral communities in Taiwan's offshore waters.

The most spectacular diving in Taiwan is found near **Oluanpi** at the southernmost tip of the island. The rocky, shallow shoreline here also permits excellent snorkeling.

In the north, divers like to explore underwater coral kingdoms off the coast of **Yehliu**, which is famous for the bizarre formations of coral-rock pro-

truding from its seaside promontory.

Air refilling facilities for divers are available in both northern and southern Taiwan, and several local diving clubs organize regular excursions to popular diving areas. For further information regarding scuba diving in Taiwan, equipment rental, contact the **ROC Diving Federation**, 123 Chiuchuan St, Taipei. Tel: (02) 596-2341; fax: (02) 593-6405. Or contact: **Friendship Divers Association International**, 2-1 Taishun St, Taipei. Tel: (02) 362-9658; fax: (02) 362-9658.

Barber Shops & Asian Bath

The Chinese are a sensual people given to creature comforts, and two of the favorite comforts of some Chinese are to relax in the pampered luxury of barber shops and bath houses. In Taiwan, bathing and grooming – like eating and drinking – are regarded as far more than mere neccessities: they are approached as part of the grand art of living.

"Luxurious Tourist Barber Shops" abound throughout Taipei and are easily identified by braces of electrified barber-poles spinning madly by their neon-lit entrances. Stepping inside the automatic doors, you will be greeted by a bevy of young barbermaids clad in long gowns. They will guide you to an empty chair, refresh you with a hot handtowel, offer you hot tea and cigarettes, then proceed to groom you in a style you surely would like to become accustomed.

If you prefer to let your own barber do your hair-cutting and styling, then just go in for a shampoo, manicure and massage. Taipei barbermaids shampoo your hair like nobody else, combining a stimulating scalp massage with the shampoo. While she's blow-drying and combing your hair, you may call for a manicure, pedicure, or whatever other grooming you require. Finally comes the massage – a curiously refreshing finger-pressure massage which covers scalp, neck and spine and sends energy coursing through your nervous system. Those with the time and inclination may then stretch out in reclining position with a towel wrapped over their eyes and indulge in the great Chinese tradition of *hsiou-hsi* ("short rest"). Depending on which services from the girls you require and how long you stay, a visit to a "Luxurious Tourist Barber Shop" in Taipei will run between NT$500 to NT$5,000.

These barber shops cater exclusively to men, but women can get the same stimulating treatment at any Chinese beauty parlor, where shampoos, permanents, hair-styling, manicures and massages are performed in the same luxurious comfort. Almost all international tourist hotels in Taipei have both barber shops and beauty parlors, but these offer contemporary Western-style service and less Chinese flavor. You'll find "Tourist Barber Shops" in all the popular entertainment and shopping districts.

Bath houses and saunas are about as numerous in Taipei as cafes in the West. The Chinese are fanatics about bathing and personal hygiene, and they devote much time to it, often spending hours scrubbing, soaking and relaxing themselves in well-appointed bath houses. Facilities vary from place to place, but generally they include showers, hot and cold pools, whirlpools, saunas, professional massage, snack-bars, lockers and lounging areas. Many a multi-million-dollar deal in Taipei has been concluded in terry-cloth robes or lawyers soothing their weary bones in whirlpool-baths. It's a great way to relax, and it really gets the grit and grime of city air out of your hair and pores.

Remember that in an Asian bath house, you are always expected to thoroughly wash yourself with soap and water before stepping into any of the communal baths or whirlpools. Remember also that modesty is unnecessary, no matter what shape you're in, because the Chinese do not regard nakedness in a bath house as embarassing. Beyond that, simply plunge in and out of the hot and cold pools as the mood strikes you; bake yourself in the sauna; lose yourself in a swirling hot whirlpool; call for a massage and pedicure; relax in the lounge with a cool drink and magazine. A visit to a Taipei bath house will rejuvenate your body and spirit, all for only NT$500–1,500, depending on the services you request.

Almost all bath and saunas in Taipei have separate sections for men and women, and the facilities and services they provide are the same. A number of leading hotels in Taipei have their own sauna and bath facilities.

Language

Chinese is at once the most complex written language and the simplest spoken language in the world. This may sound like a contradiction to Westerners, who are accustomed to alphabetic writing systems based on spoken sounds, but the Chinese system of writing operates wholly independently of the spoken language, and you can learn one without any knowledge of the other.

The Written Language

Chinese writing is based on ideograms, or "idea-pictures", which graphically depict ideas and objects with written characters derived directly from actual diagrams of the subject. The oldest recorded Chinese characters appeared on oracle bones excavated this century in China and dating from the ancient Shang dynasty (1766–1123 BC). At that time, questions of vital interest to the emperor were inscribed upon the dried shells of giant tortoises, which were then subjected to heat. The heat caused the shells to crack, and diviners then interpreted Heaven's answers to the emperor's questions by "reading" the cracks. The answers were then inscribed on the shells, and they were stored in the imperial archives. Based on the number and complexity of the characters inscribed on these oracle bones, Chinese historians concluded that Chinese written language was first invented during the reign of the Yellow Emperor, around 2700 BC.

The written characters reached their current stage of development about 2,000 years ago during the Han dynasty, and they have changed very little since then, which makes Chinese the oldest ongoing writing system in the world. The importance of China's unique written language cannot be overstated: it held together a vast and complex empire composed of many different ethnic groups, and due to its non-phonetic nature, it formed a written common denominator among China's various and sundry dialects. Once the symbols were learned, they gave the reader access to an enormous wealth of historical and literary writings accumulated in China over five millennia of continuous cultural development. Unlike Egyptian hieroglyphics, for example, which died with the Pharoahs, thereby cutting off subsequent Egyptian generations from their own roots, the Chinese written language evolved continuously from generation to generation, transmitting with it the accumulated treasures of Chinese culture right down to the present era. Small wonder that ancient traditions are so deeply ingrained in the Chinese mind. For example, the simple act of writing one's own surname in Chinese immediately recalls and identifies one with a host of historical and literary heroes, spanning five millennia, who shared the same name.

There are about 50,000 Chinese characters listed in Chinese dictionaries, but the vast majority are either obsolete or used in the highly specialized branches of learning. Three thousand characters are required for basic literacy, such as reading newspapers and business documents, and about 5,000 are required for advanced literary studies. About 2,000 Chinese characters are still used in the written languages of Korea and Japan. Few scholars, however, are capable of using over 6,000 characters without resorting to dictionaries.

The Spoken Language

There are only several hundred vocal sounds in the Chinese spoken language, which means that many written characters must share the same pronunciation. To somewhat clarify matters, the Chinese developed a tonal system which uses four distinctive tones to pronounce each syllable. Even so, many characters share both common syllables and tones, and the only way to be really sure which words are meant when spoken is to consider the entire context of a statement, or demand a written explanation.

Grammatically, spoken Chinese is so simple and direct that it makes other languages seem cumbersome, archaic, and unnecessarily complex by comparison. There are no conjugations, declensions, gender distinctions, tense changes, or other complicated grammatical rules to memorize. The spoken language consists of simple sounds strung together in simple sentence patterns, with the basic "subject/verb/object" construction common to most Western language. Tones, while foreign to Western tongues, come naturally with usage and are not difficult to master. Even within China, the various provinces give different tonal inflections to the various sounds. Proper word-order and correct context are all you need to know about the Chinese grammar.

In Taiwan, the Mandarin dialect (known as *guo-yu*,National Language) has been declared the official lingua franca by the government. Mandarin, which is based upon the pronunciations which prevailed in the old imperial capital of Peking, is by far the most melodious dialect of China.

In addition to Mandarin, there is a local dialect called "Taiwanese" derived from China's Fujian province, ancestral home of the vast majority of Taiwan's Chinese populace. Taiwanese is commonly spoken among locals, especially in the rural regions, and one of Taiwan's major television stations broadcasts programs in that dialect for their benefit. The older generation still speaks some Japanese – a remnant influence of Japan's colonial occupation – and younger people tend to understand at least some basic English. Though English is a required subject for all Chinese students in Taiwan throughout mid-dle and high school, it is spoken fluently by very few.

It helps immensely to learn a little spoken Chinese before traveling in Taiwan. Not only will it help you get around, it will also give you "big face" among the Chinese, who are always surprised and flattered to find a foreigner who has bothered to learn a bit of their language. The correct way to romanize Chinese sounds for foreigners has been a matter of dispute among linguists and sinologists for centuries, but this need not concern the layman, who simply requires a spelling system which at least approximates Chinese pronunciation. The pinyin system used in mainland China is, to some foreigners, an arbitrary and confusing system, with "x" used to denote "s" sounds, "c" for "zh" for "j", and other inexplicable anomalies. For the reader's convenience, the Chinese words, phrases, and sentence patterns introduced below are phonetically spelled according to the most common English pronunciations.

Greetings

Hello, how are you?/*Nee-how-mah?*
Fine; very good/*Hun-how*
Not so good/*Boo-how*
Goodbye/*Dzai-jyen*
See you tomorrow/*Ming-tyen jyen*
Good morning/*Dzao-an*
Good evening/*Wan-an*
You; you (plural)/*Nee; nee-men*
I; we/*Wo; wo-men*
He, she, it; they/*Ta; ta-men*
Who?/*Shay?*
Mr Lee/*Lee syen-sheng*
Miss Lee/*Lee shiao-jyeh*
Mrs Lee/*Lee tai-tai*
Thank you/*Shyieh-shyieh*
You're welcome/*Boo keh-chee*

Time and Place

Where?/*Nah-lee?*
What time?/*Jee dyen joong?*
What day?/*Lee-bai jee?*
Today/*Jin-tyen*
Tomorrow/*Ming-tyen*
Yesterday/*Dzou-tyen*
One o'clock/*Ee dyen-joong*
Two o'clock/*Liang dyen-joong*
Very far/*Hun yuan*
Very close/*Hun jin*

Food and Beverages

Restaurant/*tsan-ting*
Bar/*Jiou-bah*
Let's eat; to eat/*Chir-fan*
Let's drink; to drink/*Huh-jiou*
Ice/*Bing*
Water; cold water/*Shway; bing-shway*
Soup/*Tang*
Fruit/*Shway-gwo*
Tea/*Cha*
Coffee/*Ka-fay*
Hot/*Reh*
Cold/*Lung*
Sugar/*Tang*
A little bit/*Ee-dyen*
A little more/*Dwo-ee-dyen*
A little bit less/*Shao-ee-dyen*
Bottoms up!/*Gahn-bay!*

Settle the bill/*Swan-jang*
Let me pay/*Wo ching-keh*

Numbers

One/*Ee*
Two/*Erh (liang)*
Three/*San*
Four/*Ssuh*
Five/*Wu*
Six /*Lyio*
Seven/*Chee*
Eight/*Bah*
Nine/*Jiou*
Ten/*Shir*
Eleven/*Shir-ee*
Twelve, etc/*Shir-erh, etc*
Twenty/*Erh-shir*
Thirty/*San-shir*
Forty, etc./*Sshu-shir*
Fifty-five/*Wu-shir-wu*
Seventy-six/*Chee-shir-lyio*
One hundred/*Ee-bai*
One hundred twenty-five
Ee-bai erh-shir-wu
Two hundred, etc./*Liang-bai*
One thousand/*Ee-chyen*
Ten thousand/*Ee-wan*
Fifty thousand/*Wu-wan*

Transportation

Hotel/*Fan-dyen*
Room/*Fang-jyen*
Airport/*Fay-jee-chang*
Bus/*Goong-goong chee-chuh*
Taxi/*Jee-cheng-chuh*
Telephone/*Dyen-hwah*
Telegram/*Dyen-bao*
Airplane/*Fay-jee*
Train/*Hwo-chuh*
Reservations/*Ding-way*
Key/*Yao-shir*
Clothing/*Ee-fu*
Luggage/*Shing-lee*

Shopping

How much?/*Dwo-shao?*
Too expensive/*Tai-gway*
Make it a bit cheaper
Swan pyen-ee-dyen
Money/*Chyen*
Credit card/*Shin-yoong kah*
Old /*Lao*
New/*Shin*
Big/*Dah*
Small/*Syiao*
Antique/*Goo-doong*
Red/*Hoong*
Green/*Lyu*
Yellow/*Hwang*
Black/*Hay*
White/*Bai*

Blue/*Lan*
Gold/*Jin*
Jade/*Yu*
Wood/*Mu*
Proprietor, shop-owner/*Lao-ban*
Wrap it up/*Bao-chee-lai*

Basic Sentence Patterns

I want.../*Wo yao...*
I don't want.../*Wo boo-yao...*
Where is...?/...*dzai nah-lee?*
Do you have...?/*Nee yio may-yio...?*
We don't have.../*Wo-men may-yio...*
I like.../*Wo shee-hwan...*
I don't like.../*Wo boo-shee-hwan...*
I like you/*Wo shee-hwan nee*
I wish to go.../*Wo yao choo...*

Further Reading

General

The Anthropology of Taiwanese Society by Ahern and Gates, editors. Stanford University Press, Stanford, 1981.

Foreigners in Formosa, 1841–74 by Carrington, George Williams. Chinese Material Center, San Francisco, 1977.

Taiwan, An Economic and Social Geography by Chen Cheng-Siang. Taipei, 1963.

Doing Business in Taiwan by Cheng, Jame. Cheng Cheng Law Offices, Taipei, 1982.

Island China by Clough, Ralph N. Harvard University Press, Cambridge, 1978.

The Island of Formosa, Past and Present by Davidson, James W. Macmillan, London, 1903.

Formosa by Goddard, William G. China Publishing Co., Taipei, 1958.

Formosa, A Study in Chinese History by Goddard, William G. Macmillan, London, 1966.

Economic Development of Taiwan, 1860–1970 by Ho, Samuel P.S. Yale University Press, New Haven 1978.

From Far Formosa by Mackay, Rev. Geoge Leslie. Fleming H. Revell Co., New York, 1895.

Leadership and Values: The Organisation of Large-Scale Taiwanese Enterprises by Silin, Robert H. Harvard University Press, Cambridge 1976.

Wine for the Gods, An Account of the Religious Traditions of Taiwan by Wei,

Henry and Suzanne Countanceau. Cheng Wen Publishing Co., Taipei, 1976.

Women and the Family in Rural Taiwan by Wolf, Margery. Stanford University Press, Stanford, 1972.

Taiwan in China's Foreign Relations, 1836–74 by Yen, Sophia Yu-fei. Shoe String Press, Hamden, Connecticut, 1965.

Taiwan: A Beautiful Island by Yu Juchi, editor. TTV Culture Enterprise, Taipei 1981.

Gods, Ghosts and Ancestors: Folk Religion in a Taiwanese Village. University of California Press, Berkeley, 1966.

Republic of China: A Reference Book. United Pacific International, Taipei, 1983.

Other Insight Guides

269

Index